D0899883

SOCIAL ISSUES IN COMPUTING

This is a volume in
COMPUTER SCIENCE AND APPLIED MATHEMATICS
A Series of Monographs and Textbooks

Editor: WERNER RHEINBOLDT

A complete list of titles in this series appears at the end of the volume.

SOCIAL ISSUES IN COMPUTING

C. C. Gotlieb and A. Borodin

Department of Computer Science
University of Toronto
Toronto, Canada

ACADEMIC PRESS New York San Francisco London

A Subsidiary of Harcourt Brace Jovanovich, Publishers

ACADEMIC PRESS, INC.
111 Fifth Avenue, New York, New York 10003

United Kingdom Edition published by
ACADEMIC PRESS, INC. (LONDON) LTD.
24/28 Oval Road, London NW1

Library of Congress Cataloging in Publication Data

Gotlieb, C C
Social issues in computing.

Includes bibliographies.
1. Electronic data processing. 2. Computers and civilization. I. Borodin, Allan, joint author. II. Title.
QA76.G65 301.24'3 73-802
ISBN 0-12-293750-3

PRINTED IN THE UNITED STATES OF AMERICA

CONTENTS

Chapter 3. Computer Use: Where and Why

Chapter 4. Files, Data Banks, and Information Systems

Chapter 5. Information Systems and Privacy

Chapter 6. Surveying and Predicting

Chapter 7. Systems, Models, and Simulations

Chapter 13. Values, Technology, and Computers

PREFACE

The social implications of technology have come to be of crucial interest to the public at large. Evidence of this interest is readily apparent in writings for the mass media, the orientation of research programs, the content of university curricula, and the continued growth of an already extensive literature. Although the debate on the effects of technology has been longstanding, computers inject a new element into it. Attention to this element is relatively recent (except perhaps for the philosophical speculations on thinking which have been a fascinating subject from the beginnings of computer development), and recognition of it as a legitimate subject of study in a computer curriculum is just beginning. The present text is offered as a contribution to the discussion.

The structure and content of this book have evolved through two periods during which we taught a course on Computers and Society at the University of Toronto. The sequence of chapters corresponds to a progression of topics which proceeds from the technical to the social, ethical, and philosophical, as explained in Chapter 1.

There has been a serious attempt to discuss most of the nontechnical problems in which computers play a role, even though not all topics are treated with the same depth. We have tried to indicate the diversity of issues and opinions, providing enough references to allow the reader to pursue any subject which interests him. Some topics have been deferred to the problems.

Strictly speaking, there are no prerequisites for reading and understanding the book. The student who has had some exposure to computers, programming languages, or computer systems (possibly on as low a level as high school) will be better prepared to appreciate the force of the issues. The book is by no means meant to be restricted to computer science students. Our experience has been that class discussions are much more stimulating when there are students from the social sciences and the humanities, as well as from the physical sciences. Although the main interest is computers and society, we hope that the book will also serve as a supplemental text for interdisciplinary courses concerned with science, technology, and society. The intended use has influenced the presentation in several ways.

- The text primarily concerns issues, and we have usually avoided methodology. In certain places we have discussed techniques. Sometimes, this has been done to provide a basis for assignments and projects; sometimes, because the material is considered central to the discussion.
- There are no explanations about the components of a computer, about how computers work, or about technical matters such as operating systems. There are some details about files and about the computing industry, since these topics are not usually included in introductory computer science courses. Some of the background material (e.g., in Chapters 2 and 4) may be temporarily bypassed in favor of proceeding directly to the issues.
- There are elementary introductions to concepts in economics (e.g., the production function), in law (the common law), in philosophy (values), and in other disciplines with which those who concentrate on the physical, mathematical, and management sciences are not likely to be familiar.

We regard it as of the greatest importance to elicit interactive participation from the students as early as possible. Tutorial sessions with small groups will, of course, further this. A difficulty is that for each of the many topics there is a historical and semitechnical background which must be mastered before interchange of views can take place at a nontrivial level. We have found, however, that when the lecture presentation is supplemented by other techniques, the students do become genuinely involved in the subject. Examples of these additional techniques can be found in the problems. They include designing and conducting surveys, preparing oral and written statements of position, writing computer modeling and simulation programs, as well as participating in Delphi experiments, computer-assisted instruction programs, and business games.

Just how intense and widespread are the attempts to reappraise science and technology can be inferred from the references and from the bibliographies given at the end of each chapter. Debates are taking place in every one of the many disciplines which computers touch. Moreover, the fact that so many of the citations are to writings which have appeared only in the last three or four years shows that interest is still heightening. The result is that the interaction between computers and society is a highly dynamic one. For example, there were new developments with respect to patents and antitrust suits and a new major report on data banks just as the manuscript was being completed. For these reasons many of the opinions we express must be regarded as tentative; we like to think that there are others which can continue to be held for some time. In an introductory text such as this it is essential that a balance of opinion regarding each issue be presented. We make no claims to being unbiased, but we have tried to mute our own advocacy.

It will be noted that most of the issues have been presented as they arise in the United States. This is inevitable, for as is so clearly seen in Chapter 2, the United States has by far the largest concentration of computers, and it is here that so many of the issues first come to the fore. Yet the issues and problems are important enough that they deserve to be treated in a wider perspective. We have done our best to provide this by drawing upon examples and data from other countries, and by posing questions and answers in ways which are generally applicable.

ACKNOWLEDGMENTS

We are grateful to our many friends, colleagues, and students who, during the writing of this book, helped us sort out our ideas by discussing them with us, providing us with materials, criticizing the manuscript, and participating in the courses. Included among them are: P. Armer, I. Auerbach, B. Barg, J. Berry, M. Brodie, D. Chevion, E. Drumm, R. Fabian, J. Fagbemi, B. Gilchrist, R. Gwyn, E. Hehner, J. Helliwell, E. and M. Horowitz, T. Hull, A. Lehman, D. D. McCracken, L. Mezei, G. Mulligan, I. Munro, D. Parker, A. Ralston, P. Roosen-Runge, P. Sorensen, R. Tennent, P. Walsh, D. Weisstub, and H. Zemanek. We are indebted to the Department of Computer Science, University of Toronto, for its continued support and encouragement. We thank I. Farkas and J. Metzger for performing the calculations in the simulation examples of Chapter 7. Stephanie Johnston, Yvonne George, and Jane Gotlieb were all helpful in the extensive bibliographic work involved in finding and checking the many references. Our reading and thinking, particularly for the subject matter of Chapters 11 and 13, have been considerably influenced by the reports and publications of the Harvard University Program on Technology and Society. Sections of Chapter 9 originally appeared in the

July 1972 issue of the *Communications of the Association for Computing Machinery,* and these are reproduced with permission. Part of Chapter 11 appeared in the *Proceedings of the Fifth Australian Computer Conference, Brisbane, 1972,* under the title "Computer Weights in the Balance of Power."

Our special thanks go to Margaret Chepely, who learned to cope with computers so that the manuscript could be prepared with a text-editor, and whose dedication was a constant reminder of the importance of people in a computing system.

Finally we thank our wives, Phyllis and Judy, for being, among other things, attentive listeners and sympathetic critics.

SOCIAL ISSUES IN COMPUTING

Chapter

1

PROBLEMS AND ISSUES

The questions raised by the presence of computers range from technical problems, which can be posed rigorously and solved mathematically or experimentally, through social issues, which can only be resolved, if at all, after there is agreement about goals, to philosophical probings, whose answers are essentially discussions of the meanings of the terms being used. In this chapter we outline the problems, demarcate the areas on which attention will be focused, and attempt to indicate some of the viewpoints, assumptions, and biases from which the discussion is undertaken.

1.1. The Spectrum

An indication of the number and range of problems associated with computers can be given by attempting to classify the kinds of problems which arise. Such an attempt is shown in Fig. 1-1. The areas which designate the types are shown as overlapping to indicate that the sub-

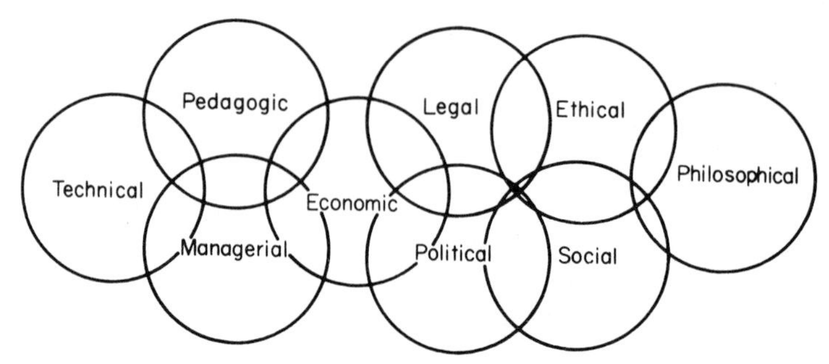

FIG. 1-1. *Problem areas with regard to computers.*

ject matter overlaps, and to convey the fact that the answers to a problem will depend on the context in which it is raised. Thus the answer to the question of whether certain regulations ought to be made applicable to the computer industry will depend on considerations which may be primarily economic, legal, social, or political. In each of the areas there are problems which fall mainly within the area, and others which could be placed in several categories. But in all of the areas the interest in computers has been great enough to warrant the publication of books and journals devoted to computer-related problems. The bibliography at the end of this chapter lists some representative books and periodicals attesting to this interest.

Although the areas of Fig. 1-1 are diffuse, there is a progression or scale from the technical, pedagogical, management problems at one end, to the social, ethical, and philosophical problems at the other, to form what might be called a *spectrum.* The primary concern of this book is with these latter problems. The spectrum shades from well-structured, unambiguously formulated problems at one end, to those which are more loosely defined and not understood as well at the other. Where there are clearly defined abstractions of physical systems, or when the actual system can be studied and modified, it is possible to pose technical questions. Mathematical reasoning or experimental techniques can be applied to answer such questions and we can look for solutions with measurable accuracies. Moving to the right takes us from the physical and mathematical sciences into the social sciences of economics, sociology, and political economy. Here the problems in which we are interested might better be described as *issues,* for they are stated as debates on the advantages and disadvantages of different courses of action. The solutions, or better the *resolutions,* depend on agreements about values, goals, and techniques. At the end of the spectrum are ethical and philosophical questions, which rather than answer, we can only hope to illuminate by examining the semantics of the terms involved.

1.2. Issues

Figure 1-1 is *not* intended to portray areas or disciplines in which computers are used, for such a figure would have to include a representation for almost every discipline. In each discipline there are specific problems about using computers effectively, problems which are largely conceptual, technical, or managerial. Although the computer is an instrument in the *solution* of problems, it is not difficult to pose problems which the computer *creates* rather than solves. Table 1-1 lists for each of the areas identified earlier, some problems and issues regarding the use of computers, including problems on how to use them effectively and issues arising from their use.

The problems about computers which have received the most attention to date are the technical ones, and the majority of books and journals about computers are at this level. There has also been a great deal written about management problems, and to a lesser but still significant extent, about economic and pedagogical problems. We shall consider questions in these areas mainly as they relate to legal, political, social, ethical, and philosophical issues. The focus is on *issues,* questions which are subject to debate and which cannot be decided only on technical considerations. We identify these issues as a subset of the questions listed above, posed here deliberately in terms calculated to provoke a reaction in order to emphasize the controversy which surrounds them.

- *Does the whole world, including the lesser developed countries, really need computers?*
- *Are data banks a threat to freedom?*
- *Can we trust plans made with computers?*
- *Will man's thinking be replaced by machines?*
- *Will computers create massive unemployment?*
- *Do we need to regulate the computer industry?*
- *Are computers upsetting power balances?*
- *Is the computer profession (assuming that there is one) aware of its responsibilities?*
- *Are computers helping to destroy our values?*

In the text which follows two chapters are devoted to each of the first three issues; the remaining six issues are discussed in the last six chapters.

TABLE 1-1

SOME QUESTIONS ASSOCIATED WITH COMPUTERS

Technical:

1. How can the time for searching large files be minimized?
2. What is the best way to organize hierarchical stores?
3. How can communication lines be used efficiently?
4. How should language interfaces between users and machines be designed?

Pedagogic:

1. How should basic concepts be identified and presented?
2. Which computer languages should be adopted as teaching instruments?
3. How can students be familiarized with equipment and software from different suppliers?
4. How can computer skills be transmitted to persons in the lesser developed countries?

Managerial:

1. What are the trade-offs between centralization and decentralization of staff, equipment, and authority?
2. To whom should the data processing manager report?
3. How should cost–effectiveness for computer systems be measured?
4. What charging procedures should be adopted for computer services?

Economic:

1. What effects have computers had on employment levels?
2. Do computers demand more or less in the way of skills from the labor force?
3. Should there be any restrictions against entry into the computer service bureau field?
4. How does the international computer market affect trade balances?

Legal:

1. Should computer software be protected by copyrights? patents? other methods? at all?
2. How can responsibility for malfunctions be assigned?
3. Should data banks be regulated and if so, how?
4. Should computers be used to predict the outcome of court decisions?

Political:

1. Do computers further the concentration of power in governments and large institutions?
2. Should social insurance numbers be adopted as universal personal identifiers?
3. Do computers help promote a technocratic society, managed by experts?
4. Should computers and communications systems be used to make politicians and public officials instantly aware of popular opinion on current issues?

Ethical:

1. Are there *new* ethical considerations in the use of computers?
2. Is there an ethical code appropriate to the computer profession?
3. Are there computer applications which should not be undertaken on ethical or moral grounds?

TABLE 1-1 (*Continued*)

4. Is it fair for a programmer who transfers from one company to a competitor, to apply his knowledge in the new situation?

Social:

1. If computers, along with other technological changes, bring about a great increase in leisure, what effects will this have on society?
2. Do computers increase or decrease the freedom to make important choices in our daily lives?
3. Do computers contribute to the alienation of individuals?
4. What changes in values are likely to occur as computers become more prevalent?

Philosophical:

1. Can machines think?
2. Does technology dehumanize man?
3. Is the conception of the world adopted for modeling purposes, as a single system with many components which grow and decay, adequate for planning purposes?
4. Is man–machine symbiosis desirable?

1.3. Viewpoints

The issues involving computer subjects are so broad, and in some cases changing so rapidly, that it is not possible to consider them all in the same detail. Our choices have been governed by what we regard as important or interesting, by the degree to which there has been recognition of the issues and serious contributions on them in the literature, and by our own experiences.

In any presentation of issues, especially controversial ones, it is well to make explicit the underlying assumptions. The assumptions which have influenced the presentation in this book can be summarized as follows.

1. Computers have effects which are similar to those of other (but not all) technological innovations. In particular the changes being brought about by industrial automation, the growth of communications, and the emergence of system planning as a general tool are closely related to changes induced by computers, and it is necessary to study computers in the context of these other technological developments.

2. The secondary effects of computers can be as important, or even more important, than the primary ones. For instance, the primary effect of the changes in productivity computers bring to office automation is on the number of persons employed and in the nature of their work; secondary effects on attitudes toward work and on the increase of leisure

are of equal significance. Again, the primary effect on centralizing data processing activities in business or government is on efficiency, but secondary effects on the control of information and distribution of authority are fully as important in the long run.

3. In presenting a topic it is best to start with the factual, historical, and technical aspects, and proceed to prediction and debate, so that issues will not be confused by poor terminology or by speculations with no basis in fact. Within each chapter there has been a conscious attempt to proceed from the factual to the debatable, from the past to the present to the future.

Finally it is necessary to admit to a bias which is probably apparent throughout the text, but which deserves explicit mention. We speak of our belief in the positive aspects of computer use. Paramount among the problems facing humanity are the control of population, the equitable distribution of wealth, balancing individual freedom against the authority of governments, preservation of the world's resources, and the peaceful resolution of conflicts. It is naive to think that there is a primarily technical solution to any of these multifaceted problems. But even though all of the problems involve conflict of basic values (for example, desire for security versus desire for independence), any answers must be found in the light of what is technically feasible. It is not necessary to maintain that computers will have a major role in all of the problems. Through their use in government administration and in the distribution of social services, computers enter into the solution of the major problems and affect the way these problems are attacked. Our belief then, without dismissing present and potential dangers, is that computers have already contributed and will continue to contribute positively toward the solution of difficult social problems.

General Bibliography

TECHNICAL

Communications of the Association for Computing Machinery (Monthly). Association for Computing Machinery, New York.

Knuth, D. E. (1968). "The Art of Computer Programming," Vol. 1. Addison-Wesley, Reading, Massachusetts.

PEDAGOGIC

AEDS Journal. Association for Education Data Systems, Washington, D. C.

Finerman, A., ed. (1968). "University Education in Computing Science." Academic Press, New York.

MANAGERIAL

IAG Communications (Quarterly). IFIP Administrative Data Processing Group, North-Holland Publ., Amsterdam.

Withington, F. G. (1969). "The Real Computer; Its Influence, Uses and Effects." Addison-Wesley, Reading, Massachusetts.

ECONOMIC

Harman, A. J. (1971). "The International Computer Industry." Harvard Univ. Press, Cambridge, Massachusetts.

Shepard, J. M. (1971). "Automation and Alienation, A Study of Office and Factory Workers." MIT Press, Cambridge, Massachusetts.

LEGAL

Freed, R. N. (1969). "Materials and Cases on Computers and Law." 2nd ed. Boston Univ. Book Store, Boston, Massachusetts.

Law and Comput. Technol. (Monthly). World Peace Through Law Center, Washington, D. C.

POLITICAL

Gilchrist, B., and Wessel, M. R. (1972). "Government Regulation of the Computer Industry." Amer. Fed. of Information Processing Soc. (AFIPS) Press, Montvale, New Jersey.

Westin, A., ed. (1971). "Information Technology in a Democracy." Harvard Univ. Press, Cambridge, Massachusetts.

ETHICAL

Computers and Automation (Monthly). Berkeley Enterprises, Inc., Newtonville, Massachusetts.

McCracken, D. D. (1971). "Public Policy and the Expert." Council on Religion and International Affairs, New York.

SOCIAL

Parkman, R. (1972). "The Cybernetic Society." Pergamon, Oxford.

Rothman, S., and Mosmann, C. (1972). "Computers and Society." Science Res. Associates, Chicago.

PHILOSOPHICAL

Anderson, A. R., ed. (1964). "Minds and Machines." Prentice-Hall, Englewood Cliffs, New Jersey.

Jaki, S. L. (1969). "Brain, Mind and Computers." Herder and Herder, New York.

Chapter

2

COMPUTER USE: EXTENT AND GROWTH

Before examining the effects of computers on society in detail we wish to document how prevalent computers have become and how computer use is growing, for the rate of growth is itself of major significance. To do this several different ways of describing the extent of computer use are presented. Disparities in computer use between different countries, as well as the degree to which different countries are able to share in the market for computer products and services, are also examined.

2.1. The Number of Installations

The obvious way of describing the growth of computer use is to tabulate the number of installations each year. In compiling censuses on computers it is common to omit small desk calculators and count only machines on which some "substantial" calculation or data processing can be carried out, for example, stored-program computers, for which the sequence of instructions can be stored in memory.[1] Even after agreeing on

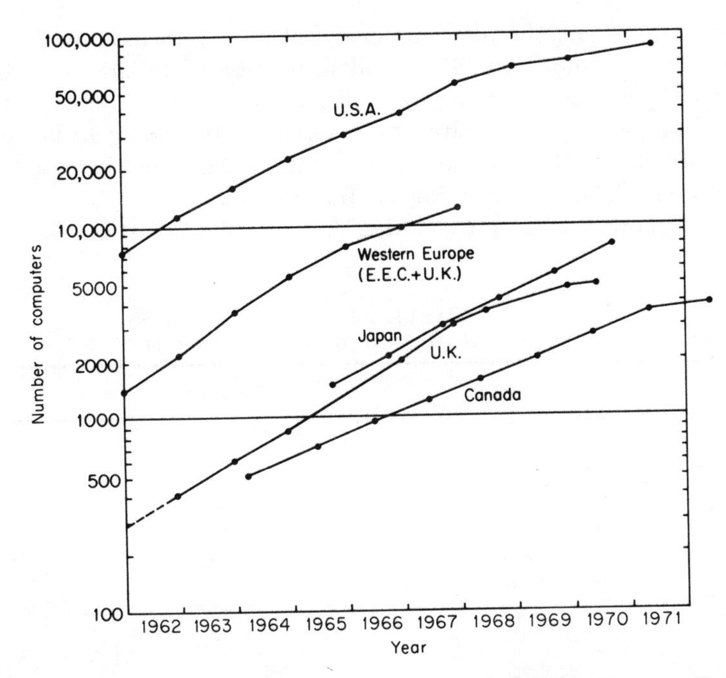

FIG. 2-1. *Number of computers installed.* (*Sources: OECD, "Gaps in Technology." Paris, 1969; Canad. Information Processing Soc., "Canadian Computer Census." Whitsed, Toronto, 1971; Japan Computer Usage Development Inst., "Computer White Paper." Tokyo, 1971.*)

what a computer is, it is difficult to obtain accurate counts on the number of installations. In countries with many computers the machines are spread widely throughout government, institutions, and private business, and it is not yet usual to include counts of them in governmental economic and statistical surveys. Data coming from manufacturers are inadequate, especially because IBM, the largest supplier of computers, holds such data confidential. Estimates on the number of computers must therefore come from trade magazines, national professional societies, international organizations, or companies that specialize in making such estimates.[2] Other uncertainties arise in comparing the statistics because

[1] Essentially this is the definition taken in Canad. Information Processing Soc., "Canadian Computer Census," p. 9, Whitsed, Toronto, 1970.

[2] An annotated summary of the sources for such statistics in OECD countries is given in OECD (1970). Sources in the United States include Computers and Automation, EDP Industry Report, the American Federation of Information Processing Societies, and International Data Corporation.

some reports on the number of computers, but not all, include machines on order as well as those actually installed, because of variations in the times at which the counts are taken, and because in some countries the number of computers being retired from service is beginning to be significant. Notwithstanding all these uncertainties, charts of the number of computer installations against time are informative.

Figure 2-1 shows the graphs for the United States, Western Europe

TABLE 2-1
COMPUTER INSTALLATIONS IN SOME DEVELOPING COUNTRIES (1970–1971)[a]

Country	Number
Africa	
Ethiopia	9
Ghana	13
Kenya	17
Madagascar	15
Nigeria	30
Senegal	12
Zaire	19
Asia	
India	183
Malaysia	28
Philippines	120
Singapore	34
Thailand	27
Middle East	
Algeria	63
Iran	49
Iraq	7
Israel	257
Lebanon	29
Morocco	52
Turkey	73
United Arab Republic	27
South and Central America	
Bolivia	6
Brazil	750
Chile	57
Colombia	82
Mexica	402
Nicaragua	14

[a] Source: United Nations (1973, Appendix).

(the European Economic Community plus the United Kingdom), the United Kingdom, Japan, and Canada. The first thing to be noted is the much greater numbers for the United States compared to those for other industrialized countries. The second observation is that in all countries the growth curve is approximately a straight line, which corresponds to an exponential growth in view of the logarithmic vertical scale. Finally we note that only in the United States is there any sign of appreciable diminution in the growth rate, and that the rate is (very approximately) the same for all the countries shown, corresponding to a doubling in a period which varies from two to four years—a remarkably short time.

For comparison it may be noted that for 1969 the number of computers in the Soviet Union and in seven Eastern European countries (Bulgaria, Czechoslovakia, East Germany, Hungary, Poland, Roumania, and Yugoslavia) has been estimated as 5000 and 777, respectively.[3] As is to be expected, in developing countries the number of computer installations is very much smaller, Table 2-1 gives an indication of the situation as of 1970–1971. Most of the countries shown, excepting Israel and perhaps some in South America, are in the early stages of computerization, and time series are not usually available. What data there are, however, confirm that the rate of increase is not very different from the doubling in two or three years as observed in the developed countries. As examples, the comparative numbers of installations in 1969 and 1971 are for India 111 and 183, for Israel 160 and 257, and for Nigeria 12 and 30.

2.2. Other Measures

The number of installations in a country is only a rough guide to computer utilization, and some obvious adjustments to it should be made. It can be normalized by dividing by the population, for example, or by dividing by the Gross National Product (GNP). Table 2-2 shows these normalized statistics for the United States and for some developed and developing countries.

Alternatively, installations might be weighted by their cost so as to obtain the value of the computers installed. As an example, Table 2-3 shows how the 3548 computers installed in Canada in 1971 were distributed according to their monthly rental cost (and also according to industry). For 1969 the *total* value (as measured by purchases) of computers installed in the United States is estimated to have been $21 to

[3] Amer. Fed. of Information Processing Soc. (AFIPS) (1971, p. 210). See also I. Berenyi, Computers in Eastern Europe. *Sci. Amer.* **223** (4), 102–108 (1970).

TABLE 2-2
COMPUTERS, POPULATION, AND GNP—1969[a]

Country	Number of computers	Population millions	GNP billions	GNP $ per capita	Number of computers per million capita	Number of computers per $ billion of GNP
Canada	2037[3]	21.1	72.9	3455	97	27.9
France	4803	50.3	139.6	2775	95	34.4
Germany	6400	58.7	132.7	2802	110	39.1
Japan	4577	102.3	166.4	1628	45	27.5
United Kingdom	4321	55.5	109.5	1973	78	39.5
United States	62,685[1]	205.9[2]	931.3	4523	305	67.3
Brazil	401	90.8	24.4	269	4.4	14.9
India	110	537	Not available		0.2	
Israel	118	2.8	4.7	1679	42	25.1
Yugoslavia	116	20.3	11.9	586	5.7	9.7

[a] Sources: Amer. Fed. of Information Processing Soc., "World Markets for Electronic Data Processing Equipment." Montvale, New Jersey, 1971; (1) Amer. Fed. of Information Processing Soc. "EDP Industry Report." Montvale, New Jersey, 1970; (2) OECD, "Demographic Trends." Paris, 1966; (3) Canad. Information Processing Soc. "Canadian Computer Census." Whitsed, Toronto, 1971.

TABLE 2-3
COMPUTERS INSTALLED IN CANADA, MAY 1971,
BY INDUSTRY AND MONTHLY RENTAL[a]

Industry	Up to $1999	$2000 to $9999	$10,000 to $49,999	$50,000 and over	Total
Primary resource	31	55	35	1	122
Construction	30	17	1	0	48
Manufacturing	338	397	96	15	846
Transportation	60	53	15	3	131
Utility	34	64	40	9	147
Communication	49	25	15	0	89
Distribution	133	127	38	3	301
Financial	74	78	105	11	268
Other services	444	190	67	13	714
Service bureaus	68	116	81	20	285
Government	232	133	78	10	453
Petroleum	24	30	25	3	82
Others	31	28	3	0	62
Total	1548	1313	599	88	3548

[a] Source: Canad. Information Processing Soc. "Canadian Computer Census." Whitsed, Toronto, 1971.

$21.8 billion, as compared to a value of $30.5 and $31.5 billion for the rest of the world.[4]

2.3. The Change in Quality

In assessing the growth of computing facilities we must also take into account the changes in the quality of data processing devices due to continued improvements in design and manufacture. There has been a systematic trend to faster central processors, larger capacity storage units, and more versatile peripheral attachments. The steady reduction in the cost per unit of computation for computers which have been marketed since 1955 can be seen in Fig. 2-2.[5] To illustrate the increase

[4] Source: Internat. Data Corp., Industry Rep. as quoted in OECD (1970, p. 52). These figures should be compared with the estimated values for 1975, which are given as 54.0 to 54.4 billions for the United States, and 92.0 to 96.4 billions for the rest of the world.

[5] There are several ways of defining a unit of computation, or computing power. A simple scheme is to take a weighted average of the times required to execute a number of basic instruction types; for a more realistic value it is necessary to take input–output operations and processing overlaps into account. [See K. E. Knight, Changes in computer performance 1963–1967: A historical view. *Datamation* **12**,

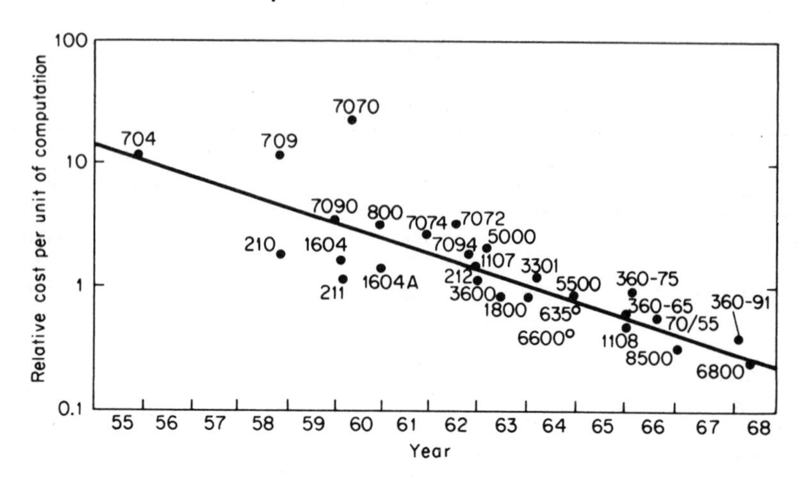

FIG. 2-2. *Cost per unit computation trend; load mix—75% scientific, 25% business. (Reprinted with the permission from F. R. Heath, Factors for evaluation of integrated on-line information system, in "Computers and Communications—Toward a Computer Utility," (F. Gruenberger, ed.). Prentice-Hall, Englewood Cliffs, New Jersey, 1968. Copyright 1968 by Prentice-Hall, Inc.)*

in storage capacity, the IBM 650 computer which appeared in 1954 had an internal store of 1000 to 4000 ten decimal digit words; the high-speed store of the CDC 3600, appearing in 1963, has 32K to 262K 48-bit words; the store of the IBM 370/165, first delivered in 1970, contains 512K to 3 million bytes.[6]

This is not the full story on the changes in the quality of computing. The current emphasis in computers is on time-sharing systems, on-line data processing, and minicomputers, and this means that computer power is being distributed to a much larger community of users.[7] The initial growth of time-sharing systems, following their introduction in 1961, has shown the usual exponential pattern,[8] and with the larger more recent systems, the number of time-sharing users continues to in-

---

40–54 (1966); Evolving computer performance 1963–1967. *Datamation* **14** (1), 31–35 (1968).] The assessment becomes very difficult with multiprogramming and multiprocessing systems.

[6] For a review of cost/effectiveness trends see Knight[5]; Sharpe (1969): "The Economics of Computers," Chapter 11; and Harman (1971): "The International Computer Industry," Chapter 4.

[7] See A. C. Gross, Accessibility and the small computer. *Datamation* **17**, 42–48 (1971) for a discussion of the relative advantages of minicomputers (under $25,000 in cost) and small computers ($25,000 to $100,000).

[8] J. T. Glauthier, Computer time-sharing: Its origins and development. *Comput. Automat.* **16** (10), 24 (1967).

crease rapidly. The installation rate of minicomputers, which started to appear in significant numbers in 1968, is exceeding that of larger computers, and it is estimated that by 1975 the population of minicomputers will equal that of other types of systems.[9]

The growth in minicomputers and time-sharing reflects the fact that the computer industry is becoming much more diversified. A distinct market has developed for peripheral components such as disk memories, plotters, and microfilm output devices. In addition totally new services based on software are emerging. These include the sale of software through contracts and packaged systems, the provision of services centered on specialized data bases, programs made available through online terminals, and undertakings to manage whole computer facilities. It is sufficient to note here that they illustrate the rapidly changing nature and increase in complexity of computer technology.

Thus the continued increase in the number of computers is being accompanied by an increase in the power of the facilities, increases in accessibility to computing systems, by more versatile services, and by a general evolution of the computer industry. The result is a very rapid growth in the number and variety of computer applications, to the point that in the industrially developed countries there are few people who do not have some direct or indirect contact with computers.

2.4. Projections

Is this rate of computer expansion likely to continue? Technological forecasting in general is discussed in Section 6.2, but at this point we examine the prospective developments for the aspects of computers we have just considered.[10]

Computer Speed

Limitations on the switching rate of electronic circuits and on the speed of propagation of signals along wires make it clear that the times for basic arithmetic operations will not be decreased substantially. But important miniaturizations are being realized through the use of large-scale integrated circuits. These, along with more complex computer organization and more sophisticated software which render the com-

[9] D. Sharpe, Minis are outstripping the maxis in the computer market place. *Canad. Data Systems,* pp. 32–38, November (1970).

[10] For more complete discussion see W. R. Graham, "The Impact of Future Developments in Computer Technology." P4401. Rand Corp., Santa Monica, California, June 1970.

plicated hardware invisible to the user, make it possible to introduce greater parallelism in computer calculations, and so effectively increase the speed. It is likely therefore that in the short term, the curve of cost per unit of computation shown in Fig. 2-2 will continue to decrease at a rate not too different from that shown.

Storage

In a similar way the storage capacity can be projected for the next five to ten years. Magnetic cores, the form of high-speed storage most commonly used now, have already undergone intensive development, and it seems unlikely that great changes in them will occur. But semiconductor memories based on large-scale integrated circuits are just coming into commercial use, and these along with other developments on the horizon seem to assure that high-speed memories will continue to show significant improvements in cost and performance. As for intermediate-speed large-scale memories, once again the present devices, magnetic drums and fixed head disks, are not likely to be improved greatly. But there are possibilities that other devices, such as optical systems and magnetic bubble memories, will come into use to offer larger capacities at higher speed and lower costs. For very large computing storage, microfilm and microfiche readers, attached to computers, are already important supplements to magnetic tape devices.

Interfaces

By mass production alone, the costs for terminals will decrease somewhat, but more important, there will be a continued proliferation of types. We are already seeing many new types of impact printers, display units, and simple devices for recording specialized transactions; eventually we can expect to see devices which will allow data entry from the home, for example, from telephones and television sets.

Software

This segment of the computer industry is at an early stage of development. Its direction will depend in part on how certain practices relating to proprietary rights, warranties, and standards evolve; these are discussed at greater length in Section 10.3. Management consultant firms and those who make industry forecasts are in general agreement that the rate of expenditures will double or triple in the next five years, thus showing the same type of growth that has characterized hardware in the past.[11]

INFORMATION UTILITIES

The way in which computer services grow will depend on developments in electronics and communications, on innovations in the production of computer components, and on economic and regulating factors which encourage or discourage particular directions of growth.

Projections on how communication costs will affect the development of computer networks, and through this the growth of computer utilities, are difficult to make. It is suggested[12] that the costs for long distance transmissions will decrease greatly, as will also the costs for data sets and other units which couple computers into the telephone system. But the traffic generated by computer data on communication lines represents at present a very small percentage of the telephone traffic. For telephone circuits the costs both for connecting local lines into branch exchanges and for switching are significant; therefore no anticipated growth of computer communications is likely to affect overall communication costs very much in the near future.

As computing systems have become larger, they have come to resemble utilities in that they provide a variety of services to a large body of customers (Gruenberger, 1968). Networks for interconnecting computers are also being formed, and the term *information utility* is being applied to computer systems and networks which provide widespread service (see Section 4.3). The economic and legal questions on how control of information utilities ought to be shared among computer users, hardware and software suppliers, communication carriers, and the public are turning out to be extremely complicated. Some of these questions are also discussed in Chapter 10 on the distribution of computer services. It is generally accepted that any controls which are applied must ensure that the computer industry will continue to grow in new ways, and enable it to interact strongly with other technological developments; there is every reason to believe that this will happen.

The expectation, then, is that technological improvements in computers will continue at a rate comparable to that recently experienced,

[11] See F. Withington, "The Computer Industry 1970–1975." R710402. Arthur D. Little, Inc., Cambridge, Massachusetts, 1971; I. L. Auerbach, Technological forecast 1971. *Proc. IFIP Congr., 1971* **1**, 764–775, 1971.

[12] Zeidler, N., *et al.*, Patterns of technology in data processing and data communications. Rep. No. 7379B-4, p. 132. Stanford Res. Inst., Menlo Park, California, February 1969.

for the next five years and possibly for the next decade.[13] It does not necessarily follow that increases in the number of computer installations will continue in the same way, but substantial growth is foreseen in every country. Eventually of course economic factors which limit the growth rate must come into play. These factors can arise from restrictions on the amounts which companies and governments are willing to spend on computers, limitations on the trained people available to make effective use of computers,[14] or from a decrease in the number of new applications for which it is economically feasible or possible to use computers. As will be seen, for example, in Chapter 8, some of these factors are already operative in specialized situations, but in the short term they are not restricting expansion significantly.

2.5. Disparities

Although computer use is spreading steadily throughout the world, there are disparities in growth which pose problems. These problems are primarily economic; they are encountered in other technologies but they are especially noticeable in the computer industry. We have already seen the disparities in computer use by the industrially advanced and the developing countries. This is of course only one of the many gaps between developed and developing countries, gaps which can be found documented, for example, in "Partners in Development" (Pearson, 1969), along with an outline of international efforts, current and proposed, to bridge them. Recognizing computers as key instruments in applying technology generally, in December 1969 the General Assembly of the United Nations directed the Secretary-General to prepare a report which would examine how computers might accelerate the process of social and economic development, with emphasis on the transfer of technology, on the training of personnel, and on technical equipment. The result was the report on "The Application of Computer Technology for Development" (United Nations, 1971).

[13] For a summary see J. C. Madden, "Technological Forecast." Report prepared for the Canad. Privacy and Comput. Task Force, Dept. of Comm. and Justice, Ottawa, 1972.

[14] In the United States there is evidence that the number of people being trained for working with computers is now greater than the number of jobs which can be foreseen for them. See B. Gilchrist and R. E. Weber, Sources of trained computer personnel—A quantitative survey, and Employment of trained computer personnel—A quantitative survey, *AFIPS Conf. Proc.* **40**, pp. 633–640, 641–647, respectively (1972).

In surveying the applications of computers the report affirmed their importance for development. It identified the lack of trained personnel as the principal impediment to the effective use of computers in developing countries, and recommended actions to alleviate the shortage. These recommendations included establishing and strengthening national and regional training centers, mounting training and education programs for the many kinds of staff needed (operators, programmers, scientists, systems analysts, managers, and policy-makers), creating special teaching materials, and setting up better means for the exchange of technical information. As important as education, the report stated, is the need for a developing country to formulate a broad policy, consistent with its national goals, on the application of computer technology. It emphasized the careful planning which is necessary to ensure that computers are used effectively and that they are not introduced until there has been adequate experience, analysis of the intended application, integration with other projects, training, and data preparation.[15]

It is not only the developing countries which have been concerned with the inequalities which have taken place in the way the computers have evolved. The industrialized countries have also been faced with problems. These have not been primarily in the application of the technology; for although computer use in Western Europe has been appreciably less than that in the United States, it has been growing steadily, and it is bound to keep increasing. The problems arise because there is a very rapidly growing industry centered around computer products and services, one which is by all predictions destined to become one of the four or five principal industries in the world. And yet the market share in the *sale* of computer products for all countries other than the United States has been almost insignificant. The immediate consequences are that even countries which have highly developed electronics and communications industries are finding that computer imports are large enough to affect their trade balances significantly. The longer term consequences may be still more serious; since computers are closely coupled with other technological developments, especially communications, process control, and manufacturing, there is a fear that modern industries

[15] On accepting the report in December 1970, the UN General Assembly expressed its continuing interest in the subject of computers for development and requested a follow-up. The second report affirmed the importance of computers to national planning in developing countries and reemphasized the need for national policies with respect to computers, and for education and training at all levels. Evidence was presented that in the two years which had elapsed since the preparation of the first report, a significant number of developing countries had entered into an initial phase of computer growth. See United Nations (1973).

TABLE 2-4
COMPUTER SHIPMENTS 1969[a]

Country	$ billions
West Germany	0.85
Japan	0.68
United Kingdom	0.63
France	0.54
Italy	0.27
Other	0.43
Total	3.40
United States	5.20

[a] Source: M. J. Stevenson, '71... the year EDP goes multinational, *Datamation*, p. 32. March 15 (1971).

will generally suffer if computer components and computer techniques cannot be incorporated into their development. The long-standing difficulties which major European companies have had in establishing themselves in the computer market, even with creative research and design, government aid, and intensive marketing efforts, are well documented. (See OECD, 1969; Harman, 1971.) Table 2-4 shows the estimated exports of computer products for 1969.[16] Persistent efforts and national policies favoring domestic producers are slowly making it possible for manufacturers in some countries to build up a competitive computer industry, particularly in the United Kingdom and Japan. It is expected that most countries will double or triple their computer installations in the next five years, but that a very large fraction of the machines will continue to be supplied from the United States or from U.S. subsidiary plants (AFIPS, 1971).[17]

Within the United States itself there has been one inequality which has had an enormous influence on the computer industry. Since the very beginnings of commercial applications of computers a single company, IBM, has consistently captured from two-thirds to three-quarters of the

[16] It should further be noted that for all the non-United States countries except Japan and the United Kingdom, more than half the shipments originate from United States subsidiary companies.

[17] See M. J. Stevenson, '71 . . . the year EDP goes multinational. *Datamation* **17**, 32–36 (1971), for a five-year prediction of computer use and shipments in the United States and other countries. A similar set of forecasts is given in, F. G. Withington, "The Computer Industry, 1970–1975." Arthur D. Little, Inc., Cambridge, Massachusetts, 1971. These forecasts predict that the slow decline in IBM's domestic market *share* (74% in 1965 to 70% in 1969) will continue, although their *volume* of sales will increase.

domestic sales.[18] As examples of the many effects, favorable and unfavorable, that this near-monopoly has had on computer practices we mention the following.

- IBM standards for input devices, tape densities, communications equipment, and programming languages have tended to become industry and hence international standards; at first this benefited the development of computers; now it is regarded as an undue influence.
- IBM hardware has been consistently reliable and this set performance standards which other manufacturers have had to meet.
- IBM for a long time had a policy of only renting (and not selling) its machines. When a company can rent its products there is little incentive for replacing them. This has resulted in a tendency to keep obsolete equipment in service, but rapid changes in computer technology and competition have introduced strong counteracting forces.
- For a long time IBM offered very large educational discounts which made it easy for universities to acquire equipment and helped computing become a recognized discipline in the North American educational system. It also meant that almost everyone formally educated in data processing learned on IBM equipment.
- Because IBM has a large multipurpose market it developed unified programming and operating systems to serve a very broad spectrum of computers and applications. This has led to very large software systems, unnecessarily inefficient, often clumsy and obscure.

Initially, the large economies of scale in hardware construction and in software made it very difficult for others to compete with IBM. The more recent developments in software, minicomputers, and peripheral devices can often be undertaken by companies not possessing large capital funds. IBM prices have in general been high enough to serve as an "umbrella," allowing other companies to market new products profitably. But competitors have had limited success and it is certain that IBM will continue to have a major, if not dominant, influence on the computer industry within the foreseeable future. (See Section 10.1 for further discussion.)

The position with respect to computer use and its rate of growth can be summarized as follows:

[18] OECD (1969, p. 39). The market share of IBM World Trade in countries outside the United States has varied through a wider range, but it has likewise been very high, consistent with the large fraction of computer sales made by United States companies (AFIPS, 1970).

1. For the past 20 years computer use in the United States and throughout the world has increased at a rate which is unprecedented when compared with other new developments, as witnessed by the doubling of the number of installations about every four years.

2. The growth of computers is even more significant when allowance is made for the increased speed and capacity of more recent machines, the greater accessibility through new modes of use, and the diversification of services.

3. Outside the United States, use in the industrialized countries is less but it is following the pattern of the United States in growth; in developing countries computer use is just beginning.

4. Detailed study of the changes in cost and quality of machines and services suggests that the current trends will continue for some years. Projections on the rate of increase of installations indicate that the number of computers will continue to increase rapidly; eventually there must be a leveling off, which is beginning to be apparent in the United States at least.

5. United States manufacturers have had a dominant share of the world markets for computers, and among them IBM has had by far the largest fraction. Recently, other companies both within the United States and outside are becoming more important, especially as new components of the computer industry, based on the production of software, minicomputers, communication devices, and peripheral devices, assume greater importance.

For these reasons it is safe to predict that the issues centering on the use of computers, as outlined in Chapter 1 and discussed in the rest of this book, are not temporary. Countries not experiencing them now will find themselves grappling with them before long.

Bibliography

AFIPS (1971). "World Markets for Electronic Data Processing Equipment." Amer. Fed. of Information Processing Soc. Montvale, New Jersey.

Gruenberger, F., ed. (1968). "Computers and Communications—Toward a Computer Utility." Prentice-Hall, Englewood Cliffs, New Jersey.

Harman, A. J. (1971). "The International Computer Industry: Innovation and Computer Advantage." Harvard Univ. Press, Cambridge, Massachusetts.

OECD (1969). "Gaps in Technology: Electronic Computers." Org. for Economic Cooperation and Develop., Paris.

OECD (1970). "Computer Utilization in Member Countries." Examination of surveys carried out in member countries on computer systems and personnel as of October 1969, Directorate for Scientific Affairs, Org. for Economic Cooperation and Develop., Paris.

Pearson, L. B. (1969). "Partners in Development," Rep. of the Commission on Internat. Develop. Praeger, New York.
Sharpe, W. F. (1969). "The Economics of Computers." Columbia Univ. Press, New York.
United Nations (1971). "The Application of Computer Technology for Development." Dept. of Economic and Social Affairs E/4800, New York.
United Nations (1973). "Report Prepared in Response to General Assembly Resolution 2804 (XXVI)." E/6.8/11, New York.

Problems and Further Work

1. Besides GNP many other statistics have been proposed as indicators of economic wealth or standard of living, for example, power consumption per capita, education level, infant mortality rate, and so on. Suggest others which one might expect to be correlated with computer usage. Look these up for some countries and see how they compare with the number of computers.

2. Look up the statistics on the rate of installation of telephones in the United States. How does the growth curve compare with that for computers? What factors are there which justify an analogy to be drawn, or which would make an analogy inappropriate?

3. Suggest a unit which might be used to describe the physical size of a computer or of a computer circuit. Look up data which will enable you to plot how physical size has been reduced in successive computers. Is the curve logarithmic?

4. Look up the ogive curve and explain why it is a form which is often used to describe a growth process. To what extent is it applicable to growth of the number of computers?

5. Show by plotting how Memory capacity/Add time has changed with time as computers have developed. It there any discontinuity in the curve where successive generations have appeared? See

M. J. Cetron, "Technological Forecasting—A Practical Approach," p. 153. Gordon and Breach, New York, 1969.

6. Choosing some suitable measure of computer power show how the successive computer models marketed by IBM have changed. Do the same for CDC computers. Obtain pricing data and show how cost per computation has decreased. How does the curve compare with Fig. 2-2? For pricing data, see, for example,

Comput. Characteristics Rev. (three issues per year). GML Corp., Lexington, Massachusetts.

7. Suggest how estimates might be obtained of (1) the number of people using computers, (2) the number of people employed in the computer industry, and (3) the number of people being trained to work with computers. (See footnote 14.)

Chapter

3

COMPUTER USE: WHERE AND WHY

The goal in this chapter is to understand the driving forces which have led to the rapid and widespread adoption of computers. Besides offering direct savings through lower production costs and better deployment of resources, computers make possible better methods of scheduling, planning, and control. All of these can be translated into dollar benefits so that such assessments of computers are essentially based on technical and economic criteria. There are other considerations, not strictly economic, which may enter into a decision as to whether computers can or should be used. It may be, for example, that only by using computers will it be possible to implement administrative procedures consistent with approved policies. Notwithstanding the benefits derived from computers there are factors which limit their use. Some of these are examined here, but those involving controversies about the advantages and judgments about values other than economic are postponed to later chapters.

3.1. Areas of Use

To explore the consequences of the increased use of computers we must know more about *why* they are used. This will help reveal the forces that give rise to change and provide some indication about which sectors of the economy and of society are likely to change next. Before looking at reasons it is helpful to list briefly the major areas of use.

It is usual to classify computer usage into a number of categories, for example, data processing and administration, management, scientific applications, education, and process control, to which might be added a miscellaneous category of library studies, artistic creations, entertainment, and so on. Since computers are general-purpose devices, in most installations they are used for a variety of applications. In any actual site, it is usually only possible to identify the company or institution using the computer rather than the use itself, and the computer will be applied to different tasks at different times. But computer jobs which originate in the categories listed above do differ enough in their characteristics to justify the groupings.

Although the first uses of computing were largely for military and scientific computations, the major use today is for data processing and administration. This usage is characterized by large volumes of input and output and relatively simple computations. Data processing entails, among other things, creating, updating, and deleting records, recording transactions, sorting, and printing statements (Bohl, 1971). These processes arise in the normal operation of business, institutions, and government. This is the function of computers with which we are most familiar: the generation of payroll checks and accounting statements, the processing of bank records, inventory maintenance, and the printing of mailing lists. In the industrialized countries a very large fraction of clerical work has been computerized. Sixty to eighty percent of all computer use is standard data processing according to any reasonable measure (hours, dollars, volume, number of installations, etc.).[1]

[1] Most computer censuses list the principal responsibility of the company or institution where the computer is installed (see, for example, Table 2-1), and this is one way of estimating the distribution of use. The distribution can also be obtained directly from questionnaires. In a survey carried out in 1964 in the United Kingdom (Manpower Ser. No. 4. "Computers in Offices." H. M. Stationery Office) it was estimated that 21% of the computer time was used for payroll, 18% for management accounting, 21% for financial accounting, and 12.5% for billing, making a total of 72.5%.

Of the national surveys on the growth of computerization, those undertaken by the Japan Computer Usage Development Institute are the most detailed and comprehensive. (See Japan Computer Usage Development Inst. "Computer White

During the 1960s data processing by computers became routine and in the latter part of the decade attention focused on the use of computers for management purposes. In spite of continued publicity and emphasis on management information systems, the extent and success of this computer application have been limited. There has been success with the preparation of summaries, statistics, and economic indexes, with timetables and production schedules, and with simple extrapolated projections. More generally, one envisions the techniques of operations research, modeling, and simulation used in conjunction with imaginative data displays to aid in planning and decision-making. Thus far, computers have been able to provide information to management in a more complete manner, but the decision-making process itself has not been replaced or revolutionized. Management information systems are being adopted gradually and with warranted caution, but the potentialities of using computers for planning remain one of their greatest attractions.

Scientific calculations continue to be one of the most successful areas of computer application. Here complex computations replace or shorten costly experiments in nuclear physics, meteorology, quantum chemistry, space exploration, and so on. Scientific calculations are characterized by the need for very fast and very large machines, so-called number crunchers; in addition, sophisticated interfaces (analog–digital converters, plotters, etc.) are often required for recording and transforming experimental data. At the other end of the computer scale, minicomputers are being used increasingly with data logging devices such as those for monitoring air and water pollution in environmental studies. Although computers are vital to scientific applications, such applications account for only about 5% of usage.

There are many disciplines, professions, and technologies where computers have become of central importance. In some, as in education at the university level, computers are completely accepted into the mainstream activity; in others, for example, in library or information science, an important beginning has been made and it is clear that computers will play an increasingly large and eventually dominant role. As further examples, we may cite printing and typesetting, telephone switching, tool production by numerically controlled machines, automated process control, medical monitoring and diagnosis, and legal research. It is the diversity and number of such new applications that account for the

---

Paper." Tokyo, 1969, 1970, 1971 ed.) In these there is much detailed information on the extent to which different Japanese industries use computers, and which applications are most common.

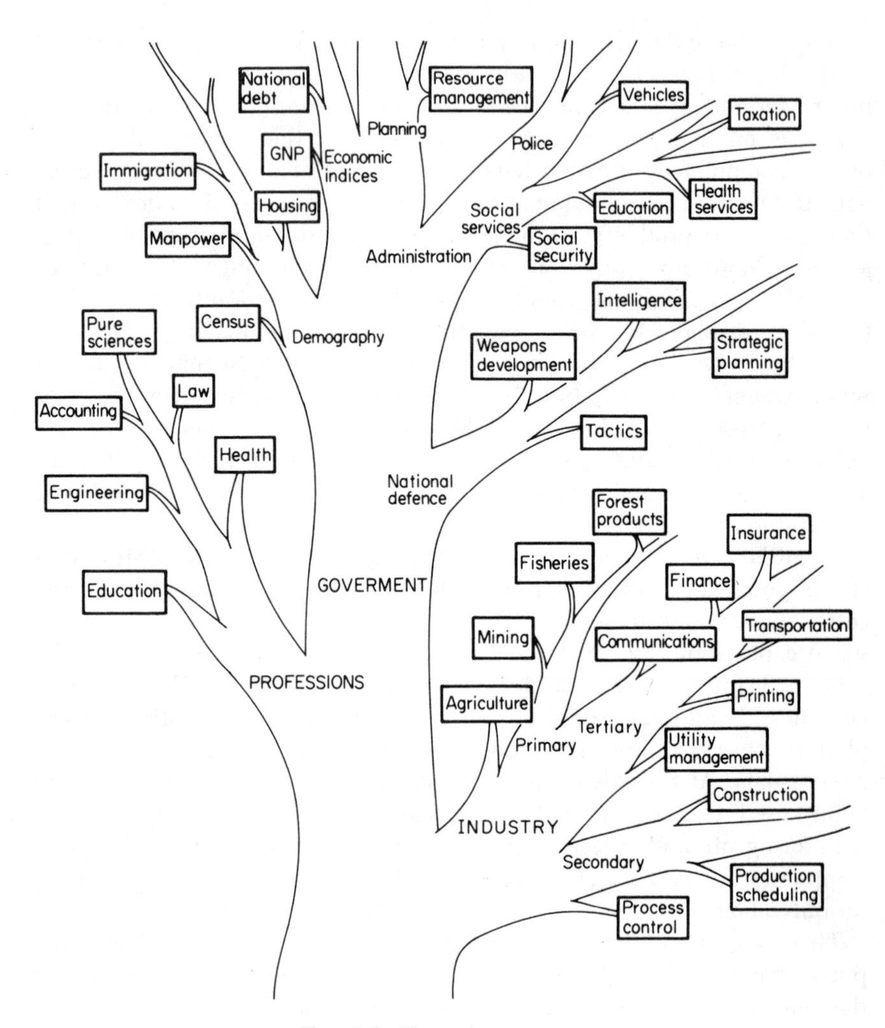

FIG. 3-1. *Uses of computers.*

continuing exponential growth observed in Chapter 2. Each specific technology usually requires its own special-purpose input devices, programs, and display systems, and sometimes (for example, in telephone switching) its own special-purpose computing machines.[2]

In the categories of use outlined above the emphasis has been on how computers are used in the private sector, where most computers are to

[2] See Fenichel and Weizenbaum (1971) for a collection of articles which illustrate the scope and range of computer applications in technology, science, education, and the arts.

be found. However, almost without exception, governments are the single largest users of computers, and in the public sector emphasis is on applications for social and economic development. Particularly important are government applications to census and demography, taxation, social insurance, public health, economic planning, and resource management.[3] Figure 3-1 illustrates the special importance of computer use in the public sector. In the developing countries these applications are of fundamental importance, and more computers which are devoted to these are likely to be found in the public sector than in private industry.

3.2. Motivating Forces

The first computers were constructed because they posed intellectual and engineering challenges, and because their usefulness for mathematical and scientific calculations was evident. Military applications spurred many of the subsequent developments. Faster and larger machines were designed because they were wanted first for ballistic calculations, then for calculations relating to atomic weapons, and later for the space program. In the United States especially, machines built for these purposes on behalf of the armed services, the Atomic Energy Commission, and the space agencies served as prototypes from which commercial versions were marketed. Important as these factors have been in the history of computers, to account for the enormous growth of the computing industry it is necessary to understand the economic and other benefits computers offer in business and administration.

One of the clearest lessons of the last decade is that economic growth per se is no longer a sufficient national objective, and by extension, economic advantage is no longer in itself sufficient justification for change. This viewpoint is expressed in everyday newspaper articles on the effects of industry on the ecology, in national reviews of economic performance, and in international reports on the relations between economic growth, science, and technology. (See OECD, 1971b; UNESCO, 1970.) Yet these same reports remind us "that measurable real gross

[3] A bibliography on the uses of computers in government is given in "The Computer in the Public Service." Public Administration Service, Chicago, Illinois, 1970. For computer use in the U. S. federal government, see "Inventory of Automatic Data Processing Equipment in the United States Government." U. S. Gov. Printing Office, Washington, D. C., 1969. Detailed enumerations of the uses in state and municipal governments are given in "Automated Data Processing in State Government" and "Automated Data Processing in Municipal Government," Public Administration Service, Chicago, Illinois 1965 and 1966.

national product per person is probably the dominant criterion of enhanced well-being for most nations".[4] Required are measures that promote physical well-being and not merely economic well-being. These must meet collective needs (clean air and water, aesthetically satisfying urban surroundings, the amenities of nature), needs formerly regarded as goods or services to be sold but now considered necessary for social justice (health care, universal education, public housing, social welfare services), *and* individual economic needs. But if individual needs are not sufficient in themselves, they cannot be dissociated from collective needs and the requirements for social justice. We will examine in later chapters the problems of reconciling these needs, but for now we can agree that there is a continuing case for economic growth and for technological improvements which increase the efficiency of production and rendering service.

The computer is an invention which has a *multiplier effect* on growth,[5] that is, one which induces a chain of effects in other industrial sectors. Thus at the national level, as well as at the level of the individual enterprise and institution, there is strong economic motivation for installing computers. This motivation comes out in the replies to questionnaires, from which some of the best evidence about the reasons for acquiring computers is to be obtained.[6] Direct cost savings, however, are not the only reasons cited. In approximate order of importance they are given as follows.

1. to reduce the costs of production and services
2. to carry out data processing within set schedules and with acceptable dependability
3. to carry out large calculations which would otherwise not be possible
4. to make more efficient use of resources
5. to provide compatibility between different components of a system
6. to facilitate planning and orderly growth.

In addition, although it is not always admitted openly, considerations of competition and prestige and the influence of persistent salesmen alter the decision in many cases. Tables 3-1 and 3-2 show the results of a survey on the advantages computers have to offer, as expressed by

[4] J. B. Quinn, Scientific and technical strategy at the national and major enterprise level, *in* "The Role of Science and Technology in Economic Development" (UNESCO, 1970, pp. 83–102).

[5] J. B. Quinn, (UNESCO, 1970, p. 85).

[6] See Section 6.1 for a discussion on surveys and questionnaires.

TABLE 3-1
DIRECT EFFECTS OF COMPUTER USAGE[a]

Effect \ Item	Number of firms	Percent replying	Yield of replies[b] (%)	1969 (%)
Reduction in inventory	132	6.1	12.0	12.6
Reduction of delivery period	101	4.7	9.2	9.4
Efficient use of funds	83	3.9	7.6	Not surveyed
Better customer service	257	12.0	23.4	Not surveyed
Reduction in personnel expenses	515	24.0	46.9	62.3
Reduction in nonpersonnel expenses	123	5.7	11.2	19.6
Accuracy and speed in processing business	740	34.4	67.5	83.0
Simplification of file management	162	7.5	14.8	30.4
Other	37	1.7	3.4	2.1
Total number of firms	2150	100		

TABLE 3-2
INDIRECT EFFECTS OF COMPUTER USAGE[a]

Effect \ Item	Number of firms	Percent replying	Yield of replies[b] (%)	1969 (%)
Improved company image	339	19.8	30.9	34.0
Greater accuracy and speed in judgment and decision making	262	15.3	23.9	38.2
More accurate measurement of work efficiency	162	9.5	14.8	13.1
Easier to grasp business situation	390	22.8	35.6	23.8
General increase in morale	190	11.3	17.7	17.0
Prevention of unfair acts	58	3.4	5.3	6.8
Better information flow in firm	280	16.4	25.5	43.2
Other	26	1.5	2.4	3.4
Total number of firms	1707	100		

[a] Source: Japan Computer Usage Development Institute, "Computer White Paper." Tokyo, 1971.

[b] The "yield of replies," is the percent who indicated the specified effect as a result of computerization. Since some firms gave two or more replies, the total yield comes to over 100%. The number and percent replying represent the data when normalized for multiple replies.

Japanese businessmen.[7] Increases in speed, accuracy, and reduction of labor costs are grouped closely together as being most important. The survey also shows the concern for less quantitative issues such as prestige.

[7] "Computer white paper," 1971 ed., see footnote 1.

The extent to which the advantages will be realized depends on many factors, including readiness by management and operational staff to look at new ways of doing things, the presence of trained and experienced people, the availability of good data, and so on. When the prerequisites are met, computers can yield better statistics, better information in the form of more timely and reliable data, better decisions, and lower costs. These in turn can lead to better qualities of products and new and better services.

Although the term "cost/benefit analysis" is commonly used in conjunction with the installation of computers, it is surprisingly difficult to obtain case studies with exact data on such analysis. Computer costs are relatively easy to measure, but it is much more difficult to place quantitative evaluations on the benefits in speed, accuracy, and other factors related to users' satisfaction. Figures on cost–effectiveness such as those in Fig. 2-2 and those given by Sharpe[8] are based on rather narrow definitions of effectiveness (for example, a weighted average of the time for a number of arithmetic operations).

It is not difficult to show that in many data processing applications, especially within government, the volume of transactions is such that they could not be processed by any reasonably sized clerical staff without computers. For purposes of social security payments, Denmark has maintained a Central Register of Persons since 1968. From a population of approximately five million people, about 100,000 entries are generated every week for input into the system. Without computers even in this relatively small country some different form of the social security system would have to be adopted, one not based directly on earnings. In the United States the social security system covers 193 million people. The basic earnings file is held on 1600 reels of magnetic tape and some 330 million transactions are entered each year. It is estimated that there are seven million people in the United States for whom the monthly social security payment is necessary to meet the immediate costs of food and shelter, and for whom failure in delivery of a check would be tragic.[9] In such cases, the accuracy and reliability of computers are paramount. Furthermore, in these cases of straightforward data processing, with which the majority of computer installations are occupied, it is often possible to document the savings in costs due to the use of computers. These savings are mainly from savings in labor, resulting in perhaps the most sensitive issue of computer use.

In some cases, it is possible to show savings because computers con-

[8] W. F. Sharpe, "Economics of Computers," Chapter 9. Columbia Univ. Press, New York, 1969.

[9] Security in numbers. *Data Processor* **10** (2), 3–7 (1967).

serve costly resources other than labor. This is particularly true in the process industries where, for example, computers have long been used for scheduling refinery operations. Here the improved performance has been well demonstrated.[10] Similar situations arise in the production scheduling of assembly lines, as in the auto industry. Computers also produce savings and contribute to economic stability by making it possible to maintain smaller, balanced inventories, and in the case of airline seats, by ensuring that a volatile inventory is not wasted.

Another major benefit is the compatibility that can be brought about in the different divisions of a company or in related operations. Advantages such as compatibility or the availability of better statistics which facilitate planning for changes and growth are again extremely difficult to evaluate. One of the most important but intangible aspects of computers is that in the course of their introduction for some tasks, they require a total reassessment of the way the task should be done. Often, they even bring about a reevaluation of why the task is being done.

When we look at computers in government rather than in private enterprise, the order in the list of reasons for acquiring them, given on page 30 has to be revised. The last reason, "to facilitate planning and orderly growth," should undoubtedly rank much higher. As indicated at the beginning of this section, the driving force leading all governments toward more planning and policy-making is the desire for greater social and economic benefits. Almost every recommendation resulting from national and international studies has planning implications. Thus in the OECD (1971b) report we have:[11]

> Governments of Member States should channel their technological policies into areas capable of producing alternative, socially oriented technologies, i.e., technologies capable of directly contributing to the solution of present infrastructural problems, of satisfying so far neglected collective needs, and finally of replacing existing environmentally deleterious technologies.

Planning in turn imposes requirements for data gathering and information processing which have direct bearings on the need for more computers. In "The Role of Science and Technology in Economic Development" (UNESCO, 1970) we have (part of) Recommendation 5 to developing countries:[12]

> In all countries emphasis should be laid on the need to perfect methods of collecting reliable data which can be used for the specific purpose of

[10] A. R. Dooley and T. M. Stout, Rise of the blue-collar computer, *Harvard Business Rev.* **49** (4), 85–95 (1971).

[11] OECD (1971b, p. 99).

[12] UNESCO (1970, p. 15).

assessing in an increasingly objective manner (a) the national and scientific technological potential and (b) the impact of research and development on the economy . . . .

Further, in "Information for a Changing Society," an OECD (1971a) report which examines the policy consideration for acquiring and using information, Recommendation 8 states (in part):[13]

> We recommend that government authorities reexamine their needs for professionally specialized information for management decisions, in order to ensure that they are aware of the possibilities inherent in new information technology, and at the same time sensitive to the difficulty of ensuring coverage, internal consistency, credibility, and utility of the information received . . . .

Consistent with these exhortations, governments at every level seek to use computers in planning, and as part of this process they set about systematically to gather and process large amounts of information. To give an example, consider an urban authority responsible for a waterfront development. It will need information about land use and values, transportation, population densities, recreational facilities, commercial possibilities, and so on. To avoid duplication, to organize the data collection, prepare reports, and apply modern statistical techniques upon which it can base conclusions, it will want to have a computer available and consolidate the information it gathers into a data bank. This need for data in planning is not, of course, confined to government. Private enterprise collects data for product and market research; social scientists require very large amounts of data, much of it of the type collected by governments, for their research. In the next chapter we examine in greater detail the types of files and data banks assembled by governments, social scientists, and private companies, and in later chapters we shall return to the issues surrounding planning. But for now we may note that one of the strongest motives for installing computers is to further the acquisition, organization, and processing of data for research and planning on the part of government, social scientists, and private enterprises. In fact it is impossible to see how the large-scale planning which is today necessary for effective use of human and other resources can be undertaken without computers. Therefore the increased use of computers envisaged in Chapter 2 is not simply a projection of a historical trend, it is based on computers being needed to do work which must be done.

[13] OECD (1971a, p. 45).

3.3. Limiting Factors

There are factors which inhibit the installation of computers and limit the effectiveness of those already installed.

One factor which is becoming less and less prohibitive is the cost for purchase or rental of equipment. Time-sharing, service bureaus, and minicomputers allow computing to be carried out in an almost continuous range of costs. The price of some minicomputers is under $10,000 and it is possible to do useful computing on a time-sharing terminal for $100 per month. On the other hand, data transmission rates remain relatively high, limiting the dissemination of time-sharing services.

Until recently, process control computers have been relatively expensive, costing in the range of half a million dollars. The benefits of process control computers have long been established, but the dollar savings they offer may represent only a small percentage improvement in an already well-organized process; initially, only large industries were able to benefit from them. But now minicomputers are being incorporated into the production process of such industries as mining and paper manufacturing.

In industrially advanced countries, unlike the situation in the developing countries, earlier shortages of trained personnel are disappearing in many levels of computer-related employment. However, qualified systems analysts and, to a lesser degree, programmers and operators continue to be needed even when other technical openings are scarce.[14] It should be noted that in commercial installations, the budget for personnel and supplies is often significantly greater than that for hardware.[15]

As mentioned, certain prerequisites must be met before computers should be installed and before they can be used effectively. In addition to the education and training of staff, good planning is required to define goals. Many applications need reliable data, which must be first collected, verified, and prepared in a suitable form, often by converting files which were previously maintained manually. Finally, site preparation and testing of specially prepared computer programs have to be carried out before a computer arrives. These activities require a long

[14] "Employment Outlook—Programmers, Systems Analysts, Electronic Computer Operating Personnel." Bur. of Labor Statistics, Dept. of Labor, Bull. 1650-41, 1970–1971 Edition.

[15] This is generally true in the United States and Canada, but does not hold in Europe where salaries are lower.

lead time, and an installation will only be partially effective (or even counterproductive) without sufficient planning.

Besides the economic and management considerations just outlined there are other reservations which may be inhibiting factors. While it is difficult to assess to what extent these restrict use, the concerns are real and widespread, and at least one is proving to have some force. This is the belief that altogether too much information is being collected by governments, by social scientists, by almost everyone, that much of the data is redundant and unnecessary, and that the result is a serious infringement on personal rights and liberties. Westin gives voice to it in drawing attention to the "quantitative persuasion, the belief that collecting large amounts of personal and individual data and subjecting it to quantitative analysis is necessary to learn why people or groups behaved a certain way in the past, and to enable analysts of such data to construct reliable predictions of how people will behave in the future."[16] The objection centers mainly but not wholly on the collection of personal data, and the issue will be examined in detail in Chapter 5.

Beyond the issue of privacy other concerns about computers are the fear that they will cause widespread unemployment; the fear that man is being rendered obsolete by an intelligent, infallible device; the fear that computers are depersonalizing our society, and the fear that computers are propelling us toward a society run by technocrats. We discuss these at length in later chapters.

3.4. Computers in Developing Countries

All the previously mentioned uses of computers are of potential importance to developing countries. The arguments about science, technology, and computers hold for them as well but as is constantly being pointed out, it is necessary to take special factors into consideration. In Chapter 2 reference was made to the United Nations report "The Application of Computer Technology for Development" (1971). In that report four general levels of computing activity are described (see Table 3-3); all but a very few of the developing countries are in the first or second of these levels, that is "initial" or "basic."

Behind the resolution of the United Nations General Assembly and the recommendations of the report lies the implication that some computer activity is appropriate for the lesser developed countries, and that

[16] A. F. Westin, Information systems and political decision-making. "The Computer Impact" (I. Taviss, ed.), pp. 130–144. Prentice-Hall, Englewood Cliffs, New Jersey, 1970.

TABLE 3-3
LEVELS OF COMPUTER DEVELOPMENT[a]

Level	Characteristics
Initial	There are no operational computers in the country. A few nationals have had contact with computing. The only local sources of information are computer salesmen
Basic	There is some understanding of computers in government (and private) decision centers. A few computer installations are to be found. There are some nationals involved in computer operations. There is some education and training in computer technology in the country. Computers are used in basic government operations
Operational	There is extensive understanding of computers in government (and private) decision centers. Among the numerous computer installations there are some very large machines. There are centers for education and training in computer technology and some are of excellent quality. They offer degree programs in computer or information science. There is design and production of software and some manufacture of hardware. Computers are affecting many disciplines, particularly science, engineering, and medicine
Advanced	Most government and administrative work is carried out by computers. There are well-established professional activities and national meetings on computers. There is a complete range of quality education and training programs. The number of computers, of all sizes, is increasing rapidly. Time-sharing, teleprocessing, and remote job entry are common. There is design and production of both hardware and software. Many technologies have been changed or are in the course of being changed. New applications of computers are found regularly. There is strong participation in and contribution to international activities

[a] From United Nations, "The Application of Computer Technology for Development." Dept. of Economic and Social Affairs, E/4800, 1971.

they should be actively seeking how they can make use of computers. This is a matter of importance. Sometimes officials in the developed countries are inclined to regard computers as technologically advanced, prestige devices to which the developing countries should give low priority so that they can concentrate on more urgent needs. But this viewpoint is definitely rejected, if not resented, by planners, officials, and educators from the developing countries. They regard computers as stepping stones to social and economic development, necessary for national planning, industry, and resource management. They show this in many ways—through their determination to acquire computers, through their responses to surveys and questionnaires, through their continuing interest in educational programs, and through their participation in computer meetings and conferences.

Given this outlook, it is clear why planners and managers in developing countries must be capable of making decisions about the acquisition of computers on the basis of their own knowledge of needs and not on the arguments of computer salesmen. Beyond this there is the need to ensure that national priorities are considered when initial computer applications are selected, and that each application is supported by the physical and personnel resources necessary to make it successful. There are certain kinds of development and applications which might best be postponed in many cases. Applications which have had mixed success in "computer-advanced" nations, such as information retrieval and computer-assisted instruction, should probably be postponed in favor of more specific data processing needs. Time-sharing would seem to offer substantial advantages to countries in the initial and basic stages, but unless communications are reliable and inexpensive this mode of use had better be deferred. In a description of the experience of a management consultant in developing countries, Kamman emphasizes the fact that there is no "model" or "average" developing country nor is there any "average" computer application.[17] Each potential application must be analyzed separately by a detailed process of which the key component is a feasibility planning study. A separate statement is needed for four different aspects of feasibility: technical, economic, acceptability to users, and legal acceptability. Further, the study team must include computer experts, management, and user members from the developing country.

In countries such as India and Brazil where there are large populations and skilled technical and scientific infrastructures, questions about embarking on the production of computer hardware and software arise. The difficulties which even developed countries have experienced in this regard suggest caution, but a three-tiered strategy which has been proposed for India may be feasible. For minicomputers, requiring as they do relatively modest resources, an indigenously based industry is suggested; for medium-sized computers it is recommended that collaboration with foreign firms be worked out so as to promote a future transfer of technology to local manufacturers; for large computers a strategy to minimize the drain on foreign currence should be adopted. For most developing countries, however, these possibilities of computer design and manufacture are not open, and they must concentrate on computer applications.

Finally, all the reservations about the use of computers can be serious issues at any level of development. Some issues will be of lesser im-

[17] A. B. Kamman, Development of computer applications in emerging nations. *AFIPS Conf. Proc.* 39, 17–26 (1971).

portance initially (for example, privacy is not an issue in India), while others will be much more chronic in the developing nations. The most important issue will undoubtedly be the human and social costs of unemployment. In this regard, the experience of highly industrialized nations is simply not applicable in view of the substantial differences in the nature of the economy and the labor force.

In conclusion, the difficulties economically poor countries have in trying to apply computers to their industrial and social development provide another illustration of how the gap between the industrially advanced countries and those which are still developing is widening. Conferences, studies, and reports on how to narrow the gap with respect to computers have had only limited success so far.[18]

Bibliography

Bohl, M. (1971). "Information Processing." Science Res. Assoc., Palo Alto, California.

Fenichel, R. R., and Weizenbaum, J., eds. (1971). "Computers and Computation." Freeman, San Francisco, California.

Gould, I. H., ed. (1971). "IFIP Guide to Concepts and Terms in Data Processing." North-Holland Publ., Amsterdam.

OECD (1971a). "Information for a Changing Society." Org. for Economic Cooperation and Develop., Paris.

OECD (1971b). "Science, Growth and Society." Org. for Economic Cooperation and Develop., Paris.

UNESCO (1970). "The Role of Science and Technology in Economic Development," Science policy studies and documents, No. 18. Paris.

United Nations (1971). "The Application of Computer Technology for Development." Dept. of Economic and Social Affairs, E/4800, New York.

Problems and Further Work

1. For the university or business computing installation with which you are most familiar, try to assess the proportionate use of the system with respect to the groupings indicated in Section 3.1.

2. Survey the use of computers as applied to a specific field (e.g., medicine, library science, law). For ongoing surveys see

R. W. Stacy and B. Waxman, eds., "Computers in Biomedical Research," vols. I–III. Academic Press, New York, 1965–1969; "Advances in In-

[18] For example, *Proc. Jerusalem Conf. Informat. Technol.*, Iltam Corp. for Planning and Res., Jerusalem, 1971; *Proc. Rio Symp. Comput. Educ. Develop. Countries, Rio de Janeiro* (C. Bussel, ed.), Ao Livro Tecnico, Guanabara, Brazil, 1972.

formation Systems," vols. I–III. Plenum Press, New York, 1969–1970; also R. P. Bigelow, ed., "Computers and the Law," 2nd ed. Commerce Clearing House, Chicago Illinois, 1969.

3. List in order of importance, insofar as you can see them, the advantages of using computers in (a) the insurance business and (b) university administration. How does your ranking compare with what can be inferred from published descriptions of such installations? See for example,

C. C. Gotlieb and J. N. P. Hume, "High Speed Data Processing," Chapter 11. McGraw-Hill, New York, 1958; R. W. Gerard (ed.), "Computers and Education." McGraw-Hill, New York, 1967.

4. The installation of a computer is often preceded by a feasibility study in which an analysis is made of the costs and benefits which might accrue as a result of the installation. List the factors which should be considered in a feasibility study. Systems study and an implementation stage follow the feasibility study. What considerations should enter into these? See

J. Kanter, "Management Guide to Computer System Selection and Use." Prentice-Hall, Englewood Cliffs, New Jersey, 1970.

5. List four instances where records or documents you possess have been produced by computers. What are the advantages (and disadvantages) to the agency or institution providing these records in having them prepared by computers? What advantages and disadvantages do you perceive for yourself?

Chapter

4

FILES, DATA BANKS, AND INFORMATION SYSTEMS

At the heart of conventional data processing lie files stored in manila folders or 3 × 5 cards; at the heart of computerized data processing applications lie machine-readable files stored on punched cards, magnetic disks, or in other forms. So many of both the benefits and problems associated with computers stem from files that it is necessary to understand them in some detail in order to judge the issues. In this chapter we examine the characteristics of the files used in routine billing, record-keeping, integrated files, and management information systems. At first the emphasis is on physical and technical features; later, and also in the next chapter, aspects related to personal information systems are examined along with resulting implications for confidentiality and privacy.

4.1. System Requirements

The components of a file are its *records* (the set of data items associated with each thing or individual to which the file pertains), the *fields* (the numbers and words which describe one item in the record), and the *keys* (those fields which identify records). The number of components and the ways in which they are interrelated are determined by the requirements of the system for which the file is maintained.

Storage

From many points of view a data processor can be regarded as a system for updating and maintaining a collection of files, and the problem of making a system efficient is equivalent to matching the very high speed central processor unit (c.p.u.) to the relatively slow speed for file access. To aid in this matching, the physical devices on which files are stored are arranged hierarchically. The fastest, smallest (and most expensive, in cost per character) contains those parts of the programs and other files which are needed immediately by the c.p.u.; other levels of storage, larger and slower, store the files needed less urgently until a storage medium which is essentially external to the computer (e.g., punched cards or documents read by an optical scanner) is reached.

Table 4-1 shows representative sizes, access speeds, and cost for a number of storage devices. For almost two decades the main long-term storage device for large files has continued to be magnetic tape; during this time there have been significant improvements in tape densities, reading and writing speeds, and costs. Removable disk packs, attachable to multidisk storage devices, continue to be the most widely used file

TABLE 4-1
Approximate Performance Characteristics for File Storage Devices

Storage medium	Type	Access time	Data rate (bytes or characters/sec)	Module capacity (bytes)	Cost ($/byte)
High-speed magnetic core	Random read–write	0.5 μsec	10^7	10^5	0.01
Slow-speed magnetic core	Random read–write	10 μsec	10^6	10^6	0.003
Magnetic drum	Random read–write	10 μsec	10^6	5×10^6	0.01
Moving head[a] disk	Random or sequential read–write	35 μsec	5×10^5	2×10^7	5×10^{-5}
Magnetic tape[a]	Sequential read–write	10 sec	10^6	2×10^7	5×10^{-6}
Microfilm[a]	Random or sequential read	10 sec	5×10^5	10^9	10^{-7}

[a] The cost given is for the media (i.e., disk pack, tape, or film). There is an additional cost for the driving unit.

storage for on-line systems; they are, for the present, successfully holding their own against the various magnetic and photographic devices which appear from time to time as possible replacements.

In most files the record size lies between 100 and 1000 characters. A small file for a modest inventory system might consist of 10^3 to 10^5 records; a medium-sized file found in a passenger reservation system might have 10^4 to 10^6 records, and a large file such as would be needed for a widely accessed data bank or a document retrieval system might contain 10^5 to 10^7 records. Files once considered large are now medium sized, and the general rule that every three or four years the file size can be doubled without appreciably increasing the physical size of the store or the processing speed continues to hold.

Response Time

The required response time to changes is, next to the size, the most important characteristic of a file, and it is this which determines whether the file will be maintained by batch processing, by queuing, by an on-line system, or by means of a real-time computer (see Table 4-2). *Batch processing* corresponds to a cycling of the files at periods which may be as long as a year and which seldom are less than a few hours. In *queued processing* there is no batch of transactions to be processed against the file in any recognizable sense. Instead transactions are queued as they arrive, to be processed according to some scheduling algorithm (e.g., first-come–first-served, highest priority first, etc.). This is the normal, multiprogramming mode of operation for most large computers today, and the response time is usually measured in hours, sometimes in minutes. *On-line systems* are used to process transactions when there is a customer waiting for a reply, as happens in a reservation system of in on-line banking. This corresponds to the time-shared mode of operation. *Real-time processing* is used when computers are dedicated to special tasks

TABLE 4-2
Response Time for Processing Modes

Processing mode	Response time	Example
Batch (periodic)	>2 hr	Simple billing systems
Queued	1 min to 6 hr	Document retrieval system
On-line	0.5 to 5 sec	Reservation or banking system
Real-time	1 μsec to 0.1 sec	Telephone switching system, process control

where immediate response is needed for reasons of safety or to control some manufacturing process, such as a paper mill.

Permanence

Files may be regarded as *static* or *volatile* according to the permanence of the records. A customer account file for a department store is a permanent file, while a list of computer jobs currently being processed in a multiprogramming system is volatile. Closely related to the permanence of the files in a batch system is the transaction ratio, that is, the fraction of records which undergo change on a scan of the complete file. It is usual to keep two or three generations of back-up files so that the records can be reconstructed in case of an accident.

Reliability

The reliability imposed on the file processing by the system is another characteristic which greatly affects the type of processing, particularly with respect to duplication of processors, cost, and so on. A system which has to be fail-safe, such as a real-time air traffic control system, presents major problems which require special solutions. On the other hand, a system where a small percentage of errors is tolerable, such as a telephone switching network, can be designed according to probabilistic principles, thereby reducing expenses. Most computing systems lie between these cases; processing errors must be few or there are unacceptable costs in checking and loss of confidence. Some errors are inevitable even if only because they are always present in the source data.

Interfaces

The input and output interfaces of a file influence the system design. It matters, for example, who will be entering data into the file or making inquiries of it—system personnel, trained operators, or the general public. The number of terminals from which the system can be accessed, the average and maximum numbers of terminals which can be active at any time, the type and speed of the communication devices—all these are important. Further, the requirements and practices for protecting records impose operating conditions, which are discussed in Section 4.5.

4.2. Organization

Most important to the organization of a file is whether records will be processed (and therefore accessed) at random or whether there will be some systematic order in the processing so that batched or queued processing can be used. The expected number of accesses to find a random record in an unordered file of N records is $N/2$, and this is prohibitively high for any but the most trivial case. When the file is sequenced according to the identifying keys, the expected number of accesses is proportional to $\log_2 N$, and this is still too high to permit random accessing for large files. In heavily used files, records are continually being created and deleted, and the behavior of the file with respect to addition and deletion (i.e., the ability to reuse storage and the necessity to rearrange the file) is also important.

Sequential Access

For applications where the response time permits batch processing, the records can be accessed serially according to ascending or descending values of the key, in which case the file is said to be in *sequential access form.* The file can be stored on magnetic tape; Fig. 4-1 illustrates an employee file stored on tape in sequence according to the social insurance numbers of the employee.

Sequential file processing is efficient where the transaction ratio is high. Insertions and deletions are handled easily by creating a new record or failing to recopy the old one onto the new tape created during the file

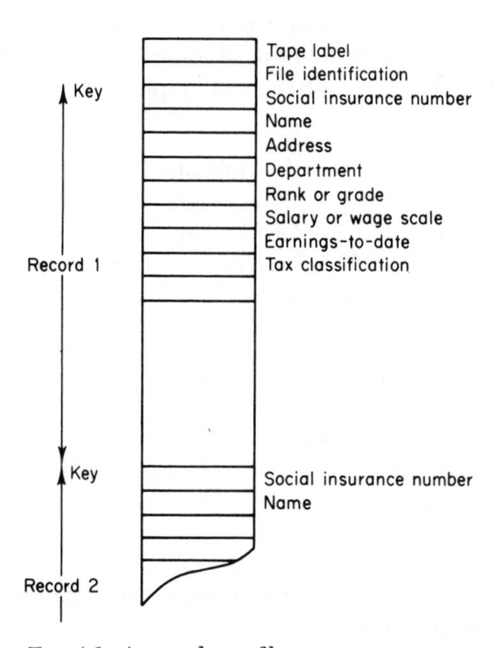

Fig. 4-1. *An employee file on magnetic tape.*

processing run. This is the simplest method of file organization and completely adequate in the many situations where a fast response time is not needed. Common examples are processing sales to produce monthly account statements, and processing an employee file to produce payroll checks.

Direct or Random Access

If the application is such that records must be processed in random order with a response time measured in seconds, then a file organization which allows records to be accessed directly will have to be used. The usual form is a random access disk maintained on-line to the central processor unit. In storing the records some method of associating the key with an address in storage is needed. Only occasionally will there be an obvious correspondence between keys and the address of the record in memory; that is, the key will determine a unique address with little or no calculation. This is because the address space, the number of locations reserved for record addresses, is essentially determined by the number of records in the file, whereas the key is usually some existing name or number and there are many more possible names than addresses in storage. The problem is to arrange the file so that the search time for a random record is short, and also to retain good characteristics with respect to addition and deletion of records. A variety of techniques are available to maintain the correspondence and facilitate searches. These include the use of directories, hash storage, inverted lists, linked lists, and special structures based on trees and graphs.[1]

4.3. Complexity

Different terms are used to describe files as the complexity grows—integrated files, data banks, information systems, information retrieval systems, information utilities, and so on. An *information system* is a set of files with the following properties.

1. There is a method for storing, retrieving, and updating information in the system.
2. There are different methods of searching the files.
3. There is a cross-referencing scheme which allows information about a subject to be extracted from different files.

[1] See R. Morris, Scatter storage techniques. *Comm. ACM* **11** (1), 38–44 (1968); also M. E. Senko, File organization and management information systems. *Annu. Rev. Informat. Sci. Technol.* 4, 111–143 (1969).

Where the information is intended for management purposes it may be called a *management information system;* when the files are machine-readable and computer-based we call the system a *data bank* or an *integrated file system.* The *data base* is the data in a data bank, as distinct from the storage and processing system. An *information utility* is an on-line data bank; it may be private or public.

Single Files

A single file such as that used to compute payrolls can require a system with many capabilities if it is to be processed smoothly. Among the complicating factors are the following.

1. The reliability requirements may be very severe; a failure to produce the checks on time can be highly damaging and will certainly undermine morale and confidence in the data processing system.
2. The records may not be uniform; there may be many fields which are absent or present in different situations. Thus employees might be categorized according to their method of payment—monthly, fortnightly, hourly, on a piecework basis, part time, and so on. For each of these the subsequent record might be different—for example, "overtime" may not be applicable to all employees.
3. The file may be highly dynamic—that is, large numbers of changes are being continuously generated for it. In addition to periodic changes such as tax or pension rates there are irregular changes in the number of dependents, in salary, address, charitable contributions deducted from the source, and so on.
4. Although the processing may be carried out as a batch run, the flexibility to make immediate corrections and changes may be needed. Thus a new employee or one going on vacation may need a check before the regular processing cycle. This flexibility is valuable in order to prevent the system from appearing impersonal and inhuman to the employees.
5. The security requirements may be high.

Even when factors such as those listed above are present, making it necessary to have long, detailed programs for processing, a file is conceptually simple as long as it is used mainly for a single purpose and as long as access to it is limited, as is the case with serial processing. The master file of the Social Security Administration of the United States consists of some 1600 reels containing the earnings record for almost 200 million people; the whole file is searched every day and updated quarterly.[2] We would regard this as a file rather than an integrated system or a data bank because of the single function and limited access.

Data Banks and Integrated File Systems

It follows from the previous definition that a data bank is a computerized information system based upon a set of files relating to common subjects, from which questions may be answered and a variety of tables may be printed or displayed. The system will have many users, and we shall use the term data bank to include both systems where users submit their work through on-line terminals and those which operate in the batch processing or queued processing mode. Accompanying the system there will be a set of programs for query, information retrieval, and output, written in a language understandable to prospective users without need of a programmer or librarian. The data bank can be expected to have a long life because of the high investment in accumulating data for it, and changes have to be introduced with caution and only after ample notice since any change will affect many users.

The Data Bank and Information System of the Bureau of Labor Statistics,[3] Washington, D. C., consists of a large number (over 30,000) of time series on statistics related to employment originating from the monthly current population surveys conducted by the Census Bureau. It contains data on individuals, such as employment status and duration, occupation, industry, sex, age, color, marital status, education, and household relationship. In addition, there are summary statistics gathered for local, state and federal regions. With the system, there is a problem-oriented computer language which allows a social scientist or statistician (as distinct from a computer programmer) to query the data, print out tables in a wide choice of formats, to carry out analytical and regression calculations, and to produce economic indicators on productivity, trends in employment, and so forth. Since the system was established in 1964, it has been a research and planning tool of proven value for it contains data which are real, reliable, and accessible.

The Bureau of Labor Statistics data bank is in effect a library or archival system for specialized quantitative information. The data bank built up for the Bay Area Transportation System (BATS) and that for the Wisconsin Assets and Income Studies Archive (WAIS) are other

[2] U. S. Department of Health, Education and Welfare For the Employer: Reporting Social Security Earnings Data on Magnetic Tape, Social Security Administration, Baltimore, Maryland (1968).

[3] R. C. Mendelsohn, The systems for integrated storage, retrieval and reduction of economic data of the Bureau of Labor statistics, *Social Sci. Informat.* 6 (4) (1967).

examples of this type of system.[4] Social scientists, recognizing that achival data banks complement conventional libraries and enormously extend the research possibilities in their disciplines, have urged that more be established, and have set about to make the information from those which exist more generally available.[5] In spite of the agreement about the need and value of these, they are being assembled only slowly because of the expense in gathering and validating data, the absence of standardized formats, the frequent changes in computer systems, the problems in arriving at a pricing system for the services, and the general tendency of researchers to depend on their own sources, neither making use of nor providing data for other workers. These difficulties notwithstanding, archival data banks for social science research are growing steadily in number and importance.

But the main thrust toward data banks comes from governments wishing to carry out their operational and planning functions. The Bureau of Labor Statistics data bank contains statistical or aggregated information. In many of the information systems assembled by governments it is necessary to identify the individual or subject whose data is recorded, and this leads to the necessity of maintaining confidentiality, a problem which is examined in later sections of this chapter and in Chapter 5.

In looking at data banks in public administration it is also possible to classify them as specialized or multipurpose. A specialized system contains data primarily relating to one type of application; a multipurpose data bank is used in different ways, and because it is open to many persons or agencies the security problems for it are more severe. Westin classifies data banks used by an executive branch of government into five types, depending on whether they are statistical (type 1), used by many agencies (type 2), used for general administration (type 3), used by a single agency (type 4), or used both by public and private groups (type 5).[6] Thomas (1971) discusses the problems posed by computerized data banks in public administration in some depth; they are in large

[4] See R. J. Miller and N. J. Roberts; R. A. Baumann *et al.*, Working with Complex Data Files, *in* "Data Bases, Computers, and the Social Sciences" (R. L. Bisco, ed.), Chapters 6 and 7. Wiley (Interscience), New York, 1970.

[5] Many of the efforts are centered at universities, for example, the Inter-University Consortium for Political Research at the University of Michigan, the Data and Program Library Science of the Social Systems Research Institute at the University of Wisconsin, the Roper Public Opinion Research Library at Williams College (Williamstown, Mass.), and the Social Science Research Council Data Bank at the University of Essex, England.

[6] A. F. Westin, "Information Technology in a Democracy." Introduction, pp. 15–22. Harvard Univ. Press, Cambridge, Massachusetts, 1971.

measure the social problems of computers discussed throughout this book.

On-Line Systems and Information Utilities

On-line information systems introduce new major complexities. To illustrate these we consider airline reservation systems, and in particular the SABRE system developed for American Airlines.[7] Features of the SABRE system which make it complex are as follows.

- The system must not only be accurate but extremely reliable since interruptions of even a few minutes bring about an accumulation of transactions which are hard to cope with and are extremely costly; longer interruptions are disastrous.
- The system is large. There may be up to 600,000 passenger records stored simultaneously for 27,000 flight segments. At the time of installation there were 1000 offices in 100 cities with access to the system, all requiring on-line response.
- Part of the file is static, but much is extremely dynamic. As an example seats can be reserved up to a year in advance but most of the activity on a flight with regard to reservations takes place in the day or two before flight time. The file structure is complex; since passenger records may be related to other records in many ways they do not have a uniform format.
- Although the primary function of the system is to manage the seat reservation there are many secondary tasks. These include the generation of lists to be used for schedule and fare information, billing, passenger service requirements (car rentals, hotel reservations), boarding manifests, ticket mailing, wait-listed passengers, messages to connecting airlines, and so on. The system also handles flight plans, log records, parts inventory control, and air cargo control.

The reservation systems were developed jointly by the airlines, the Bell Telephone Company, and the computer manufacturers (different airlines have worked with different manufacturers). As remarkable as the complexity of the systems themselves is the smooth way in which some have been implemented from the point of view of the public. A long time was spent in planning these systems, but the care and thought that went

[7] Computers in airline reservation systems, *in* "Computer Usage/Applications" (E. A. Weiss, ed.), pp. 139–168. McGraw-Hill, New York, 1970.

into their development are evidence that large new computer systems do not necessarily entail inconvenience, massive disruptions, and loss of public confidence.

The SABRE system took 11 years to implement (1954–1964). The general process by which the function requirements of American Airlines were translated into operating computer program contained seven major stages.

1. The requirements were determined by airline personnel experienced in reservations work.
2. The functional requirements were translated by computer-oriented analysts into preliminary program specifications.
3. Airline personnel, the analysts, and a programming group maintained continuous discussions to produce the final program specifications.
4. A list of functional descriptions was written to describe how the system would carry out reservation functions. The list was submitted to and accepted by the airline staff.
5. A massive programming effort produced the 500,000 lines of symbolic code required.
6. An extensive program was established to train airline staff in the use of the system.
7. The system was tested in several developing stages. Before the hardware arrived, simulation programs allowed preliminary testing. Later the basic logic was tested by constructing test situations; basically this allowed the program to be tested in segments. More elaborate programs permitted the simulation of agent consoles. Then a package of current system records (the pilot system) was developed to simulate the data for more complete and efficient testing. Finally, one city at a time was converted from the manual to the automated system (the first city was converted in April 1963, and all cities by December 1964).

To automate the airline reservation systems it was necessary to apply techniques in communication engineering and electronic data processing to the reservation problem. From communications came methods of collecting and queuing messages, and maintaining conversational continuity between the central system and the terminals. From data processing came methods of authorizing users and maintaining audit trials of entries so that files could be cross-referenced and reconstructed if necessary. Eventually several independent reservation systems were constructed. Even though there was an appreciable amount of information about these systems in the open literature, the implementation problems were difficult enough so that the experience of one computer manufacturer and airline was not easily transferred to a different manufacturer and airline.[8]

Reservation systems are private information utilities providing a clearly defined service to a single company. On-line banking services are similar, and another example is the large-scale interactive administrative system which IBM uses for its own orders.[9] More far reaching are the information systems designed to provide a service to a large number of subscriber customers through inquiry terminals. Examples are the data bases developed by credit reporting agencies and by companies furnishing information for health and casualty insurance applications. These operations are very large, extending to a national or continent-wide scale.[10] For all of these systems which contain personal data about individuals, the privacy considerations to be discussed in Chapter 5 are vital. There are also on-line information systems which provide information not of a personal nature to their subscribers, for example, data on stock market transactions or legal data about legislation and court actions. On-line systems are evolving at a steady rate and it is clear that they represent what may be the major force in the whole computer technology. Whether the systems will evolve so that multiple-type services will be available on a single communication device, as is perhaps implied by the term "information utility," remains to be seen. So far the different companies have tended to concentrate on distinct services, and the market for a multipurpose information utility has neither materialized nor been developed.

Natural Language Information Retrieval Systems

As a final example of a file complexity we consider a general-purpose, computerized information storage and retrieval system. The elements of

[8] Several lawsuits developed out of the dissatisfaction of some airlines with the reservation systems built for them. [TWA vs. Burroughs reported in *Computerworld,* Oct. 28 (1971); United Airlines vs Univac, discussed in *Datamation,* March, p. 131 (1970).]

[9] This system, using 1500 terminals located in 320 geographical sites, carries out order entry, delivery scheduling, commission accounting, inventory maintenance, billing, and many other functions. It was developed along the lines of the SABRE system, and a particular feature is the computer-assisted instruction for user training. See J. H. Wimbrow, A large-scale interactive administrative system. *IBM Syst. J.* **10** (4), 260–282 (1971).

[10] Examples of companies providing nationwide credit reporting services on-line in the United States are the Retail Credit Company (based in Atlanta, Georgia) and the Credit Data Corporation (a subsidiary of TRW in Los Angeles). The Medical Information Bureau (Boston) and the Casualty Index (Morristown, N. J.) provide health data to their insurance company clients throughout the United States and Canada.

the system are the file, the query (i.e., the search prescription), the search, and the response.

We may imagine the file as a large growing collection of documents (which may be books, reports, journal articles, abstracts of books, etc.) consisting in the extreme of millions of items. The documents cover many subjects and topics.

In the previous applications the file system or data base was expected to produce answers to a set of specific, carefully formulated questions; here document retrieval must provide answers to an unlimited number of very different and very general questions. For this reason it is desirable to have the machine language as close as possible to natural language. In Section 8.1 we consider the present status of computer translation of natural languages and the problem of having a computer extract the semantic content in a sentence or query. But aside from the serious limitations which presently characterize computer treatment of natural language, our system supposes, on behalf of the user, a considerable knowledge of file classification and cataloging. The problem is further complicated because different persons might classify the same document in significantly different ways. Still further, the query should be able to describe not only what is wanted but also what is not wanted.

The purpose of the search is to return to the user a set of useful documents. Two measures of its success are the fraction of relevant documents retrieved and the fraction of retrieved documents that are relevant. In a working retrieval system we might imagine the user at a console submitting a query. He indicates which documents yielded by the response are satisfactory, and perhaps modifies his query. These changes permit the system to deliver new response documents, and this continues until the user is satisfied in a reasonable time.

With the present status of retrieval systems, there are serious problems in the search. Assume that each document is classified according to some scheme (e.g., subject headings, key words, author, related documents, etc.). Even if the document abstracts and indexes are stored on-line and the fastest large storage devices available are used, it would take several hours to search the whole document file, an obviously unacceptable response for on-line retrieval. There are basic problems in knowing how to cluster documents so as to allow access to a small but useful subset, and how to construct indexes which will guide the search.

The system we have just described is in effect an automated library. So far computerized information systems have not been constructed to behave like a large library, nor is there any immediate prospect that this will be done. The successes in information retrieval systems have been achieved in applications which were limited in important respects, for example, full-text documents were not stored (only abstracts), the subject matter was limited to special topics, the query language was restricted in format and content, the queries were batched so that the response time is long, and so forth. With such restrictions it has been possible to construct useful management information systems (Salton, 1968) or systems for searching legal statutes.[11] But systems which correspond to libraries in the manner discussed here are a long way off; the main attention so far has been focused on automating the library catalog rather than the library itself (Dolby *et al.*, 1969).

4.4. Record Linkage

In different files which contain information about the same entity it is necessary to provide a method of cross-referencing, that is, to provide a method of record linkage. Linkage can be accomplished through geographic identification,[12] but the aspect we are particularly interested in is linkage through personal data. Such linkage is needed in longitudinal studies where the history of an individual is recorded in different files over a period of years. The fact that records might be linked with a high degree of certainty even when record linkage has not been deliberately built into the system is fortunate in certain situations, for example, in population and genetic studies based on searching hospital records; but in others it is a cause for concern because it makes it possible to nullify attempts to maintain confidentiality.

When a file is maintained by a single agency the simplest way to identify records and provide for linkage is to assign a unique identifier (numeric or alphanumeric) to each individual when a record for him is created the first time. An individual's name is not an adequate identifier simply because there are too many different persons having exactly the same name and too many instances when names are misspelled. The identifier may be structured so that different parts of it are coded descriptions of features possessed by the person or it may simply be a serial accession number, but the important thing is that it be unique. This common technique of creating an identifier for each new application gives rise to a multiplicity of numbers—the student number, the hospital insurance number, the driver's license number, the employee number, and so on, a proliferation which is widely regarded as a depersonalizing

[11] For an overview of management systems see, "A Survey of Generalized Data Base Management Systems," Codasyl Syst. Committee Tech. Rep., Assoc. for Comput. Machinery, New York, 1969.

[12] See W. T. Fay, "Problems of Area Identification"; E. M. Horwood, "Grid Coordinate Systems," Chapters 12 and 13 in Bisco (1970).

influence in which people are turned into numbers. From a public administration (and from a research) point of view this multiplicity creates serious inefficiencies in data collection and verification and in communication between departments.

It is tempting to seek a single identifying number which would be adopted as a permanent identifier for each individual. An obvious candidate for such a number is that used in connection with the social security schemes which have been adopted in many countries. When social security became universal in the United States and social security numbers were assigned, there were assurances that the number would *not* be used as a universal identifier to replace names, among other reasons because it was recognized that this would facilitate the collection of personal dossiers (see Section 5.3). But the fact that it is the most widely assigned number has inevitably led to its use for purposes other than social security. The acceptance of social security numbers is not universal, however, because usually it is assigned only when a person enters the labor force and therefore may not be available for students or foreigners, because it is long and easily forgotten or misquoted, and because there have been cases of identical numbers being assigned to different persons. For these reasons many companies and institutions in North America continue to use their own numbering for individuals. The objections to a single identifying number are not held with the same force in other countries, and in Scandinavia, Belgium, the Netherlands, and the Federal Republic of Germany such identifiers have already been adopted or are in the process of becoming so.[13]

Since neither names nor numbers are in themselves certain to distinguish individuals, standard identifiers, using a combination of the two, have been proposed where it is imperative that individuals be positively identified. As an example, the Canadian standard identifier[14] contains three fields:

1. a single character identification Code Designator which identifies the type of numeric code in the second field: 0 for independent users; 2 for social security number (U. S.); 4 for social insurance number (Canada);

[13] See Thomas (1971, pp. 21–23) for a brief summary of the position in European countries.

[14] Draft CSA Standard Z243.9, "Identification of Individuals for Machine to Machine Information Interchange." Canad. Standard Assoc., Rexdale Ontario, January 1971. For the United States the corresponding proposal is "Proposed USA Standard for Identification of Individuals for Information Interchange." X3.8.3/55 October 24, 1968 X3.8/128, 68-10-25. Amer. Nat. Stand. Inst., New York.

2. the identification number (social security number, social insurance number, etc.);
3. surname, first name, middle name.

For John Smith (no middle name) whose Canadian social insurance number is 419044730, the standard identifier would be:

4419044730SMITH,JOHN . . .

In the absence of standard identifying numbers there are well-established techniques for bringing together data about an individual from different files, even though there may be different identifiers for the individual and inconsistencies in the information which characterizes him.[15] These techniques have been used to very good effect in studies of family history, genetics, and vital statistics. Newcombe[16] shows how four-character strings, easily constructed by contracting surnames, can be used as a preliminary method of tagging a family, and then additional information, derived from the initial letters of the Christian names, year and place of birth, and so forth, can differentiate individuals within the family with a very high degree of certainty. Thus when there are different files containing information about an individual, it is certainly possible to combine all the data into a single file. The recognition of this capability played a large part in the rejection of a proposed national data bank in the United States (see Section 5.3).

Even when information consists of aggregated data and there has been a deliberate attempt to prevent the identification of individuals, there has been concern voiced that it is not difficult to apply techniques which circumvent this. Data from the U. S. and Canadian censuses are available for purchase in magnetic tape form. The census bureaus are bound by legislation not to reveal information in a form which will permit identification, and go to great pains to maintain confidentiality. Nevertheless objections have been raised that for census tracts where the number of individuals is not large, statistical techniques and the powerful searching

[15] For a review see J. Steinberg, "Some Aspects of Statistical Data Linkage for Individuals," in Bisco (1970). For a bibliography see G. Wagner and H. B. Newcombe, Record linkage: a Bibliography. *J. Methodol. Med. Res., Informat. Documentation* **IX** (2), 121–138 (1970). See also M. A. Jaro, UNIMATCH—A computer system for generalized record linkage under conditions of uncertainty. *AFIPS Conf. Proc.* **40,** 523–530 (1971).

[16] H. B. Newcombe, Record linkage: The design of efficient systems for linkage records into individual and family histories. *Amer. J. Human Genet.* **19** (3), Part 1, 335–359 (1967).

methods which computers offer will actually make it possible to identify individuals.[17]

Where it is essential that confidentiality be maintained, as in social science surveys where subjects are asked questions on drug abuse or other questions to which the replies might be incriminating, special techniques have been worked out to prevent the answers from being associated with individuals.[18] If the research is based on a single study, the replies can be simply given anonymously; but in longitudinal studies, where it is necessary to go back to the subjects again, identifiers must be included. One possibility is to include deliberately, at random, a small number of incorrect answers, on the principle that the uncertainty so introduced would make it impossible to take punitive action on the basis of the replies. Another is to attach an identification number, ID1, to the answers, and a different identification number, ID2, to the names of the respondents. The link file, which is a list of ID pairings, is stored in a completely separate file, not accessible to the researcher or to those who have the name and address list of the respondents. Not only does this protect against breach of privacy by browsing, but it is possible to store the link file in a foreign country and thereby protect against release of information even by a court subpoena.[19]

4.5. System Security

Data security is the protection of data from accidental or intentional but unauthorized destructive modification or disclosure. It is distinct from *confidentiality,* which is determined by policy decisions defining right of access, and *privacy,* which is associated with the individual to whom the records pertain. It is a matter of importance to determine exactly how files are accessed and to incorporate devices and procedures which will safeguard their security.

Security has to be assured for many kinds of files: payroll and medical records for personnel, financial records, customers' lists, national defense

[17] L. J. Hoffman and W. F. Miller, Getting a personal dossier from a statistical data bank. *Datamation* **16** (5) (1970).

[18] R. F. Boruch, Maintaining confidentiality of data in educational research: A systematic analysis. *Amer. Psychologist* **26** (5), 413–430 (1971).

[19] In the "Decennial Census": Rep. to the U. S. Secretary of Commerce, July, 1971, it is suggested that the name be removed in the microfilm copies of the census record and be maintained in a separate link file. This technique will not, of course, provide any greater protection than removing the identifier altogether, so that if statistical techniques permit identification from the data itself, no security is afforded.

information, product data, census data, and so on. Even when these files are in machine-readable form, it will be necessary to take all the normal precautions for handling confidential materials. Such precautions, which might be designated as external security, must include limiting access to places where the files are stored and processed. This limitation can be effected by means of locks, guards, sign-in and sign-out procedures, by controlling the number and distribution of printed lists bearing sensitive information, by carrying out security checks on those who have the responsibility for working with the files, and by providing back-up copies of important files. This could mean substantial changes in working habits, and the computer room, often a glass-enclosed showplace for visitors, may have to become much less prominent. In addition, accounting and auditing controls normally applied to financial data for preventing and detecting fraud must be maintained.[20]

These measures are necessary for the security of any type of information system, manual or automated. Beyond these there are measures using both hardware and software which can be taken with computerized systems. These special measures can be applied to users, terminals, jobs, and files. Table 4-3 shows a classification of types of threats which can be directed against computer systems, along with possible countermeasures. This table was first suggested by Petersen and Turn, and it has been adopted by others who have subsequently discussed system security.[21]

The threat types are grouped under accidental and deliberate. These latter include attempts to obtain information by such methods as wiretapping, picking up electromagnetic radiation, examining carbon papers, and impersonating an authorized user. The deliberate, active techniques are those which might be used in time-sharing or remote job entry systems. They include "between-lines" entry in which an infiltrator enters the system when a legitimate user is inactive but continues to hold the communication channel, "piggyback" penetration in which the infiltrator intercepts messages between the user and the computer, and "trapdoor" entry where there is some loophole in the operating system, allowing access without going through the normal sign-on routine. As shown in the table, the countermeasures can be grouped under five headings (includ-

[20] See Section 12.1; also J. J. Wasserman, Plugging the leaks in computer security. *Harvard Business Rev.*, pp. 119–129, Sept.–Oct. (1969); and Van Tassel (1972, especially Chapters 3–5).

[21] H. E. Petersen and R. Turn, System implications of information privacy. *AFIPS Conf. Proc.* **30**, 291–300 (1967). See also L. J. Hoffman, Computers and privacy: A survey. *Comput. Surveys* **1** (2), 85–104, (1969); Data security in the corporate data base, *EDP Analyzer* **8** (5) (1970).

ing integrity management, which has already been considered under external security).

ACCESS MANAGEMENT

All systems, batch and time-sharing, have some kind of control in connection with the job accounting program which computes the cost of services. The simplest control is a directory which lists secret passwords assigned to the users, but more sophisticated methods are necessary to provide more careful monitoring both of the users and of the privileges they have. Since passwords are easily revealed, mislaid, or even guessed if they are chosen thoughtlessly, it is not uncommon to construct changeable or one-time passwords. It may also be desirable to exercise control over the terminal by requiring terminal identification, and security for both the terminal and user can be increased by instituting call-back procedure whereby the computer calls the terminal back once initial communication has been established. Still higher levels of access control are achieved by storing security tables which define the privileges of each user.

PROCESSING RESTRICTIONS

One of the most effective ways of improving security is to limit the operations of users. This can be implemented at several levels. At the lowest or machine language level there may be privileged instructions which can only be executed when the computer is in a special supervisor state, open only to the operating system; or there may be a memory protect feature which confines users to a bounded set of storage locations.

Stricter conditions can be enforced by insisting that users work in a high-level programming language which allows only limited kinds of operations. For example, in text-editing systems users can manipulate only files and have no access to the assembly language, the operating system, or even the general instructions of a high-level language. Usually restrictions are also established on the type of file operations open to users. The directory includes indicators which show for each user and file what operations may be performed—read-only, write-only, read–write, copy, change the list of authorized users, and so on.

THREAT MONITORING

There are ways of detecting attempts to gain access to the system. The appearance of rejected passwords or of attempts to carry out forbidden operations can be logged, unusual activity in files may be noted, and in

TABLE 4-3
SUMMARY OF COUNTERMEASURES TO THREAT TO INFORMATION PRIVACY[a]

Threat \ Countermeasure	Access control (passwords, authentication authorization)	Processing restrictions (storage, protect, privileged operations)	Privacy transformations	Threat monitoring (audits, logs)	Integrity management (hardware, software, personnel)
Accidental:					
User error	Good protection, unless the error produces correct password	Reduce susceptibility	No protection if depend on password; otherwise, good protection	Identifies the "accident prone"; provides *post facto* knowledge of possible loss	Not applicable
System error	Good protection, unless bypassed due to error	Reduce susceptibility	Good protection in case of communication system switching errors	May help in diagnosis or provide *post facto* knowledge	Minimizes possibilities for accidents
Deliberate, passive:					
Electromagnetic pick-up	No protection	No protection	Reduces susceptibility; work factor determines the amount of protection	No protection	Reduces susceptibility
Wiretapping	No protection	No protection	Reduces susceptibility; work factor determines the amount of protection	No protection	If applied to communication circuits may reduce susceptibility

Waste basket	Not applicable	Not applicable	Not applicable	Not applicable	Proper disposal procedures
Deliberate, active: "Browsing"	Good protection (may make masquerading necessary)	Reduces ease to obtain desired information	Good protection	Identifies unsuccessful attempts; may provide *post facto* knowledge or operate real-time alarms	Aides other countermeasures
"Masquerading"	Must know authenticating passwords (work factor to obtain these)	Reduces ease to obtain desired information	No protection if depends on password; otherwise, sufficient	Identifies unsuccessful attempts; may provide *post facto* knowledge or operate real-time alarms	Makes harder to obtain information for masquerading; since masquerading is deception, may inhibit browsers
"Between-lines" entry	No protection unless used for every message	Limits the infiltrator to the same potential as the user whose line he shares	Good protection if privacy transformation changed in less time than required by work factor	*Post facto* analysis of activity may provide knowledge of possible loss	Communication network integrity helps
"Piggyback" entry	No protection but reverse (processor-to-user) authentication may help	Limits the infiltrator to the same potential as the user whose line he shares	Good protection if privacy transformation changed in less time than required by work factor	*Post facto* analysis of activity may provide knowledge of possible loss	Communication network integrity helps

(*Continued*)

TABLE 4-3 (*Continued*)

Countermeasure / Threat	Access control (passwords, authentication authorization)	Processing restrictions (storage, protect, privileged operations)	Privacy transformations	Threat monitoring (audits, logs)	Integrity management (hardware, software, personnel)
Entry by system personnel	May have to masquerade	Reduces ease of obtaining desired information	Work factor, unless depend on password and masquerading is successful	*Post facto* analysis of activity may provide knowledge of possible loss	Key to the entire privacy protection system
Entry via "trap doors"	No protection	Probably no protection	Work factor, unless access to keys obtained	Possible alarms, *post facto* analysis	Protection through initial verification and subsequent maintenance of hardware and software integrity
Core dumping to get residual information	No protection	Erase private core areas at swapping time	No protection unless encoded processing feasible	Possible alarms, *post facto* analysis	Not applicable
Physical acquisition of removable files	Not applicable	Not applicable	Work factor, unless access to keys obtained	*Post facto* knowledge form audits of personnel movements	Physical preventative measures and devices

[a] Reprinted by permission from H. E. Petersen, and R. Turn, Systems implications of information privacy, *AFIPS Conf. Proc.* **30** (1967). Copyright 1967 by Amer. Fed. of Information Processing Soc., Inc.

general, if norms can be established for any kind of activity, it may be useful to record deviations from these norms. Although certain of the responses may be automatic, for example, a remote terminal might be disconnected if three invalid passwords were presented in succession, it is of course necessary that the logs be read and follow-up action taken if monitoring is to be effective. The first prosecution for theft of a computer program in California was a result of noting an unusual action. The operating system of Information Systems Design, a company which sells time-sharing services, included a provision for simultaneously punching any program for which a program listing was requested. When a punched program with no forwarding address turned up, it was possible to trace the request to a former salesman who was charged with copying and selling the program without authorization.[22]

PRIVACY TRANSFORMATIONS

These are enciphering systems which encode data as they are read into the computer, and reversibly decode them as they are printed out. Hardware devices similar to those which code and decode diplomatic messages can be used, or the ciphering can be carried out under program control. Any standard cryptographic technique can be used, substitution (replacement of characters or groups of characters), transposition (rearrangements of the message), or addition (combining characters with those of a key supplied by the user or the system). The well-known method of Vernan, where the plain text characters (i.e., those of the original message) are combined with the key by carrying out an exclusive OR addition, is easily adapted to computers by generating the keys from pseudo-random numbers.[23] A concomitance of any cryptographic technique is the *work factor:* a measure of the work required to break the code using standard cryptographics. Codes are more secure as the work factor increases, and in the Vernan codes this can be achieved by making the key as long as possible compared to the message.

Experience has proved that many practices which should be adopted to make systems secure are consistent with those which should be put into effect in any good operating system. To take a simple example, for security purposes it is desirable to clear the working store after each user; this is also a sound practice to ensure that programs are not affected by previous programs using the same storage area. Good systems are those in which one user cannot interfere with the work of another (or

[22] *Computer World,* March 10 (1971).

[23] J. M. Carroll and P. M. McLelland, Fast infinite-key privacy transformation for resource-sharing systems. *AFIPS Conf. Proc.* **37,** 223–230 (1970).

with the system), where system crashes (i.e., loss of control by the system necessitating a restart of the job stream) are absent, and which are well documented and easily explained to prospective users. A well-designed system recognizes the need to store important directories and tables in areas where they cannot be overwritten inadvertently or by intent, the need to have privileged instructions usable by the system designers and operators but by no one else, and the desirability of building the systems up in concentric rings, with access becoming more and more controlled as the inner rings are approached. A system whose security depends instead on secrecy, that is, on users not knowing where important tables and instructions are stored, is easily penetrated.

Perfect security is unachievable; there is no unbreakable lock. All that can be done is to make the work factor large enough to deter attempts at penetration. There is general agreement that really secure systems require that the computer be dedicated to a single application.

Finally, adding security to a system increases costs. There is the cost of the software or hardware for providing the security, of storage for extra directories and extra characters which define authorization, and the overhead system cost because extra time is needed on each computer job to carry out the security checking. It is difficult to estimate these, although some attempts have been made.[24] The extra coding is probably no more than 10 to 15% of the coding which is needed in any case to identify users and perform job accounting. The extra storage requirements and the system overhead are estimated as a few percent. Some of these figures might have to be increased significantly if a decision were taken to have authorization indicators not only for files (as is now common) but also for individual records within a file.

The total cost is very difficult to estimate because in addition to the above, there are other factors, such as the cost for the external security described above and opportunity costs which may be present if programmers are required to use a high-level programming language and thereby deprived of the efficiencies that languages closer to the machine level offer. On the other hand, many of the security measures result in a better understood, better documented system with improved efficiency. Aside from the question of privacy, they produce better protection against accidental or deliberate losses so that the cost for maintaining security is recovered, in part at least, because of these gains.

[24] C. Weissman, The ADEPT-50 time sharing system. *AFIPS Conf. Proc.* **35**, 39–49 (1969); C. C. Gotlieb and J. N. P. Hume, Systems capacity for data security. Rep. for the Privacy and Computers Task Force, Dept. of Comm. and Justice, Ottawa, 1972.

Bibliography

Bisco, R. L., ed. (1970). "Data Bases, Computers and the Social Sciences." Wiley (Interscience), New York.

Dolby, J. L., Forsyth, V. J., and Resnikoff, H. L. (1969). "Computerized Library Catalogues; Their Growth, Cost and Utility." M.I.T. Press, Cambridge, Massachusetts.

Salton, G. (1968). "Automatic Information Organization and Retrieval." McGraw-Hill, New York.

Thomas, U. (1971). "Computerized Data Banks in Public Administration." Org. for Economic Cooperation and Develop., Paris.

Van Tassel, D. (1972). "Computer Security Management." Prentice-Hall, Englewood Cliffs, New Jersey.

Westin, A. F., ed. (1971). "Information Technology in a Democracy." Harvard Univ. Press, Cambridge, Massachusetts.

Problems and Further Work

1. Write a computer program for enciphering (and deciphering) a message by the Vernan method. (The clear text message and the key, repeated as often as necessary, are represented in binary form. Performing an exclusive OR enciphers the message, and a second OR operation deciphers it.) Generate the keys using a pseudo-random number generator. See

Carroll, footnote 23; also R. O. Skatrod, A consideration of the application of cryptographic techniques to data processing. *AFIPS Conf. Proc.* **35,** 111–117 (1969),

where in addition Vigenere-type transposition codes are described.

2. When surnames are part of a long record it is often useful to have an abbreviation for them. Two such abbreviations are the Russell Soundex Code and Name Compression. These are constructed as follows.

Russell Soundex Code

1. The code consists of an alphabetic prefix which is the first letter in the surname followed by three digits.
2. Ignore W and H.
3. A, E, I, O, U, Y are defined as *separators,* but they are not coded.
4. Other letters are coded according to the table shown, until three digits are reached.

Letter	Code digit
B, P, F, V	1
D, T	3
L	4
M, N	5
R	6
CGJKQSXZ	2

5. When a letter is coded with the same digit as its predecessor, it is ignored unless there is a separator between the two.
6. Zeros are added as necessary.

NAME COMPRESSION

1. Delete the second of any pair of identical consonants.
2. Delete A, E, I, O, U, Y except when the first letter in the name.

Construct the coded and compressed forms for a number of similar name pairs (e.g., Fischer, Fisher; MacLain, McLaine). What advantages are there to having these the same? What are the relative advantages and disadvantages of the two methods of abbreviation?

3. Outline the measures which should be taken to protect files against disasters and catastrophes (fire, water damage, bombs, etc.). See

Van Tassel (1972, Chapters 12 and 13).

4. Discuss file retention under the headings (1) requirements (auditing, legal requirements, recoverability), (2) procedures (mechanics, retention period, erasure), and (3) difficulties (storage, access, compatibility). What special considerations arise with machine-readable files?

5. Make a list of all the numbers which identify you in the sense that they each serve as entry to some file in which you are listed as an individual. Which of them are structured numbers? Which do you remember by heart? Would you regard it primarily as a threat or a convenience if all of them were replaced by a single number?

Chapter

5

INFORMATION SYSTEMS AND PRIVACY

Programs for achieving social and economic benefits are critically dependent on the availability of good data, especially data about people. This dependency has meant, as we have seen, that most countries, developed and nondeveloped, have methodically set about to gather population data to better carry out their administrative and planning responsibilities. The zeal for data collection has not always been accompanied by safeguards to prevent data about an individual from being used in ways which might harm him. If the data are consolidated, they can become in effect a dossier and in this form they are easily used by governments to invade privacy and enforce conformity. It is necessary to devise means of balancing the legitimate needs of government and business for personal data against the right to individual privacy. In this chapter the trade-offs between these requirements are examined. At present this balance favors those who gather the data. Guidelines and recommendations to preserve privacy are presented.

5.1. Personal Data

Governments are by no means the only agencies which collect data about individuals. Corporations, institutions, charitable groups, credit reporting agencies, advertising companies, and many other organizations maintain files for reasons which may be regarded as necessary, legitimate, or annoying, with or without the individual's consent, but often without constraint.

Table 5-1 is a partial listing of the types of data commonly gathered about individuals. This information is a direct by-product of the normal, regulatory, revenue-raising activities of government, the administrative processes of institutions and civil authorities, and the competitive drives of business. Some data will appear over and over in the files of different government jurisdictions and private agencies. The amount of detail in any one category will vary widely according to where the information is being used. In one case the personal identification may simply consist of the person's name and social insurance number, or his driver's license number; in another it may be a computer record with 50 or more fields, storing minute details about appearance, physical characteristics, family history, and identifying medical data, and be accompanied by noncomputerized material such as photographs, fingerprints, and voice recordings. These records are not necessarily in machine-readable form (although the trend to computerization is rapid), nor will they all be accurate or consistent with one another. The dispersed form of the data is actually a protection, for it prevents any one agency from believing that it has everything needed to make any decision about a person. But the tendency is toward collecting more data, and equally important, toward consolidating the collections.

As an illustration of the trend we may look at the proposal for a medical data bank described in a report of the Ontario Council of Health Care Delivery Systems.[1] The data requirements are estimated in Appendix A of the report. Two kinds of files associated with the Health Care System are described. The first, called the Active Personal Data File, contains medical information on an individual for the most recent five years, to be made available through on-line terminals to doctors and hospitals. Assuming that there would be about 2200 characters of information for each person, and that all the records in a region of 200,000 people would be stored on one computer, it is estimated that queries could be answered within three seconds. The second file, called the Lifetime Per-

[1] Rep. of the Ontario Council of Health on Health Care Delivery Systems, "Role of Computers in the Health Field," Suppl. no. 9. Ontario Dept. of Health (1970).

TABLE 5-1

TYPES OF DATA ABOUT INDIVIDUALS

1. Identification
   Name, maiden name (if applicable), social insurance number, date of birth, place of birth, citizenship, address, appearance, physical features, marital status, names of family
2. Employment
   Occupation, current employer, employment history, earnings, education and training, qualifications
3. Medical
   Current health status, medical description and history, genetic factors, reportable diseases, x-rays, immunizations, dental history, health plan participation
4. Education
   Schools attended, educational attainments, professional licenses, awards, loans
5. Taxation
   Earnings, investment income, foreign holdings, dependents
6. Financial
   Bank account history, holdings, earnings, credit and loan history, life insurance
7. Military service
   Rank and qualifications, service record, disciplinary record, medical record
8. Vehicle registration
   Owner, vehicle identification, origin, insurance, accident record
9. Real estate
   Owner, property identification, description, zoning, assessment and taxation, uses
10. License and permits
   Identification, type of license, dates, insurance
11. Travel
   Passport, visas, countries visited, customs and duty payments
12. Welfare
   Agency, history, dependents, aid received, earnings
13. Civil action
   History, court identification, dates, outcomes
14. Police records
   Offenses, warrants, convictions, confinements, probation and parole, political affiliations
15. Customer accounts
   Company, sales history, credit status
16. Life insurance
   Identification, value, history, other insurance, medical data
17. Mailing lists
   Type, source, customer profile, history of purchases
18. Biographical
   Identification, curriculum vitae, accomplishments, publications, memberships, relatives
19. Membership
   Organization, history, participation, financial, relatives

sonal Data File, would take the form of a magnetic tape containing more information but in a more highly compressed form. Assuming 100 characters per person per year it is estimated that 60 reels of tape would be needed for a district. This is compared with the 70-reel tape file held by the agency responsible for maintaining the current records (primarily financial) of the Ontario Health Insurance Plan (OHIP).

The medical records on the proposed computer system do not in the main correspond to new data. In fact much of the advantage of the system arises because it would consolidate duplicate records presently being accumulated in doctors' offices, hospitals, and in government agencies. When the records about a patient are transferred from the relatively inaccessible files of his doctor to the centralized files of a medical information system, the question of confidentiality naturally arises.

In a "Report on the Right to Privacy" prepared by the Oxford Group of Society Labour Lawyers[2] it is suggested that an on-line medical data bank would have only a marginal effect on improving medical care. A doctor, it is argued, does not need to see an entire medical record for diagnosis and treatment even on patients he has not seen before. But this view does not seem to be held generally; most hospital information systems now being designed include the computerization of patients' medical records, and the Ontario report, while discussing privacy, proceeds from the assumption that an Active Personal Data File is essential to the Health Care System. The push toward consolidation of medical records and toward a more complete data collection for the whole population is extremely strong. It is difficult to believe, given a demonstration of the technical feasibility of such a plan and the political and financial decisions to embark on it, that implementation would be withheld because of concerns for confidentiality and privacy.

The justification for collecting medical data does not apply with the same force to other data collecting. But plausible need can be established for much of the activity. It is difficult, for example, to counter the argument of the credit reporting agencies that consumer credit is an essential component of our economic system. We must expect that the volume of records of personal data will continue to grow. And as technical and financial considerations justify it, these data will be consolidated into computers and data banks. The question is, does this present real or new problems about confidentiality and privacy? And if so, what should be done about these problems?

[2] Rep. on the Right to Privacy, Oxford Group of Soc. of Labour Lawyers, March (1971).

5.2. Privacy and Information Gathering

Privacy, in one form or another, is basic to human relations. Its biological, philosophical, sociological, and psychological aspects are explored at length in an issue of *The Law and Contemporary Problems*.[3] Westin (1968), in an influential book entitled "Privacy and Freedom," traces the history of privacy, the legal framework which has grown up in the United States for its protection, and the problems which have suddenly come up because of modern techniques which make it possible to intrude on individual privacy with devastating effectiveness. Westin identifies four aspects to privacy—solitude, intimacy, anonymity, and reserve, and he defines privacy more precisely as the right of an individual to determine what information is revealed about himself.[4]

The concept of privacy is strongly dependent on the cultural and political context, and changes with time.[5] In Germany, for example, people are appalled at the size and scope of North American credit information systems, considering these to be gross invasions of privacy; but they do not object, as North Americans unduobtedly would, to reporting to the police each time they change their address. In Holland there was a long-standing opposition (eventually overcome) to social security numbers which would identify individuals, because during the Nazi Occupation of World War II the Gestapo kept surveillance on citizens by such a system. The salaries of public officials and educators, once confidential, are now matters of public record in many places.

The concern about the ways in which modern technology affects privacy centers on how information is gathered and also on the unsatisfactory practices for verifying, maintaining security on, and restricting the flow of information. Computers are primarily involved in these latter functions, but in examining the relation between computers and privacy it is desirable to look at information gathering first, partly as background, and also because computers are often involved in the subsequent analysis.

It has long been accepted that government will engage in information gathering, police in surveillance, and business in appraising its employees. But starting about 1950, spurred by the belief that more and more information was necessary and attracted by the possibilities offered

[3] Privacy issue, *Law Contemporary Probl.* **31** (1966).

[4] A. F. Westin, Computers and the Protection of Privacy. *Technol. Rev.* **71**, 32–37 (1969).

[5] See Telecommission Study 5(b), Conference Report, "Computers: Privacy and Freedom of Information." Information Canada, Ottawa, 1971.

by new devices, many agencies, private and public, went about procuring information in ways that destroyed whatever balance had existed between the need to know and the need to be free of interference. The extent to which intrusions into privacy were being carried out as a matter of course, and to which judgments about people were being accepted on the strength of highly suspect techniques, was revealed in several long series of hearings in the United States Congress held during the 1960s. When investigations into these same practices were carried out in other countries, it became apparent that they were widespread there also. Subsequently the relation of computers to privacy engaged the attention of Congress, but before that three aspects of privacy had received special attention: lie detectors, personality testing, and wiretapping and electronic eavesdropping.

Details on the misuse of lie detectors and personality tests, summaries of the Congressional testimony, and accounts on the limitations that were eventually placed on their use are given in Westin (1968) and Miller (1971). More recently computers have entered into the debate about lie detectors and personality tests because of the practice of having the charts marked by machine and the test results stored in computer memory. Since the answers are not seen by any person, it can be argued that there is no intrusion of privacy. Miller does not accept this argument because he feels that computer data banks simply do not offer satisfactory protection for the confidentiality of data.[6] If, as has also been suggested, the answers were not to be stored in the computer at all, and only the overall results conveyed to the subject and to those administering the tests, perhaps much of the privacy issue about such tests would vanish. There would still remain the question of whether they do what they purport to do—detect lies and measure personality.

Devices designed for surveillance, wiretapping and electronic eavesdropping, have been by far the most difficult to cope with in the matter of privacy. Once again it was a series of Congressional hearings that revealed to a startling extent how widespread were the techniques used not only by law enforcement offices but by private investigators on behalf of industrial clients, unions, and individuals. Computers are not directly involved, but the history of wiretapping is relevant because the laws against wiretapping which were eventually passed both in the United States and in Canada, for example, have been coupled with the right to privacy. Moreover the same problem of the balancing of public and private needs arises with these laws as it does with computerized

[6] Miller (1971, pp. 104–105).

data banks. The problem in wiretapping is that it is easy to agree about banning the sale and use of electronic surveillance devices to private users. But when crime investigation and especially national security are involved, police officers are not prepared to give up these important weapons and in this attitude they undoubtedly have public support. It is very difficult to define a "reasonable" use of wiretapping by the police. In the view of Civil Liberties Unions in the United States and Canada, federal laws regulating wiretapping in the respective countries are too permissive in granting authority to police.

5.3. Data Banks and Dossiers

In 1964 the needs for data to carry on research in the social sciences led the U. S. Social Science Research Council to set up a committee to study the preservation and use of economic and social data. The committee proposed the establishment of a Federal Data Center, and in 1965 the Bureau of the Budget, in supporting this proposal, recommended that a National Data Service Center be set up. Social scientists and officials in the Bureau of the Budget were interested only in statistical, aggregated data, but from the beginning it was clear that many records would have to be linked by the methods described in Section 4.4 so that longitudinal studies could be carried out. The proposal for the National Data Bank was attacked in a series of Congressional hearings held before the Subcommittee on Invasion of Privacy, chaired by Representative Gallagher,[7] and again in 1967 in hearings under the chairmanship of Senator Long.[8] Although the National Data Bank was eventually rejected,[9] the issues raised in the hearings have continued to receive a great deal of attention in the popular press, in journals published by law, computer, and other professional societies, and through books written by persons convinced that vital freedoms were being threatened. Investigations of personal data banks were undertaken in many countries including the United States, Canada, the United Kingdom, Germany, Scandi-

[7] "The Computer and Invasions of Privacy," Hearings before a subcommittee of the Committee on Government Operations, House of Representatives, 89th Congress, 2nd session, July 26, 27, and 28, 1966, U. S. Govt. Printing Office, Washington, D. C., 1966.

[8] "Computer Privacy," Hearings of the Subcommittee and Procedure of the Committee of the Judiciary, United States Senate, March 14 and 15, 1967, U. S. Govt. Printing Office, Washington, D. C., 1967.

[9] "Privacy and the National Data Bank Concept," Thirty-Fifth Report by the Committee on Government Operations, House Rep., no. 1842 (August 2, 1968).

navia, and also in the United Nations.[10] The book "The Assault on Privacy" (Miller, 1971) contains an historical account of the issue as well as proposals which, in Miller's opinion, would allow the United States to cope with the problems.

Although government operated data banks are seen to present the greatest problems, those operated privately, especially consumer credit reporting agencies, also attract criticism. Among the practices considered objectionable are the following:

• Recording opinions and hearsay evidence. In courts such evidence is not permissible. Law enforcement and security agencies do collect hearsay when making investigations, for informers are considered indispensable, and experience has shown that it is impossible to obtain their help if anonymity is not guaranteed. But this method of obtaining information causes uneasiness, and in other situations such as credit reporting and insurance checking it is generally regarded as unacceptable.

• A great deal of unnecessary information is collected. This is true particularly about persons who are in a poor position to object, for example, high school students or welfare recipients. It is felt that only information pertinent to the decisions being made should be recorded.[11]

• Individuals are not given access to the information held about them and have no opportunity to correct mistakes and challenge misrepresentations. Everyone having experience with computerized systems knows how easy it is for mistakes to find their way into the system. Before the privacy issue came to the fore, few if any credit agencies were prepared to discuss unfavorable reports with an individual, nor did they have adequate mechanisms for correction.

[10] For an annotated bibliography see Harrison (1967, 1969). Niblett (1971) surveys European developments. For United Nations studies, see "Human Rights and Scientific and Technological Developments," Rep. of the Secretary-General of the United Nations, Commission on Human Rights, 26th Session, E/CN.4/1028, March 4, 1970, Part III, Uses of electronics which may affect the rights of the person and the limits which should be placed on such uses in a democratic society. This contains a list of studies in progress in various countries at the time of writing. Also, P. Juvigny, "The Right to Privacy in the Modern World." Presentation to a panel of experts convened to discuss the right to privacy. UNESCO, Paris, January, 1970.

[11] Other surveys have showed that it is not only the poor who are subjected to inordinate demands for information. Doctors are required to fill out highly detailed forms at every stage in their careers, as prospective students, before receiving license to practice, in connection with medicare programs, and so on. Executives who seek employment are expected to furnish very complete curricula vitae to placement bureaus.

• Unfavorable entries, even those of minor significance, are retained too long. It is now recognized that even many types of criminal records should be erased eventually. Computers make it possible, perhaps likely, that records of youthful indiscretions, misdemeanors, and delinquent payments will be retained indefinitely. This offers too many possibilities for judgments untempered by a recognition of human failings, and too easy justification for unfair actions.

• Records about an individual are passed too freely among agencies. In many places a bank report or a detailed high school record, including medical reports, is easily made available to a prospective employer. When an individual consents to the release of records about him this should remove liability. But there are many situations when he does not know that information about him is being circulated, or he cannot object to the release.

• Security measures to protect against unauthorized access to information are not applied.

These criticisms of the way personal data banks are managed are serious. But an even more serious objection to data banks containing personal information was raised in U. S. Congressional hearings, and it is supported by those who look at the problem from the legal and social point of view. This is that the whole practice of collecting and consolidating data about an individual is equivalent to maintaining a dossier on him—a practice repugnant to American (and British) concepts of justice. It is an invasion of privacy which is perhaps unconstitutional in the United States and is certainly contrary to the declaration of human rights in the United Nations Charter. This objection is, of course, the most wide ranging and challenging.

In the United States, Senator Ervin's Constitutional Rights Subcommittee has been a most effective forum for civil libertarian concerns. The subcommittee's hearings into "Federal Data Banks, Computers, and the Bill of Rights" revealed the extent of political surveillance by the Army and other government agencies. When does a file or a data bank become a personal dossier and what are the implications of dossiers? The book "On Record" (Wheeler, ed., 1969) describes, in detail, record keeping practices in the United States. What comes through is that by their very existence personal data files are a force which limits freedom of action. In countries where democratic freedoms are suppressed, the dossier is a basic tool for maintaining surveillance and ensuring conformity. But even if there is not an overt intention to intimidate, the existence of the files has pernicious effects on attitudes, morale, and patterns of behavior.

Clark[12] describes what he calls the "dossier-consciousness" of college students. He suggests that this leads them generally to pay more attention to the record of their passage through the educational system than to the learning process.

Most of the files described in "On Record" are not yet computerized and it is clear that the main problems are quite independent of the existence of computers or data banks. But computers are part of the problem insofar as they make record keeping simpler and less expensive, and because of remote-entry communication devices, they aggravate the problem. In fact, the argument is that they are one of the new technological factors which makes new laws on privacy imperative.

5.4. Legal Guarantees to Privacy

However basic the right to privacy may seem, rights exist only as defined by the body of laws in each country; natural laws or universal laws have at best dubious legal standing. The closest approximations to universal laws are the United Nations Universal Declaration of Human Rights, but these have to be incorporated into the laws of member states to become effective. Article 12 of the Universal Declaration states that:

> No one shall be subjected to arbitrary interference with his privacy, family, home or correspondence, nor to unlawful attacks on his honour and reputation.

Members of the United Nations subscribe to the Universal Declaration of Human Rights and many have the rights mentioned above entrenched in their constitutions, but the concept of privacy, if it is mentioned explicitly at all, is difficult to defend against electronic surveillance or computerized dossiers on the basis of the laws as they are usually stated. What rights of privacy there are usually devolve from constitutional or long recognized rights of person (freedom from arrest or from unwarranted government interference), from property rights (freedom from trespass and nuisances), or from copyright and libel laws.

In the United States, authorities on jurisprudence have based the right to privacy on rights for freedom of person embodied in the constitution, but a most important support comes from a seminal article written in 1890 by Warren and Brandeis on "The Right to Privacy."[13] The article was directed mainly against intrusions from the press and its photographers, but a general right to be "let alone" was enunciated. Subse-

[12] B. R. Clark, The dossier in colleges and universities, in Wheeler (1969).

[13] Warren and Brandeis, The right to privacy. *Harvard Law Rev.*, December 15 (1890).

quently many states legislated a right to privacy, but there has been enough variation and outright difference of opinion to complicate the issue. In countries where protections are derived from torts (rights to damages) incorporated into the common law, the right to privacy is even less clearly formulated and has to be inferred from a variety of precedents, for example, a very old case on peeping Toms (in Great Britain) or from laws pertaining to copyright and libel. There are effective laws to protect the confidentiality of census data, but these are too specific to be applicable in other situations. In countries such as France and in Quebec where the code of civil law descends from the Napoleonic code, there are no sections obviously relevant to the type of intrusions of privacy we have been considering.

Miller in "The Assault on Privacy" (1971) examines the deficiencies of the present common law on privacy. Although the arguments apply only in the United States, they illustrate the challenges that new technologies pose to laws generally. Precedents based on four recognized categories of injuries (appropriation of a person's name, intrusion upon seclusion, public disclosure of private facts, and false publicity) are simply too far removed from the kinds of damages which might arise through the use of computers. In addition the laws of libel and slander are found to be inapplicable because in most awards based on them the claimant must prove financial loss due to the injury. A major weakness in the common law, Miller notes, is the frequency with which awards are denied because of the successful assertion that the claimant waived his right by consenting to the dissemination of personal information, or by engaging in an activity which was clearly inconsistent with a desire to maintain privacy. Still more often, people give information for one purpose only to find that it has been widely disseminated and used for quite different purposes (a common example is the sale of mailing lists). Thus waiver and informed consent need to be defined much more carefully. Still another difficulty is that in damages arising out of the passing of information there is a very good possibility that the individual is not even aware of the injury. Thus some kind of protection which is not dependent in litigation is needed.

In several jurisdictions laws have been passed to regulate consumer credit reporting on the basis that this is one well-defined area in the problem of computers and data banks where injustices can be documented and where the laws can be framed clearly. Generally the laws have provided individuals with the opportunity to examine and (sometimes) have their records changed, defined rules for the dissemination of information, and in some cases set up a mechanism for licensing public data banks, all measures along the lines of those discussed later in Section 5.6. The Fair Credit Reporting Act was enacted as a U. S. federal law in 1969, but even in its later improved form it permits so many exceptions to the controls that it offers at best limited protection.[14] Although laws for regulating credit bureaus have now been passed in many of the United States, in provinces of Canada, and in other countries, these laws have not yet been tested sufficiently in the respective courts to demonstrate how effective they are.

Many who have examined the problem of protecting privacy most carefully have concluded that special laws such as those covering consumer credit agencies or wiretapping legislation are too narrow in their scope. What is needed, it is argued, is some kind of umbrella legislation which relates information systems (not just data banks) to privacy, and which creates a tort for invasions of privacy. The existence of computerized data banks aggravates the situation, but objections can also be raised against many systems based on manual methods. In most countries credit data banks are not yet computerized, and a law which exempts these from the regulations applicable to computerized credit data banks would not solve the problem it had set out to do.

5.5. Balances

Before considering specific recommendations for laws and guidelines on information systems, it is useful to review the factors to be balanced.

A Right to Privacy Conflicts with Freedom of Speech and Freedom of the Press

A right to privacy must inevitably abridge, under certain circumstances, one of the most jealously guarded rights in a free country, freedom of the press. Although this point has not been emphasized until now, it is undoubtedly one of the main reasons why governments are slow to pass legislation on privacy. Freedom to publish information which could be labeled private can be an important public protection. Thus publishing the names and salaries of public officials and civil servants, which certainly infringes on their privacy, is regarded as a necessary protection against nepotism and misappropriation of public funds. The Freedom of Information Act passed in the United States in 1967[15] is intended to ensure access to information, private or otherwise, which should be open in the public interest. The controversy about the

[14] Miller (1971, pp. 86–87).

[15] Freedom of Information Act, United States Code, Vol. 5, Para. 552, (Supp. III, 1965–1967).

New York Times' publication of the Pentagon Papers on Vietnam in June 1971 is a reminder of how difficult it is to decide when secrecy is legitimate. In a free society, secrecy, especially on the part of government, is countenanced only when it is necessary for national security, and this means that there are legitimate forces operating against privacy.

A Right to Privacy Interferes with Essential Operations of Governments, Institutions, and Business

It is very difficult to go beyond the concept of regulating computer systems to deal with information systems generally. Unless laws are very carefully framed, they will interfere with such accepted personal information systems as the telephone directory[16] or a newspaper morgue (the file on personalities a newspaper keeps in case any newsworthy story about them arises suddenly). These systems and many others work well, and it would be most undesirable to restrain or even subject them to the bureaucracy of licensing. In these two cases we have on the one hand, the consent of the person about whom the information is being circulated, and on the other, the fact that the information is a matter of public record. Laws or regulations which assure privacy must recognize and define the situations where the gathering and dissemination of personal information are legitimate.

A Right to Privacy Inhibits Planning, Research, and Other Highly Desirable Activities

We have already seen the arguments about the need for centralized information for planning and research. The case for increased centralization was cogently presented by Kaysen in defending the National Data Center in the United States.[17] He pointed out that the disadvantage of decentralization is not just duplication in collecting data, but that inconsistencies and aggregations result in loss of information and degradation of the quality of analysis.

Aside from the question of consolidation of data, much research in behavioral science, particularly in the fields of psychology and sociology, is about the attitudes and actions of individuals, and this research would be inhibited if rules about privacy were to be applied too strictly. There is general acceptance that when informed consent, confidentiality, and

[16] In the Soviet Union telephone directories are not generally available because, it is argued, they are invaders of privacy.

[17] C. Kaysen, Data Banks and Dossiers, *Public Interest* 7, 52–60 (1967), also reprinted in "The Computer Impact" (I. Taviss, ed.), pp. 161–168. Prentice-Hall, Englewood Cliffs, New Jersey, 1970.

anonymity are assured, there is no invasion of privacy. But it is not simple or even always possible to assure them (Office of Science and Technology, 1967).

The conclusion to be drawn from all of this is that a balance has to be struck between the need for privacy and the need to obtain data for government, business, and research. This balance is not easy to define or achieve, but it is not more difficult or less important than other balances which have to be sought on vital issues relating to human rights and basic freedoms. The law has to cope with these issues continuously and from time to time must be restructured as values, technology, and social needs change. The technology of gathering, storing, and processing information has changed sufficiently to make it necessary to redress some balance in favor of privacy.

5.6. Proposals and Actions

Through 1970 and 1971 public interest in data banks and privacy continued to mount, leading in many countries to the initiation of projects and studies which had as their aim the delineation of policy approaches to the issues involved. In the United States there was a Project on Computer Data Banks directed by A. F. Westin on behalf of the National Academy of Sciences; in Great Britain there was the MacLeod and Younger Committees dealing with governmental and nongovernmental matters, respectively; in Canada there was the Privacy Task Force of the Departments of Justice and Communications. Reports on all three of these studies appeared in 1972.[18] The United States and Canadian studies both included detailed investigations on practices relating to the handling of personal records, investigations conducted with the help of questionnaires, surveys, briefs, and visits to governmental, industrial, and educational institutions. The picture which emerged was of some importance, for it provided the first authoritative information on current (1971) practices and hence a much better basis for recommendations. The principal findings were the following.

1. That many systems were not yet automated, but there was a strong trend toward computerization. Many companies were still retaining the

[18] Westin (1972); Rt. Hon. K. Younger (Chairman), "Report of the Committee on Privacy." H. M. Stationery Office, London, 1972; Department of Communications and Department of Justice, "Privacy and Computers." Information Canada, Ottawa, 1971.

In the United States another study has been conducted by A. R. Miller on behalf of the National Science Foundation.

most sensitive parts of records manually, being unwilling to subject them to the uncertainties and costs of computer processing.

2. That most companies carried over to computer files the same rules of confidentiality and access they had used for manual files. Although computerization was making it possible to adopt new rules, there was relatively little consideration going on as to what these should be.

3. That computerization thus far has mostly meant file automation rather than shared interorganization data banks and general retrieval capabilities. The main effect has been better utilization of existing systems. But there are plans for more general purpose systems.

The conclusion from these findings was that there was still time to act so as to protect privacy, but that the rate of change of data bank technology made new approaches to handling personal information a matter of urgent priority.

Almost all of the studies, surveys, and reports we have mentioned have resulted in recommendations about computers and data banks, some of them very general and others very specific to the jurisdiction in which they were undertaken. But because of the complexity of the issues, the rate of adoption of proposals has been slow. Even when governmental bodies have conducted the studies, they have usually had only a semi-official status, and separate steps have been required for implementation of their suggestions. We conclude this chapter by collecting the various recommendations and actions in the form of directives to the group or body responsible for carrying them out. The main directives are to governments.

Directives to Government

Many feel that government information systems pose the greatest threat to individual liberties and that the need for protection measures is most urgent here. The fear is not just that some government will wish to assemble a vast centralized data bank containing massive information about every citizen. It is also about the unsatisfactory practices relating to the many specialized data banks which already exist, and further, that governments will fail to regulate both public and private data banks so as to protect individuals. It is useful to consider governmental actions under four headings.

Government Practices. Governments which are sincere in their stated desire to respect the rights of individuals clearly have to implement good practices in maintaining personal data banks. In the main this means guaranteeing individuals the opportunity to see their own records, to offer corrections, control dissemination, and to learn when files about them are being assembled.

The Land Parliament of Hesse in the Federal Republic of Germany is the first jurisdiction to enact legislation of this type.[19] Part I of the act defines the rules for access, storage, safeguarding, and communicating records, along with redress mechanisms for improper actions. Part II provides for the appointment of an ombudsman who oversees the observance of the rules.

Public opinion and the reaction of governments suggest that fair record-keeping procedures will in time evolve in most governmental systems, for example, school records, personnel records, taxation data, and so on.[20] The most difficult problems arise with police intelligence records and those maintained for purposes of national security. We may accept the contention of the police that the data in their systems cannot be open to the public, that the anonymity of informants must be preserved, and that unconfirmed speculation which might be forbidden in other systems must be recorded. Thus some of the essential safeguards which should in general be built into personal data banks cannot be applied here. Nevertheless it should be possible to set up guidelines which will give the public greater confidence that the systems are being operated fairly, without at the same time impairing their effectiveness. There are no insurmountable reasons against making known what information systems exist, who has access to them and under what condition, and defining the conditions under which data may or may not be stored. In cases where an individual has reason to believe that there were inaccuracies or irrelevancies in the information about him, it should be feasible to set up review of the data by third parties. The essential point is that the mechanics of operation of the system can be distinguished from the data contained in it. Being more open about the former can serve to build up public confidence in the fairness of the system, a *sine qua non* if feelings of alienation and hostility are to be checked; and it should be possible for this to happen without jeopardizing the system itself.[21]

Regulation and Licensing of Data Banks. The basic idea is to set up a regulating agency, commission, or tribunal similar to the bodies which

[19] Data Protection Act, State of Hesse, Federal Republic of Germany, October 7, 1970. For an unofficial English translation see Niblett (1971, pp. 47–51).

[20] As an example of how practices evolve in both New York State and the Province of Ontario as a result of court rulings and governmental changes, school records are being released for inspection by parents (*New York Times,* March 12, 1972).

[21] There are already moves to make police systems open in the United States—see U. S. House of Representatives (HR10892 and HR854), and U. S. Senate (S2546). See report in *Datamation,* p. 101, Dec. 15 (1971).

exist in many countries for overseeing the activities of public corporations, utilities, broadcasting companies, and other organizations where the public interest should be protected. Regulations would specify the conditions for licensing data banks and define standards of conduct for officials and employees. One of the earliest proposals of this nature was the Data Surveillance Bill, introduced as a private members Act to the British House of Parliament to regulate credit data banks.[22] Although this bill did not become law, others similar to it in spirit have been adopted in other jurisdictions.

It is significant that the Data Surveillance Bill is designed to deal with a specific type of damage, namely that arising out of computerized credit reporting. In this it is similar to wiretapping legislation which also deals with invasion of privacy in a specific situation. Questions about computerized data banks for other purposes or information systems in general are avoided. The underlying premise is that it is not necessary or desirable to approach the privacy problem as a whole. Progress can best be achieved by solving known problems in localized situations. After experience has been accumulated about credit data banks it may be possible to go on to other areas.

Computerized banking systems are just coming into use and it is likely that they will grow and become general. These are (or can be) tied to credit reporting systems, and it should be easy to extend regulations about credit systems to include banking data systems. As another example, we have seen that computerized medical information systems are being proposed and constructed. Here the problems are much less clear. They arise less out of the introduction of computers than through changes in medical practice. There is a definite tendency away from the binary doctor–patient relationship toward a team approach to delivery of health care. This is accompanied by a change of status in the health profession. Many more people are involved—clinicians, specialists, laboratory technicians, nurses—and with this change there is a requirement to produce a more generally accessible patient record system. It is reasonable to believe that only after much more experience will it be possible to arrive at workable regulations governing health records. If necessary, conditions under which patients can see, alter, or control the dissemination of their records can then be worked out.

In a similar way regulations about other information systems for personal records can develop—for example, school record systems, personnel records, and so on. These would evolve in the framework within which the records are kept, either under existing legislation, with the protection

[22] "Computers and Freedom," Conservative Res. Dept., Old Queen Street Papers, no. 8, London, December 1968, and "Right of Privacy Bill," House of Lords Bill 35, H. M. Stationery Office, London, February 14, 1971.

already present in law, or under well-defined extensions designed to meet specific needs.

This view, that regulations must be developed in the different contexts in which records are kept, is essentially that taken in the National Academy of Sciences report.[23] The overall conclusion is that the data bank issues are not primarily technological, but rather administrative, social, political, and legal, arising out of changes in the relationships between individuals and organizations. For this reason, a simplistic solution such as establishing a *single* regulatory or licensing agency is questionable, although licensing should not be ruled out in particular situations. Instead there must be a heavy emphasis on the importance of due processes in law as a general protection for the rights of individuals, that is, a reliance on the long-established administrative and legal practices in which there is insistence on well-defined procedures, on open rulings, and on opportunities for challenge and review of decisions.

A Right to Privacy. Another possibility, not necessarily opposed to regulation, is that governments should define and affirm a right to privacy. It is significant, however, that of three reports mentioned at the beginning of this section, all produced in English-speaking countries where the common law is the basis for much of the legal system, not one recommended this approach.

Apparently there are serious difficulties in it. Many of the damages which would presumably be protected by a right of privacy are already covered under existing laws. It is not at all clear how a privacy bill would operate in the presence of the numerous existing laws, or most important, how a new general right could be justified and given meaning.

Suggestions that it might be possible to extend rights of property to rights of ownership of data, or to classify information systems in ways which would make clear when regulations are applicable, have not found favor.[24] There are too many questions about how consent for release of data should operate. How long should it be good for? When should the release be obtained? What protection against coercion should be sought?

A point which is often brought up as limiting the ability of the law to offer protection against privacy invasions, and weakening the interest of governments in taking action, is that there are few proven instances of damages arising out of the misuse of personal records. This is not surprising. Public bodies such as police or immigration departments, and private companies such as insurance or employment agencies, do not re-

[23] Westin and Baker (1972).

[24] C. C. Gotlieb, Regulations for information systems, *Comput. Automat.* **19** (9), 14–17 (1970).

lease the contents of their files or information about dissemination unless they are required to do so. Under these circumstances it becomes very difficult for anyone to prove that some judgment about him or some action taken against him is unfair because of faulty information. In the case of credit records there have been documented instances of individuals being able to show evidence of mistakes and unfair treatment. There have also been publicized examples of agencies maintaining files about students and even legislators for reasons which cannot be defended.[25]

In general the law (especially the common law) works so as to respond to rather than anticipate instances of damages, and this makes it difficult to justify the need for legislative changes about information systems. Nevertheless there are still those who are convinced that the law must find a way of dealing with new technologies, and that an overall right of privacy must be affirmed, if for no other reason than to give encouragement and justification for regulatory mechanisms in specific situations.

Centralized Data Banks. Some believe that society is too committed to planning to stop centralized data banks, that the case for privacy is essentially lost, and that we all have to make new adjustments between what we may keep to ourselves and what must be made known for the common good. It is also argued that a single large data bank with good, well-defined rules for dissemination is better than the present situation in which there are multiple files, often with inadequate rules for restricting the dissemination of data. But the choice does not have to be between many poorly run systems and one good one; there is no reason why there should not be many well-run information systems. We may accept that a consolidated health system is desirable and inevitable; but there is no reason to combine a health information system with one for finances, education, or taxation. The economies of scale may lead to consolidating systems which serve the same function, but it is not at all to

[25] *Computerworld* regularly publishes news about misuse of credit and other personal records, challenges, and court hearings on data banks, and so on. Typical examples are reported in the issues of:

Sep. 15, 1971; Dec. 16, April 22, 1970 (errors in credit records)

June 7, 1972; Dec. 8, May 5, 1971; Feb. 11, 1970 (a U. S. army data bank on civilians)

March 22, Jan. 12, 1972; June 23, March 31, 1971 (F.B.I. data banks)

June 7, 1972 (Medical data bank).

See also "Federal Data Banks, Computers and the Bill of Rights." Hearings before the Subcommittee on Constitutional Rights of the Senate Judiciary Committee, U. S. Govt. Printing Office, Washington, D. C., 1971.

be taken for granted that multipurpose data banks containing personal information systems are more efficient.

One of the main concerns about a single large personal data bank is that it would inevitably become a dossier and that in times of emergency, when national security is felt to be jeopardized all rules which allow access only for certain purposes would be suspended. Admittedly if a government which was maintaining a dozen or more different personal information systems decided that the records should be made compatible and the systems combined, it could effect this. But it would take time—and during this time it is conceivable that the decision to construct the master data bank might be reappraised.

Prohibition of Single Identifier Numbers. Although there is some force to the argument for making it more difficult to assemble comprehensive dossiers, it can be claimed that the real gain in protection (as opposed to the psychological gain) achieved by prohibiting single identifiers is not worth the economic cost (see Section 4.4). Presumably Israel, West Germany, and the Scandinavian countries which *have* adopted universal identifiers have decided that the resulting effects on freedom and privacy are not damaging. Prohibiting a single number could give the appearance that an effective measure to protect privacy was being taken, whereas by itself it would be totally inadequate. If other necessary protections are not adopted, this measure probably adds little. In any case this is a good example of how considerations of efficiency and convenience may force an issue. In spite of confirmations of the policy not to encourage the use of social security numbers deliberately, and periodic reviews of practices, there is a steady trend toward adopting them as identifiers both in the United States and in Canada.[26]

Directives to Other Groups

Other directives are mainly concerned with data security as discussed in Chapter 4; we summarize them here for reasons of completeness.

Designers of Information Systems. Designers should consider every aspect of content, access, and dissemination. Only data relevant to the purpose in question should be acquired; aged data should be purged; checks should be built in, including the opportunity for individuals to check their own records; a hierarchy of access categories should be explicitly defined, possibly including categories not only for files but also

[26] See "Report of the Social Security Number Task Force," Social Security Administration, May 1971.

fields within a record. Access should be on a need to know basis. The elements necessary for maintaining system security should be built in (validity checks, passwords, logging procedures, etc.). The rules for dissemination should be explicit and open.

Operators of Data Banks. Operators should build procedures for careful handling of data into operating systems and follow them conscientiously. Besides those already outlined above, these should include appointing a person responsible for security measures; establishing user authorization; incorporating methods for identifying terminals and users; setting up and using changeable, programmed locks on files; and avoiding unnecessary printouts of sensitive data.

Professional Societies and Computer Organizations. Professional societies should help define standards for security in the design and operation of information systems containing personal information by working with government, the public, and computer software manufacturers. Analysts, programmers, and operators should be informed about regulations on information systems as they come into force, and generally made security conscious. A code of ethics for members should be established and adopted (see Chapter 12).

Manufacturers of Hardware and Software. Manufacturers should design and market hardware devices for maintaining security, for example, scramblers, shielded lines for communications circuits, terminal and user identifiers, and so forth. These should be made available on an optional basis at least, and where warranted, should become standard. Software for security (passwords, programmed locks) should be made standard and designed with low overhead so that operators will be encouraged to use them.[27]

In summing up this discussion it is helpful to return to the three concepts which were identified in Section 4.5—data security, data confidentiality, and privacy. At the risk of oversimplification it appears that the difficulties of maintaining data security are essentially technical, and these are well on the way to being overcome. The concept of privacy, on the other hand, is so complex that it is not possible at present to obtain agreement on direct actions which would establish it as a general

[27] At the Spring Joint Computer Conference held in Atlantic City, May 1972, IBM announced data security as a new "product," that is, a plan for marketing methods of assuring confidentiality of computer records.

right. Most of the effort should be directed to operational definitions of confidentiality in specific situations. It may be that the general controversy about computers and privacy will fade, to be replaced by a series of detailed technical issues, each resulting in practices and legislation within narrow confines. Conceivably, out of this a general position on privacy could yet emerge. It may be that some countries will find that a general privacy right can be defined and applied within its own legal framework. What is clear is that computers have provided the focal point for reexamining questions about privacy, information systems, and government practices relating to files about individuals. Computers, through their versatility and flexibility, permit administrative procedures which are much more sophisticated, much more able to allow for the special case, than has hitherto been possible. If this individualized view of personal data is taken, computerized information could, in the end, lead to better services. But for this to happen organizations, and above all governments, must be willing to make it happen. They must be prepared to define and adopt good administrative practices, and they must be ready to design and use both systems and the law so that computer technology provides means which harmonize with humane political and social goals.

Bibliography

Amer. Civil Liberties Union, *Civil Liberties*. ACLU, New York.

Bigelow, R. P., ed. (1966). "Computers and the Law: An Introductory Handbook." Commerce Clearinghouse, New York.

Freed, R. N. (1969). "Materials and Cases on Computers and Law," 2nd ed. Boston Univ. Book Store, Boston, Massachusetts.

Harrison, A. (1967, 1969). "The Problem of Privacy in the Computer Age: An Annotated Bibliography," RM-5495-PR/RC, vols. I and II. Rand Corp., Santa Monica, California.

Hoffman, L. J. (1969). Computers and Privacy: A Survey, *Computing Surveys* 1 (2), 85–103.

Miller, A. R. (1971). "The Assault on Privacy." Univ. of Michigan Press, Ann Arbor, Michigan.

Niblett, G. B. F. (1971). "Digital Information and the Privacy Problem." Org. for Economic Cooperation and Development, Paris.

Office of Sci. and Technol. (1967). "Privacy and Behavioral Research." U. S. Govt. Printing Office, Washington, D. C.

Westin, A. F. (1968). "Privacy and Freedom." Atheneum, New York.

Westin, A. F. and Baker, M. A. (1972). "Databanks in a Free Society—Computers, Record-Keeping and Privacy." Computer Sci. and Eng. Board, Nat. Acad. Sci., Quadrangle Books, Chicago, Illinois.

Wheeler, S., ed. (1969). "On Record: Files and Dossiers in American Life." Russell Sage Foundation, New York.

Problems and Further Work

1. Look up the laws relating to credit reporting in your state (province). What rights does the individual have? Are there any shortcomings? Is there any special mention of computers?

2. Do the same for school records and for medical records. What special circumstances arise in these cases?

3. Special arguments can be made for collecting highly personal information for research purposes. Discuss the problems centering around consent to gather and disseminate such information. What special precautions should be taken? (See Office of Science and Technology, 1967).

4. "A national data bank will offer better protection for privacy than is to be had from current systems." Prepare (1) the "pro" arguments for a formal debate on the question above and (2) the "contra" arguments.

5. Look up the controversy surrounding intelligence and personality testing; see, for example

Miller (1971, Sect. 3.3); Testing and public policy. *Amer. Psychologist* **20**, 857–993 (1965).

Are the objections to such tests met if the answers are scored by computers? What if the answers are never seen by anyone except the person being tested, and only the overall results are reported and recorded?

Chapter

6

SURVEYING AND PREDICTING

Surveys and questionnaires are the principal means of obtaining data on the use of computers and on attitudes about them. When surveys are carefully designed and executed, statistical tests can be applied to measure the significance of the results and estimate the confidence which can be attached to them. To project computer developments and speculate on their social effects it is possible to apply, with appropriate reservations, some of the new techniques which are being used to forecast technological changes.

6.1. Surveys about Computers

The fundamental role of statistics in business and government (including opinion surveys, forecasting, quality control) is well recognized; it has become an underlying methodology in all the social sciences as well as a principal tool in the experimental biological and physical sciences. Computing and statistics interact in many ways: in testing the reliability

TABLE 6-1
EXCERPT FROM OECD COMPUTER QUESTIONNAIRE

6. Number* of computers installed in the computing center ... ... [ ]

7. How many hours computing time per month do you buy from outside institutions? ... ... h/m [ ] model [ ]

8. How many hours computing time do you sell to outside institutions? ... ... h/m [ ] model [ ]

9. Total size of file library:*
   Tape reels ... ... [ ]
   Disk packs ... ... [ ]
   Others (...) [ ]
   (please specify with capacity)

D. PERSONNEL*

1. Staff of computing center:

	TOTAL	EDUCATIONAL BACKGROUND		
		UNIVERSITY AND OTHER PROFESSIONAL EDUCATION*	WITH CERTIFICATE OF SECONDARY EDUCATION*	OTHERS (TRAINED ON JOB)
—Managers*				
—Systems analysts* ...				
—Programmers* ...				
—Operators				
—Keypunchers ...				
—Clerical staff* ...				
—.................... Others* (please specify)				

2. Persons outside the computing center, working with your computers:*

	TOTAL	EMPLOYEES OF YOUR ORGANIZATION
—Systems analysts		
—Programmers		
—Others (............)		

and effectiveness of hardware and software, in computer modeling and simulation of diverse systems (see Chapter 7), and in surveying to determine attitudes about the uses and desirability of computers. The Appendix describes some of the statistical concepts employed in the interpretation of survey results.

Questionnaires about computers are generated at an unending rate by an enormous number of commercial, national, and international organizations. At least three aspects are objects of study.

1. Hardware, software, personnel, and management. This information is sought by companies and institutes planning to acquire facilities, by organizations responsible for coordinating computer use, and by suppliers of hardware and software services.
2. Practices regarding use of the computing facility. Such data are needed for planning changes in equipment, determining policies regarding access, and for studying the benefits and costs of computer use.
3. Attitudes toward computers. These are needed in attempts to gauge the social effects of computers and the acceptability of new systems.

Tables 6-1, 6-2, and 6-3 show excerpts from questionnaires which illustrate the three types. The first is from a survey undertaken by OECD to determine computer utilization among member states.[1] The second is from a Computers and Privacy Task Force carried out by the Departments of Justice and Communications of the Canadian government.[2] The third is from an attitudinal survey jointly commissioned by the American Federation of Information Processing Societies and *Time Magazine* in the United States.[3]

Designing questionnaires and conducting opinion polls for the social sciences is a highly developed technique which started with government censuses and which has been largely perfected through experience gained in election forecasting and marketing surveys. Three phases of a survey requiring technical knowledge are formulating the questions, choosing the sample, and evaluating the results; the last two in particular depend heavily on statistics (Parten, 1966; Kish, 1965).

When detailed information on individual opinions and feelings about complex subjects is sought, there is no substitute for an in-depth inter-

[1] "Computer Utilization Survey—for National Authorities." OECD, DAS/SPR/69.5, Paris (1969).

[2] Dept. of Justice and Comm., Survey Questionnaire, Information Canada, Ottawa, November, 1971.

[3] "A National Survey of the Public's Attitudes Toward Computers," a joint project of the Amer. Fed. of Informat. Processing Soc. and *Time Magazine*, AFIPS, Montvale, New Jersey, November, 1971.

TABLE 6-2
EXCERPT FROM QUESTIONNAIRE OF PRIVACY TASK FORCE, DEPARTMENTS OF JUSTICE AND COMMUNICATIONS, OTTAWA

12. A. As a general rule, can the individual examine his own record or a copy of his record from the file? (Please mark only one response.)

The individual does not know the record exists ( )
Has no understanding of the contents of his record ( )
Can examine all data in his record ( )
Can examine some data in his record ( )
Can examine no data in his record ( )

12. B. If an individual is permitted to examine any data in his record, is translation or interpretation provided to an official language which the individual understands?
Yes ( ) No ( )

12. C. Have individuals or groups representing their interests ever sought to examine their own records or complained about the adequacy of your organization's practices regarding an individual's right to examine his own record? (Please mark one response only.)

Never ( )
Occasionally ( )
Frequently ( )
Do not know ( )
Does not apply ( )

13. A. Indicate your principal means for gathering information for this file? (Please mark one response in each row.)

	None	Some	Most	All	
13. A. 1	( )	( )	( )	( )	Other information suppliers
13. A. 2	( )	( )	( )	( )	Published sources or public records
13. A. 3	( )	( )	( )	( )	Individual on whom the record is kept
13. A. 4	( )	( )	( )	( )	Information recipients (e.g., merchants)
13. A. 5	( )	( )	( )	( )	Investigators

view followed by careful analysis of the content. In other situations aggregate results from surveys are sufficient, and the less expensive method of tabulating responses to prepared questions is used. Care has to be exercised in avoiding leading questions when conducting the survey; also when opinions on an issue are sought, the responses indicating

TABLE 6-3
EXCERPT FROM TECHNOLOGY STUDY, AFIPS/TIME[a]

Question	Response	5
1. All in all, what effect do you think inventions and technology have had on life in the past 25 years—have they made life better, worse, or haven't they affected us one way or the other? (IF "BETTER" OR "WORSE," ASK:) Would you say much or somewhat (better/worse)?	Much better	☐ 1
	Somewhat better	☐ 2
	Not affected	☐ 3
	Somewhat worse	☐ 4
	Much worse	☐ 5
	Don't know	☐ 6
2. Overall, what effect do you think the use of computers has had on life—has it made life better, worse, or hasn't it affected us one way or the other? (IF "BETTER" OR "WORSE," ASK:) Would you say much or somewhat (better/worse)?	Much better	☐ 7
	Somewhat better	☐ 8
	Not affected	☐ 9
	Somewhat worse	☐ 0
	Much worse	☐ X
	Don't know	☐ Y
		6
3. Have your feelings towards computers and their uses changed very much in the past 5 or 10 years? (IF "YES," ASK:) Is your present attitude toward computers more favorable or less favorable than it was?	Yes, more favorable	☐ 1
	Yes, less favorable	☐ 2
	No	☐ 3

4. I'm going to read some statements. For each one I mention, I would like you to tell me how well you think that statement describes the nature or function of a computer. To do this, give me a number from 0 to 10. The more you think a description describes the nature or function of a computer, the bigger the number you should give me. The less you think a description describes the nature or function of a computer, the smaller the number you should give me. Now, from 0 to 10, how well does________ describe the nature or function of computers? (READ ALL ITEMS)

An electronic brain or "thinking machine"	7______
A super-fast adding machine	8______
An automatic electronic machine for performing calculations	9______
An electronic device for storing information	10______
An accounting machine used for business purposes	11______
An electronic device for controlling factory equipment	12______

[a] Reprinted with the permission of Time, Inc. and AFIPS. Copyright 1971 by Time, Inc.

agreement and disagreement should be presented equally often, to minimize the chance of bias. Scaling techniques are available to obtain measures of the intensity of belief on a subject.[4] These are arrived at by

[4] C. F. Schmid, Scaling techniques in sociological research, *in* "Scientific Social Surveys and Research" (P. V. Young, ed.), Chapter 12, 4th ed. Prentice-Hall, Englewood Cliffs, New Jersey, 1966.

presenting a battery of questions whose answers have been rated by a panel of experts according to their strength of attachment to a position, or more frequently by offering the subject a sequence of levels (usually four to six) on which he can indicate a measure for his feeling (see question 1 on Table 6-3). Questions to check the consistency of the replies can be incorporated into a survey, but it must not be assumed that the opinions (as distinct from facts) provided by a response must show consistency.

Among the methods for drawing samples are *stratified sampling* (where random samples are drawn from known subdivisions of the population being studied, usually in proportion to the size of the subdivision), *systematic sampling* (where every *k*th member of a list is chosen, the first being selected randomly), and *cluster sampling* (where members are chosen according to some frame, often geographical, superimposed on the population). Once a unit has been selected for sampling it is important that a response be secured from it, by repeated contacts if necessary. The sample size depends on the number of cells into which the responses are to be grouped (no cell must have only a few responses) and on the precision which is to be attached to the results.

We have already seen in Chapters 2 and 3 some results of surveys on the number of computer installations and the types of applications, and later we shall be discussing results of attitudinal surveys on employment and on other effects which might be observed if computer technology were to evolve along certain lines. At this point, in order to provide a basis for subject matter in later chapters, it is useful to present some of the data on attitudes toward computers which were observed in the AFIPS/Time survey mentioned earlier. The results are based on 1001 telephone interviews with a constructed sample drawn from the adult population of the United States. There were five demographic questions whose answers helped describe the respondent (political leanings, age and income group, education, occupation), three indicating experience with computers, and 14 indicating attitudes about uses (present, future, desirable), about government responsibilities, and about computing as a career. Excerpts from the tabulated replies are shown in Table 6-4. Tabulations on the 22 questions along with cross tabulations according to sex, age group, education, and income are given in the survey. Although the questionnaire is fairly simple, there is sufficient detail to see some patterns. About half of the public has had some contact with computers and although only 15% has any detailed knowledge or experience, it is generally correctly informed about the uses of computers. It is, on the whole, optimistic about the effects of technology and benefits of computers, both present and prospective, and computing as a career.

TABLE 6-4
SOME RESULTS FROM AFIPS/TIME SURVEY ON ATTITUDES ABOUT COMPUTERS

Involvement with computers	
Contact through job	49%
Knowledge required in job	15%
Worked directly	14%

Overall effects on life	Better (%)	Same (%)	Worse (%)	DK/NA (%)
Technology has improved life in past 25 years	85	2	8	5
Computers have improved life	71	5	15	9

Computers now	Agree	DK/NA	Disagree
Increase quality of products and services	68	10	22
Help raise standard of living	65	9	26
Make information about other people too readily available	58	9	33
Dehumanize people and turn them into numbers	54	6	40
May be used to destroy individual freedom	53	7	40
Create more jobs than they eliminate	36	13	51
Represent a real threat to privacy	38	8	54
Are changing our lives too rapidly	35	6	39
Increase the chance of war	17	13	70
Think for themselves	12	5	83

Computers will	Agree	DK/NA	Disagree
Provide information and services in the home	89	4	7
Create more leisure	86	2	12
Improve our lives	75	6	19
Be used for surveillance	58	7	35
Decrease our freedom	33	8	59
Disobey instructions	23	8	69
Read thoughts	17	6	77

Increase or decrease desired for selected use in	Increase	DK/NA	Decrease	Believe that computers are used currently
Keeping track of criminals	78	16	6	78
Gathering census data	70	24	6	
Medical diagnosis	74	15	11	78
Guiding missiles for defense	71	18	11	

TABLE 6-4 (*Continued*)

Increase or decrease desired for selected use in	Increase	DK/NA	Decrease	Believe that computers are used currently
Vote counting	66	26	8	
Credit card billing	52	35	13	96
Surveillance of radicals	56	27	17	54
Projecting election results	50	30	20	
Public opinion polling	47	34	19	81
Compiling files on citizens	50	24	26	95
Teaching children in school	48	27	25	64
Matching people for dating	14	31	55	
Sending mail advertisements to the home	16	21	63	69

Concern about information being kept about people	Concerned	Not concerned	DK/NA
	62	36	2

Government and regulation	Government is concerned	Government is not concerned	DK/NA
	61	36	2
	Government should be concerned	Government should not be concerned	DK/NA
	84	12	4

Computing as a career	Would advise	No opinion	Would advise against	DK/NA
	76	17	5	2

	True	DK/NA	Not true
Offers good opportunities for women	87	6	7
Offers good opportunities for professionals and scientists	81	7	12

These optimistic beliefs are held somewhat more strongly by the young and the better educated. There are some inconsistencies; although 54% disagree that computers represent a real threat to privacy, 58% believe that because of computerized information files, too many people have information about others, and 53% that such files may be used to destroy individual freedoms. Although 62% express concern about information being kept about people, there was no type of record which even half the respondents felt should not be kept in a computer file. The only computer applications which a majority wished to see reduced were computer dating and sending mail advertisements into the home, two which seem relatively innocuous.

In general these results are consistent with those obtained from other surveys on attitudes about technology and about computers. Such surveys reveal that computers are strongly associated with new technological developments, that on the whole the benefits of technology are perceived as outweighing the disadvantages, that there is *not* a general concern about the effects of computers on privacy, and that the level of education does significantly influence viewpoints (more education makes people more favorably disposed to technology, but not necessarily uncritical of it).[5]

As the computer industry and computer utilities grow, public involvement and acceptance of the developments will have to become even more pronounced than it has been hitherto. Questionnaires and surveys about computers offer a mechanism for monitoring this involvement.[6]

6.2. Technological Change and Forecasting

At this point we wish to extend the subject of discourse beyond computers to embrace technology as a whole, and particularly technological change and methods of forecasting it. In the chapters which follow we shall be interested in the effects, both observed and projected, of the increasing use of computers. It is vital to know how computer effects relate to those induced by other technologies—for example, by new modes of transportation and communication, or by new types of energy sources, materials, and services. If there is some unwanted consequence of computers (e.g., unemployment or loss of privacy) and corrective action is being considered, it is necessary to coordinate this action with steps for related technologies. Many of the recent studies of technologi-

[5] See D. Armor, S. Feindhandler, and K. Sapolsky, Public views of technology, Harvard Univ. Program on Technol. and Soc., *Res. Rev.* October (1970); R. E. Anderson, Sociological analysis of public attitudes towards computers and information files. *AFIPS Conf. Proc.* **40**, 649–657 (1972). The results are also similar to those obtained from surveys conducted as class projects in a course on Computers and Society at the University of Toronto.

[6] B. Gilchrist, Public involvement and acceptance, *in* "Planning Community Information Utilities" (Sackman and Boehm, eds.), Chapter 5. AFIPS Press, Montvale, New Jersey (to appear).

cal change center on computers and automation; conclusions about technology in general are often inferred from observations on computers, or conversely, the effects of computers are deduced from more general postulates about new technologies. In studying forecasting, we shall be subscribing to the view that a rational society is one which attempts to determine goals and plan actions which are predicted to achieve these goals. Planning and forecasting are essentially interrelated, for we must know what is feasible and what is probable within the time span of our plans. In this book, we shall reverse the natural order and discuss predicting and planning before goal-setting. This reversal is necessary because difficult as forecasting and planning are, they are far more amenable to formal study than is goal-setting; the treatment corresponds to the progression from science and technology toward politics and sociology presented in Chapter 1.

Technological forecasting is not without its own issues. Criticism has been leveled at it because some of its practitioners are seen as offering it as a normative, goal-setting approach to planning, without providing a framework for reaching goals in a broad democratic way.[7] This approach undoubtedly arises because technological forecasting had its origins in military applications where goals are obvious, but it raises doubts about the appropriateness of its methods when they are offered for corporate planning, and even more so when they are proposed for social planning. Can predictions and goal-setting be kept distinct? Another factor which makes it difficult to accept forecasting is that the proponents often appear as prophets of doom who warn about impending disasters from nuclear weapons, overpopulation, and global pollution.[8] There is at least a suggestion that catastrophes can be avoided only by adopting their techniques, and it is difficult to separate the sense of urgency from special claims. Nevertheless there is a growing recognition that it has become absolutely essential to forecast the directions of technology and the interactions between technological and social change. Computers are inextricably bound up in such forecasting, both in developing the techniques and as objects of study.

Measurement and Definition

Before attempting to catalog methods of forecasting technological change it is useful to define it, identify its constituents, and indicate how

[7] See R. Jungk, "Technological Forecasting as a Tool of Social Strategy"; L. E. Schwarts, "Technological Forecasting: Another Perspective," *in* Arnfield (1969, pp. 3–11, 71–82).

[8] See J. Maddox, The doomsday man. *Encounter,* pp. 64–68, January (1971).

it can be measured. Economists derive a measure from the *production function,* which is an expression for calculating the aggregate goods produced by an economic system. Let the production function Y depend on the capital K and labor L.[9] If we wish to emphasize the fact that, even for constant K and L, the output changes with time, we may write

$$Y = A(t) \cdot f(K, L) \tag{1}$$

$f(K, L)$ is a function of K and L and $A(t)$ is a multiplicative factor which determines the output for a given K and L; this factor is a description of the technology for the (aggregated) economy.[10]

Writing

$$\log Y = \log A(t) + \log f(K, L)$$

we have

$$\frac{\Delta Y}{Y} = \frac{\Delta A}{A} + \frac{\Delta f}{f} \tag{2}$$

Writing

$$\Delta f = \frac{\partial f}{\partial K}\,\Delta K + \frac{\partial f}{\partial L}\,\Delta L$$

and defining the labor and capital elasticities W_L and W_K by

$$W_L = \frac{L}{Y}\frac{\partial Y}{\partial L} \qquad \text{and} \qquad W_K = \frac{K}{Y}\frac{\partial Y}{\partial K}$$

we obtain

$$\frac{\Delta A}{A} = \frac{\Delta Y}{Y} - W_K\frac{\Delta K}{K} - W_L\frac{\Delta L}{L} \tag{3}$$

$\Delta A/A$ is interpreted as the technological change, and Eq. (3) states that it is equal to the (percentage) change in production not accounted for by the changes in capital and labor. A closely related variant of this definition which we shall use in Chapter 9 states that the technological change is the change in output per man-hour of input after capital changes have been replaced by equivalent labor changes.[11]

Although this economic definition based on aggregate production pro-

[9] It is usual to assume that the factors exhibit *constant return* to *scale,* that is, a given percentage change in K or L produces the same percentage change in Y.

[10] This general form of the production function was used by R. Solow [Technical change and the aggregate production function, *Rev. Econ. Statist.* (1957)] to derive the measure of technological change given here. A commonly assumed form is the Cobb–Douglas function $Y = AK^{W_K} \cdot L^{W_L}$ where $W_K + W_L = 1$.

[11] In general, the method of measuring technological change given here is too simple. Among other things, it is necessary to calculate growth industry by industry, that is, take structural effects into account, and also to allow for time variations in the elasticities. See L. B. Lane, "Technological Change: Its Conception and Measurement." Prentice-Hall, Englewood Cliffs, New Jersey, 1966.

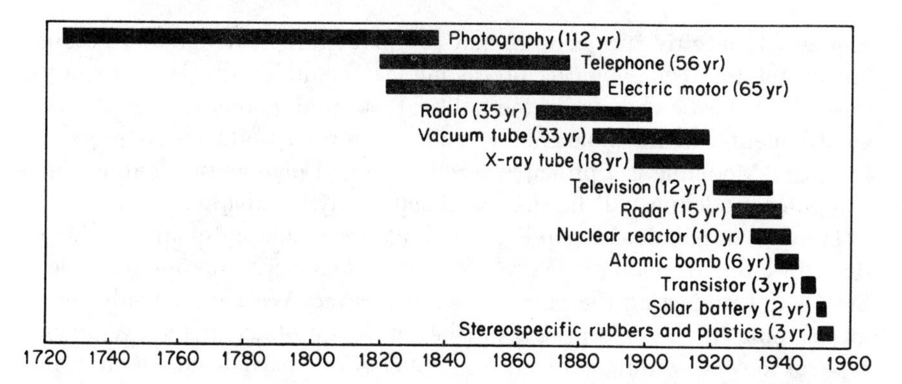

FIG. 6-1. *The speed of change; time lag between invention and innovation.* (*Reprinted with the permission from W. O. Baker, The dynamics of science and technology, in "Seminar on Technology and Social Change" (Eli Ginzberg, ed.). Columbia Univ. Press, New York, 1964. Copyright 1964 by Columbia University Press.*)

vides a useful overall measure, it is necessary to look at technological change more carefully. Of various subprocesses contributing to it, we can identify *invention, innovation, transfer,* and *diffusion*. Each of these can be studied in its own right. Although it is possible to argue that inventions occur when the time is ripe for them in response to economic and social needs, individuals play such an important role that it is very difficult to forecast them.[12] Innovation, as distinct from invention, occurs when an invention is actually applied. One of the most striking features of technology is the steady decrease in the time lag between invention and innovation. This is illustrated in Fig. 6-1. Transfer occurs when an innovation in one industry is adopted in another, and diffusion is the process whereby "best practice" gradually spreads throughout an industry.[13] Technological transfer has been the object of intense study in many countries as well as by international organizations such as OECD and the United Nations.[14]

FORECASTING

Forecasting techniques can be grouped under five headings: (1) extrapolation of trends; (2) morphological analysis; (3) heuristic rea-

[12] See Ayres (1969, pp. 29–34).

[13] See E. Mansfield, "Industrial Research and Technological Innovation," Parts III and IV. Norton, New York, 1968, for a detailed analysis of innovation and diffusion.

[14] For a study of technological innovation and transfer in the computer industry see "Gaps in Technology." OECD, Paris, 1969. Also R. Curnow, "The Innovation Cycle in the Manufacture and Application of Computer Systems," *in* Arnfield (1969, pp. 314–320).

soning; (4) intuitive projections; and (5) modeling. Although all of these are useful for technological forecasting, it should hardly be necessary to say that drastic changes in the political, cultural, military, or economic environment will invalidate underlying assumptions and all consequent forecasts. Modeling is a principal forecasting and planning technique and computer modeling will be discussed separately in Chapter 7.

Trend extrapolation depends on finding some suitable quantity which describes the technology (very often the efficiency, appropriately defined) and projecting the curve forward in time. We have already seen an example of this in Fig. 2-2 on the efficiency of computers. A given type of device within a technology, such as a particle accelerator in nuclear physics or an engine in mechanical engineering, will be improved over time until its performance levels off. The common experience is then that some new type of device is found so that the technology is escalated, and there is a performance curve at a higher level until that

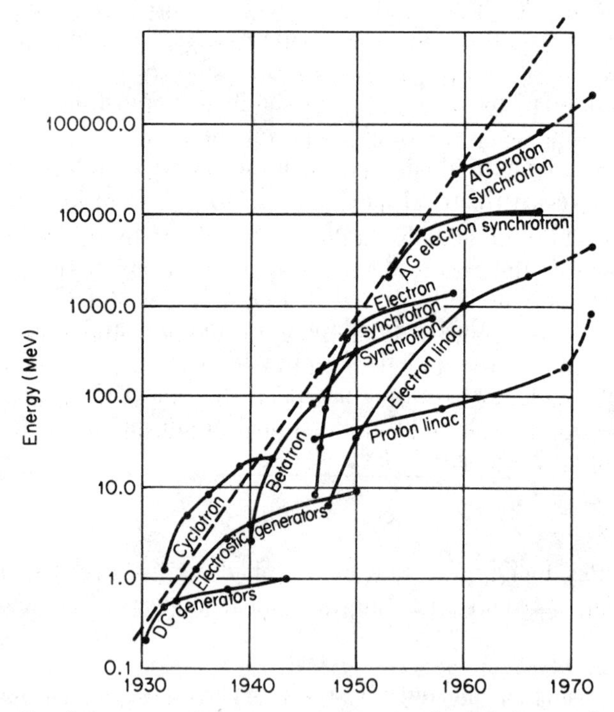

FIG. 6-2. *Envelope curve forecasting. Energies achieved by accelerators from 1932 to 1968. The linear envelope of the individual curves shows an average tenfold increase in energy every six years. (Reprinted with the permission from M. Stanley Livingstone, "Particle Accelerators: A Brief History." Harvard Univ. Press, Cambridge, Massachusetts, 1969. Copyright 1969 by Harvard University Press.)*

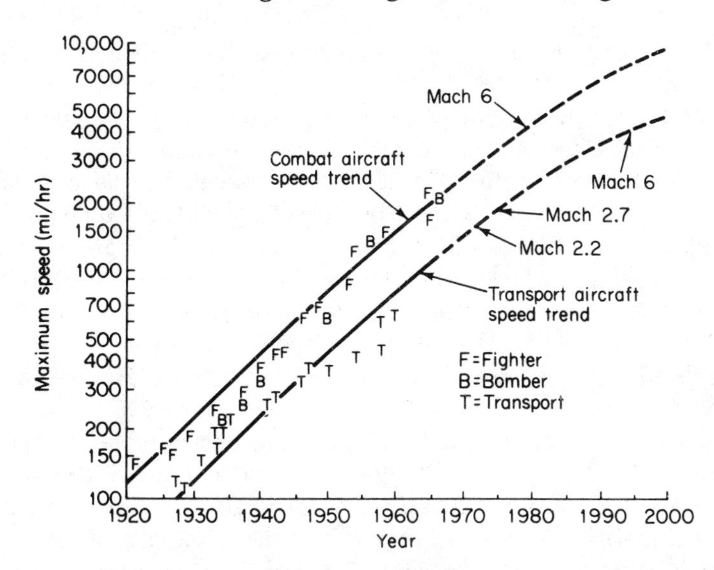

Fig. 6-3. *Forecasting by analogy. Speed trends of combat aircraft versus speed trends of transport aircraft, showing lead trend effect.* (*Reprinted with the permission from R. V. Ayres, "Technological Forecasting and Long-Range Planning." McGraw-Hill, New York, 1969. Copyright 1969 by McGraw-Hill Book Company.*)

device too is supplanted. Figure 6-2 illustrates this escalation process for particle accelerators. From such a curve it is often possible to draw an *envelope* curve which shows the progress of the technology as a whole, but of course it is not possible at any point in time to predict with certainty that a new device will be invented to maintain the envelope projection.[15]

Morphological analysis is essentially a classification. A set of devices or processes having the same function is examined and grouped into classes or types according to features which they possess or parameters which can be identified. From this grouping it is sometimes possible to recognize a missing member in the group and to set about constructing or designing such a member. This technique has been successfully used in metallurgical processing and transportation system analysis, and it has resulted in useful predictions and suggestions for exploratory research.[16]

Heuristic reasoning is the application of a rule which is plausible but which cannot be used to justify a prediction with certainty. One might

[15] R. C. Lang, "Forecasts of Exploding Technologies by Trend Extrapolation"; R. Ayres, "Envelope Curve Forecasting," in Bright (1968, pp. 57–76, 77–94).

[16] A. V. Bridgewater, "Morphological Methods: Principles and Practices," *in* Arnfield (1969) and Ayres (1969, Chapter 5).

look for a precursor event which anticipates that which is being forecast. Figure 6-3 illustrates an example which is commonly given, showing how the speed of commercial aircraft is anticipated by the speed of military planes. Or one might make a prediction based on a variable which is correlated to the one of interest. Essentially the prediction is based on analogy and it is therefore attendant with the obvious danger that the analogy may cease to hold over the range of the prediction.

Intuitive projections are derived by inviting "experts" and informed persons to speculate about possibilities, often by arranging for some interaction among them. One approach is to make "surprise-free" projections, that is, without assuming any major change in technology, political, or social structures, and extrapolate present trends.[17] Alternatively it is possible to generate a list of potential or desirable technological breakthroughs, and follow through the consequences. A technique introduced at the Rand Corporation for encouraging imaginative explorations, particularly for military purposes, is the enactment of "scenarios"[18] in which participants take various roles and improvise responses to situations with which they are confronted. Among the intuitive projections of the future must be included the numerous societies, utopias, and hells which have been envisaged by generations of authors and science fiction writers. Some, for example those of Butler, Huxley, and Orwell, have been absorbed into the consciousness of society and have had considerable influence on opinion leaders and social thought.[19]

A highly structured way to bring informed opinion to bear on long-range technological forecasting is the Delphi method developed by Olaf Helmer and Norman Dalkey at the Rand Corporation.[20] Early Delphi experiments were used to arrive at estimates for the times when events and developments considered to have high sociological significance would be achieved. Participants are given a list of such events and asked to indicate the date (if ever) when they might happen. On a second iteration they are given the average predicted date, along with the interquartile range (the interval containing 50% of the estimates) and asked if they wished to revise their predictions. If they choose to make a pre-

[17] This term is from H. Kahn and A. J. Wiener, The next thirty-three years: A framework for speculation, *in* "Towards the Year 2000." *Daedalus,* Summer (1967), where various speculations of the kind indicated appear.

[18] A term also introduced by Herman Kahn.

[19] For an account of predictions in fiction, see W. H. G. Armytage, "Yesterday's tomorrows." Univ. of Toronto Press, Toronto, Canada, 1968. For a study of science fiction, see Livingston, Science fiction as source material for futurists, *Futures* March (1969).

[20] O. Helmer, "Analysis of the Future: The Delphi Method," *in* Bright (1968, pp. 116–133).

diction outside the range, they are asked to give reasons for their differing view. In subsequent iterations summaries of the arguments for and against the majority dates are circulated. The observation, which in large measure makes it possible to have some confidence in the Delphi method, is that after a few iterations (three to five normally) a consensus is often reached. This does not, of course, provide assurance that the prediction will be correct, but it does mean that there is a measure of agreement on the part of experts about what is likely to happen. About some matters agreement is not reached, but the opinions may crystallize around two different views, and this provides a basis for further explorations.

The advantage of the Delphi method of obtaining aggregate opinion is that through maintenance of anonymity in the responses, the possibilities of coercion and the "bandwagon" temptation to join the majority are eliminated. It is also possible to set up variations in which an "elite" group, one which has special expertise in the subject, is identified, and the opinion of the elite is given special weight, allowed to influence the other participants, or examined to see whether it differs significantly from the generally held view. It was further realized in Delphi experiments that it is necessary to incorporate methods of allowing for interactions between events, and in subsequent experiments attention has been given to so-called cross-correlation impacts.[21] More recently Delphi studies have been conducted in which the participants communicate through interactive computer terminals, thereby greatly shortening the period of the experiment and providing a great deal of flexibility in the size of the participating group, the manner in which the experiment is monitored, the number of interactions, and the type of statistics gathered and circulated during the course of the interaction.

The Delphi technique is not limited to technological forecasting. It is essentially a method of communication which can be used to achieve consensus or reveal divergence of opinions. It has been used to assess historical events, poll current medical opinion, structure models, and delineate policy options, and it has been proposed as a technique for dealing with controversial issues.[22]

Predictions about Computers

Because computers are in themselves regarded as precursors of technological change, forecasts about them are made at every turn. These

[21] T. J. Gordon, "New Approaches to Delphi," *in* Bright (1968, pp. 134–143).

[22] See M. Turoff, The design of a policy Delphi, *Tech. Forecasting Social Change* **2**, 149–171 (1970–1971); J. B. Schneider, The policy Delphi: A regional planning application, *Tech. Forecasting Social Change* 3 (4), 481–497 (1972). Also see Sect. 11.3.

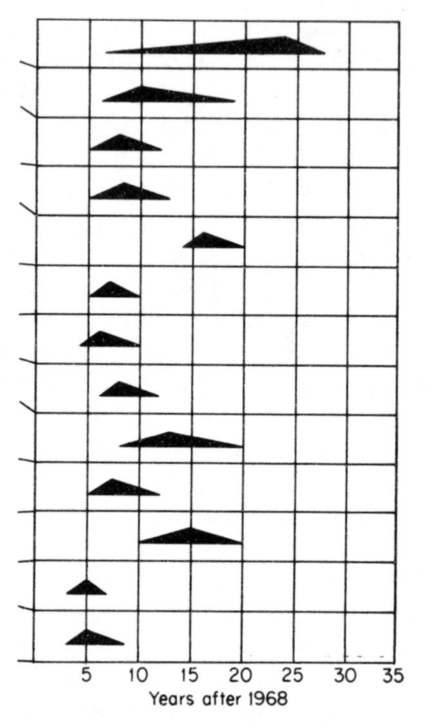

FIG. 6-4. *Forecast development of computer technology. At each entry let L, M, and U be the time for the entry start, peak, and end, respectively. Then M is the median of the responses and the interquartile intervals M–L and U–M each contain one-quarter of the estimates. (From P. H. Hall, Computer systems, in "Technological Forecasting and Corporate Strategy" (G. Wills, D. Ashton, and B. Taylor, eds.). Bradford University Press and Crosby Lockwood & Son Ltd., London, 1969.)*

range through short-range market predictions for various segments of the computer industry (see footnotes 9 and 10 in Chapter 2), trend extrapolations, intuitive predictions,[23] and Delphi exercises on developments to be expected in computer hardware, software, applications, and on the social consequences of the growth of information systems. One of the first large Delphi experiments conducted by Helmer was on the effects of automation,[24] and other related Delphi studies are cited by Bjerrum and by Hall.[25] Figures 6-4 and 6-5 from Hall are typical of the results obtained. One predicted development which has received special

[23] T. J. Rubin, "Technology, Policy and Forecasting," *in* Bright (1968, pp. 242–262).

[24] O. Helmer, "Social Technology," Appendix. Basic Books, New York, 1966.

Utilization

National U.K. Data Bank with central record of whole population
Chequeless society in U.K.
Cheques used only by private individuals
Computer-aided teaching in over 50% of U.K. comprehensive schools
Complete control of London's underground railway system
Ten fully integrated management information systems operational in U.K.
One percent residential houses in U.K. with terminal linked to information service computer
National economic forecasting and planning by computer
Large-scale information retrieval system
(a) Science and technology
(b) Patents
(c) Law
(d) Medical diagnosis

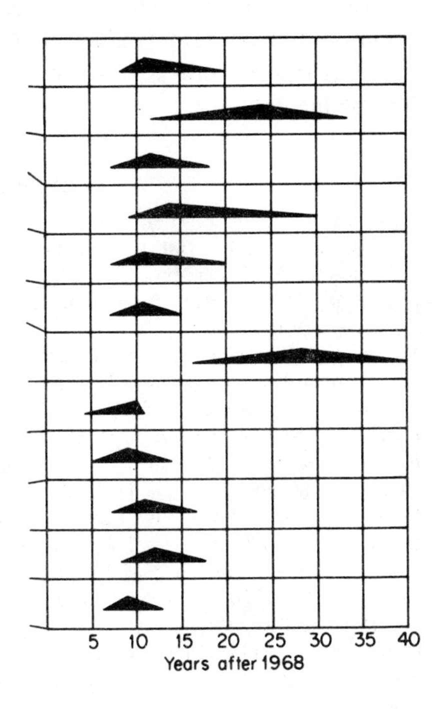

Fig. 6-5. *Forecast utilization of computers. (From P. D. Hall, Computer systems, in "Technological Forecasting and Corporate Strategy" (G. Wills, D. Ashton, and B. Taylor, eds.), Chapter 12. Bradford University Press and Crosby Lockwood & Son Ltd., London, 1969.)*

attention is the possibility of bringing computer power into the home, through the telephone or through a coaxial cable used for television. If this is accompanied by two-way transmission of signals to and from the user, it is expected to have profound social effects. These possibilities and their consequences are discussed further in Chapters 10 and 11.

In summary it can be said that, with some reservations, the studies and forecasting of technological change are becoming an accepted part of technology. The intensity of the activity both in North America and Europe is witnessed by the many books which have been published since Jantsch (1967), by the appearance in rapid succession of several journals (*Innovation, Futurist, Technological Forecasting,* and *Social Change*), by the emergence of a number of societies and companies devoted to the

---

[25] C. A. Bjerrum, Forecast of computer developments and applications, 1968–2000, *Futures* 1, 331–358 (1969); P. D. Hall, "Computer systems," in Wills *et al.* (1969, Chapter 12).

subject,[26] and by the adoption of recognized courses in universities. An extensive bibliography is given by Cetron (1969). Computers are of central importance both as a subject of technological forecasting and as a forecasting tool.

Bibliography

Arnfield, R. V., ed. (1969). "Technological Forecasting." Edinburgh Univ. Press, Edinburgh, Scotland.

Ayres, R. V. (1969). "Technological Forecasting and Long-Range Planning." McGraw-Hill, New York.

Bright, J., ed. (1968). "Technological Forecasting for Industry and Government." Prentice-Hall, Englewood Cliffs, New Jersey.

Cetron, M. J. (1969). "Technological Forecasting." Gordon and Breach, New York.

Futures (1968). First issue, Sept. Ilife House, London.

Futurist, The World Future Society, Washington, D. C.

Helmer, O. (1966). "Social Technology." Basic Books, New York.

Jantsch, E., ed. (1969). "Perspectives of Planning." OECD, Paris.

Jantsch, E. (1967). "Technological Forecasting in Perspective." OECD, Paris.

Kish, L. (1965). "Survey Sampling." Wiley, New York.

Lane, L. B. (1966). "Technological Change: Its Conception and Measurement." Prentice-Hall, Englewood Cliffs, New Jersey.

Mansfield, E. (1968). "The Economics of Technological Change." Norton, New York.

Parten, M. (1966). "Surveys, Polls, and Samples." Cooper Square Publ., New York.

Tech. Forecasting and Social Change (1970). First issue. American Elsevier, New York.

Wills, G., Ashton, D., and Taylor, B. eds. (1969). "Technological Forecasting and Corporate Strategy." Bradford Univ. Press and Lockwood, London.

Problems and Further Work

1. In a survey conducted among students the following replies were obtained to a question on whether technology has made life better or worse:

Reply	Number of respondents
Much better	52
Somewhat better	146
Not affected	22
Somewhat worse	17
Much worse	2
No answer or do not know	17
Total	256

Is this sample of student population significantly different in its answer than the sample of the AFIPS/Time survey?

2. In the student survey the following replies were obtained to questions on whether computer use should be increased, decreased, or remain the same.

	Number wishing to see			
Application	An increase	Use remain the same	A decrease	No opinion
Teaching children in school	93	61	62	38
Medical diagnosis	80	75	52	31
Projecting election results	60	96	64	33
Matching people for dating	20	51	106	61
Compiling information on citizens	47	73	93	25
Credit card billing	118	66	29	26
Surveillance of radicals	37	46	99	70
Sending mail advertisements to the home	20	35	141	35

For each question, and for the survey as a whole, determine whether the student population is significantly different than that polled in the AFIPS/Time survey.

3. If you wished to use the AFIPS/Time survey on a university population, how would you select the sample? See Kish (1965).

4. Trace the diffusion of computing technology into the typesetting and photocopying industries.

5. Plot the trend curve of computer speed (using some suitable measure) for computers of successive generations (vacuum tube, transistors, integrated circuits). Can an envelope be drawn? Is there a leveling at each generation, followed by an escalation at the next?

[26] For example, The Hudson Inst. and Inst. for the Future (United States), Internat. Futuribles Committee (France), Next Thirty Years Committee (United Kingdom), The Club of Rome (international).

Chapter 7

SYSTEMS, MODELS, AND SIMULATIONS

Of a variety of planning techniques in which computers are used, the most important is systems planning. This is emerging as a basic approach to problem solving where large, complicated structures and many factors are involved. In this approach the system under study is isolated from its environment, its components are identified, and their behavior and interactions are analyzed. Many systems under study today are so large and have so many components that their behavior cannot be calculated directly from physical or statistical principles. If improvements are proposed in a system which is difficult or highly undesirable to experiment with, to evaluate the proposals we may construct a model and carry out simulations on it. Often the models are computer models, and many such have been advanced for analyzing systems which are important socially—transportation, urban, educational, and so forth. In this chapter we consider the use of computers in systems planning to examine the advantages and limitations of this approach. From relatively simple systems and models we go on to consider some large-scale, highly ambitious simulations. How valid is the model is the essential question which must always be raised. As the systems become more complex, it becomes increasingly difficult to verify that a model represents the system accurately with respect to the properties under study. In some cases, the present usefulness of computer modeling has been oversold.

7.1. Computers and Planning

We saw in Chapter 3 that the use of computers in planning is attractive to both businesses and governments. Aside from mathematical techniques as exemplified by trend analysis, statistical calculations, and linear programming, three general planning techniques involving computers have gained currency. These are the *critical path method* (known as CPM and also as PERT, program evaluation and review technique), *planned program budgeting* (PPB), and *systems planning*, especially as carried out through computer simulation. All three of these techniques have strong advocates, particularly the first two whose use has at times been required when bidding on government contracts in the United States and Canada. Of the three, systems planning is the method which has the widest applications, and it is potentially the most important; however, it is useful to examine the other two briefly.

CPM is a method for planning and scheduling large complicated undertakings where there are many subprojects and participants.[1] The whole project is represented as a network, defined by a set of activities each of which has a given duration, and a set of precedence relations that are pairs of activities, one of which must precede the other in time (Table 7-1 and Fig. 7-1). By finding the path through the network of longest duration, it is possible to find a *minimum completion time* and also a *critical path,* that is, a path containing those activities which must be completed in their given duration if the minimum is to be achieved.

On the very large projects where PERT and CPM have had their

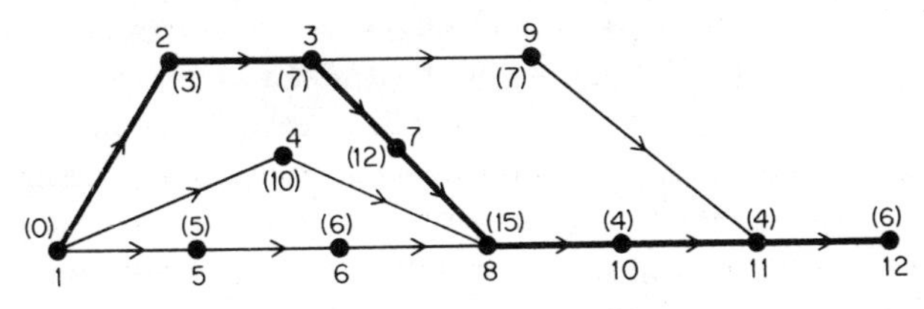

FIG. 7-1. *Activity network—critical path shown in heavy lines. Minimum completion time, 51 days.*

[1] H. J. M. Lombaers (ed.), "Project Planning by Network Analysis." North-Holland Publ., Amsterdam, 1969.

TABLE 7-1
AN ACTIVITY TABLE FOR A SURVEY PROJECT

(a) Activity number	Activity	Duration days
1	Initiate project	0
2	Formulate general questions of interest	3
3	Design questionnaire	7
4	Construct sample	10
5	Select interviewers	5
6	Train interviewers	6
7	Obtain approval for survey	12
8	Conduct survey	15
9	Formulate specific hypothesis	7
10	Record observations	4
11	Compute results and test hypothesis	4
12	Write report	6

(b)	Precedence relations
	1 precedes 2, 3, 4, 5, 7
	2 precedes 3
	3 precedes 7
	4, 6, 7 precede 8
	5 precedes 6
	3 precedes 9
	8 precedes 10
	9, 10 precede 11
	11 precedes 12

most notable successes (e.g., the development of the Polaris missile where it was first used, EXPO 67 in Montreal, and EXPO 70 in Osaka) computers are needed for systematic handling of the voluminous data which accumulate as the project goes on. Although there was a period during which CPM was overrated, it has come to be accepted as a valuable planning aid, applicable especially to the construction industry. Programs of CPM scheduling exist for all standard computers, and they are part of the repertoire of computerized management techniques. Of the three planning techniques mentioned, CPM is the most precisely described in mathematical terms; it is the least controversial in the sense that its domain of applicability is best understood.

Planned program budgeting also had its origins in military planning, but in 1965 it was adopted as a general budgeting procedure for the federal government in the United States, and since then it has become a widespread management tool, especially in the public sector.[2] One of the strongest attractions of PPB is that it offers an alternative to the traditional budgeting procedure so characteristic of institutions and government administration, in which each year departmental budgets are prepared by categorizing expenses according to salaries, equipment, supplies, and so on, and the new budget is essentially a series of incremental changes to the established categories. There are two basic objections to this conventional budgeting: (1) it bears little relation to the function and objectives of the organization; (2) the only way changes can be introduced is by adding or regrouping departments, and this gives very little information about the benefits to be derived from a change or the effectiveness of it.[3] In PPB attention is focused on the goals of the organization and on *programs* which are groups of activities directed to achieving a goal (e.g., building something or rendering a service). The budget is drawn up by showing for each program the inputs and costs, the outputs in the form of products and services, the effects as benefits or disadvantages, and the alternatives. Computers play only a secondary role in PPB, but since computers are used in the preparation of budgets, and especially since the technique spread throughout government during the same period over which computers were introduced into administration, the two are often associated. Moreover, the component technique of systems planning used to identify goals and select programs to achieve these goals depends heavily on the use of computers.

The controversy which has surrounded PPB stems from the often exaggerated claims that it is a scientific, quantitative procedure which will revolutionize management and planning. It is advocated not only for military planning but also in the budgeting of educational institutions, law enforcement agencies, and for social planning where perhaps goals are not clearly discernible and not subject to quantitative cost–benefit analysis. An example of a situation where quantitative goals are difficult to evaluate is the conduct of a foreign affairs department.[4] The Peace Corps, technical assistance, and economic aid are identifiable programs, but the important unit is the foreign country which must be recognized as a complex political, economic, and cultural whole. PPB

[2] For a general review of planned program budgeting see B. M. Gross, The New Systems Budgeting, *Public Administration Rev.* no. 29, 113–133 (1969).

[3] Even in traditional budgeting methods the reasons for increases and the benefits to be derived from changes must be outlined in supporting arguments, but the emphasis is on *incremental* budgetary changes.

[4] T. C. Schilling, PPB's and foreign affairs, *Public Interest* no. 11, 26–36 (1968).

is said to offer little or no advantage over existing budgeting and planning methods in such a situation.

Whatever the limitations, PPB has found a permanent place as a management technique in certain areas. In budgeting for military departments it is accepted as standard procedure; in other types of organizations, including educational, it is still being adopted to an increasing degree; yet in others it may never be used. The aspect of PPB which continues to attract the most attention is systems planning. In fact this has become more important than PPB itself.

7.2. The Systems Approach

It is not easy to define what is meant by a system. The concept is so general as to include a physical or mechanical system as exemplified by a motor vehicle, a biological system such as a cat, an economic system such as the steel industry, an operational system consisting of a set of computer programs, and a behavioral system whose members are political parties. A system is recognizable because it acts in some characteristic way. It has structure, that is, identifiable components, which may themselves be subsystems, and these are coordinated to accomplish a purpose or set of goals. Churchman (1968) describes five basic aspects of a system:

1. the total system objectives—including the way performance is measured so as to recognize how well the objectives are being met
2. the environment—the external constraints and inputs
3. the components—these will have their own activities, objectives, and measures of performance
4. the resources—the quantities within the system which can be changed
5. the management—those components and processes which control the behavior

As an illustration consider the system consisting of an individual who makes daily trips to work, choosing among different modes of travel: driving his own car, using public transportation, traveling with a car pool, and so on. His objective is to minimize inconvenience, measured as some function of travel time, waiting time, cost, the chance of getting wet, and so forth. The environment includes the given transportation schedule, the distance of the transit stops from his home and place of work, the weather. The components are the individual and the modes of transportation, the resources are the time and money which he may expend. The management is the set of rules by which he chooses a mode of transportation. In an urban transportation model the system just described will be one of many similar subsystems.

In systems analysis the five aspects are identified and represented; there will be external variables and parameters which describe the environment, and internal parameters which describe or are associated with the components. The goal of the analysis is to allow the performance to be predicted under varying conditions of the environment and under varying configurations, that is, interconnections of the components. Through design the system is reconfigured or the components are altered to improve the performance. A model is a representation of the system and its behavior. We choose representations which are simpler to manipulate and test than the system itself. A simulation run is an observation of the performance of the model, that is, of the behavior of the model in

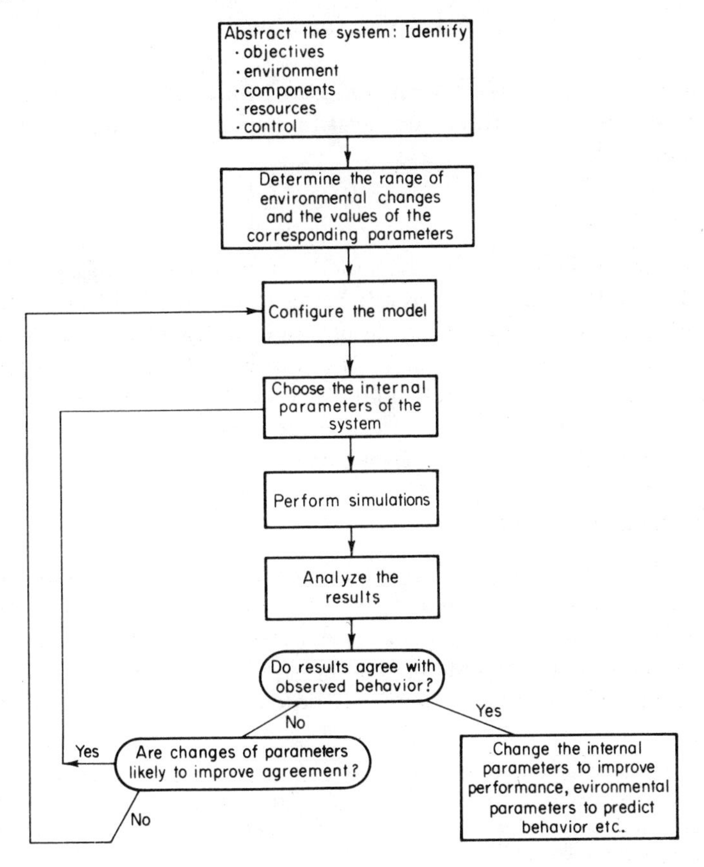

FIG. 7-2. *System design.*

its environment. There are models for any of the types of systems mentioned above, physical, biological, behavioral, or operational. One of the most important decisions to make in modeling a system is to determine the level of detail, that is, the extent to which the system and the various subsystems should be broken down into components. This depends, among other things, on which measures of system performance are chosen and on the time scale in which environmental changes take place. In building a model to represent a system, the system configuration and parameters are altered until simulations show that the model behaves like the system in response to previously observed changes in the environment. The model can then be altered to improve performance in its existing environment or to give acceptable performance in an expected new environment. Figure 7-2 illustrates the process of system design.[5]

7.3. Types of Models

Different kinds of models can be used to aid in systems analysis and design. We recognize three: physical models, mathematical models, and computer models.

Physical Models

These are scaled-down versions of the system being studied. Common examples are the models of aircraft being tested in wind tunnels to study the performance of a proposed design and models of river systems built to predict the effects of a dam. The validity of the tests depends on the laws of similiarity which hold between the actual system and the model. These are useful in those special situations where they can be built, but we will not consider them further.

Mathematical Models

Here the components of the system are represented by variables and the processes are represented by mathematical equations. Variations of the configuration or environment are achieved by varying parameters in the equations. The equations may be algebraic, differential, or integro-differential. Solving the equations is equivalent to a simulation of the

[5] If a totally new system is being designed, one for which there is no past behavior for comparison, then the label on the box "Do results agree with observed behavior?" will have to be changed, for example, to "Do the results correspond to what is expected or desired?"

system. One of the great powers of mathematics is that systems which appear very different physically are represented by the same set of equations. For example, the second-order linear differential equation

$$a \frac{d^2x}{dt^2} + b \frac{dx}{dt} + cx = F(t)$$

represents a wide variety of oscillatory systems including a mechanical system containing a spring-loaded mass, an electrical circuit with inductances, capacitors, and resistors, and an acoustical system consisting of a tuning fork and resonator. In the next section a simple biological system is represented by a pair of mathematical equations, each of which is similar to the one above, and the resulting solution describes the important characteristics of the real situation.

Unfortunately many real systems are too complex and not understood well enough to permit the formulation of a mathematical model which represents the system faithfully. It may also happen that the components of the system can be represented as abstract variables and that equations can be written to represent the interactions between the components, but that it is not possible to solve the set of equations analytically, or the number of equations may be so large as to make them unmanageable. In these latter cases computers can be used to solve the equations for particular values of the parameters.

Computer Models

A computer model is one in which the simulations are carried out on a computer. In the case we have just seen the model may be regarded as a mathematical model for which the equations are solved by computer. If the computer used to model the system is an analog machine, then the computer model may be regarded as a physical model, for analog computers are really physical representations of certain classes of equations.

The type of computer model which has achieved most widespread use by far is a *discrete event simulation.* A variable in a discrete event simulation can take on one of a given set of values. When all of the variables of the system are assigned, it is said to be in a given state. A change from one state to another is an *event.* Time also is changed in discrete steps, and events occur at one of the discrete time instances. Discrete event models may be *deterministic,* that is, each event is followed unfailingly by certain others, or there may be components governed by *random processes;* that is, there are statistical fluctuations in some events. A discrete state simulation of a parking problem is studied in Section 7.6.

The principal advantage to modeling and simulation compared to experimenting with real systems is the lower cost. To determine the number of toll booths required at a bridge it is less expensive to set up a queuing model of the bridge than to experiment by adding and deleting booths on the bridge. Sometimes it is not even possible to build a system without the benefits of models and simulation; the space program contains many such examples. Often the main benefit of computer simulation is not to produce a specific design, but rather to provide a focus for a more precise description of the system and to identify the critical parameters. The main reservations about simulations center on the validity of the results. Is the model good enough to reflect the properties and behavior of the systems under study? How useful are the results? We defer these questions to later in this chapter.

7.4. A Mathematical Simulation

In 1937, D. A. MacLulich published a book on the populations of the Varying Hare (Lepus Americanus) and the Bay Lynx (Lynx Rufus).[6] MacLulich noted that the hare population rose and declined cyclically, with a period of about ten years, and that the lynx population had a similar cycle which correlated closely with that of the hare. The hare is a herbivore while the lynx is a carnivore, whose main diet is the hare.

It is not difficult to formulate this predator–prey relationship in mathematical terms. Let x be the population size of the prey and y the population size of the predator. The first equation

$$\frac{dx}{dt} = ax - bxy$$

states that the rate of increase of hares is proportional to the number of hares already present, and that the proportionality factor is a linearly decreasing function of the lynx population. This is plausible because it indicates that if there were no lynx the hare population would increase exponentially, and that the growth rate in the presence of lynx is diminished by a factor proportional to xy, the number of hare–lynx encounters. The second equation is

$$\frac{dy}{dt} = -cy + dxy$$

and we note that in the absence of hares the lynx population would

[6] D. A. MacLulich, "Fluctuations in the Numbers of the Varying Hare (Lepus Americanus)." Univ. of Toronto Press, Toronto, Canada, 1937.

decline exponentially to become extinct, and that in the presence of hares the rate of increase has a term which is proportional to the number of encounters.

The equations are definitely a simplification of the biological system. They imply, for example, that aside from the presence of the lynx, the birth and death rates of the hare are constant, their difference being measured by the constant a. But data on population make it more reasonable to expect curves such as those shown in Figs. 7-3 (a) and (b) for these rates. Here R_b is a "critical" hare population size, beyond which the birth rate falls off sharply due to overcrowding, natural abortion, malnutrition, and abnormal sexual behavior, and the death rate increases sharply due to starvation, parasitism, and overcrowding. The equations also imply that the lynx appetite is insatiable (because of the term $-bxy$ in dx/dt) but by observation the natural appetite of the lynx is satisfied when it has killed about 200 hares. These limiting factors could be incorporated into the mathematical formulation but the equations would become more complicated, and it is instructive to examine solutions in their present form.

Even for this simple system of nonlinear differential equations, known as the Volterra equations, there is no general mathematical solution. It is necessary to assign particular values to the constants a, b, c, d and to choose appropriate initial conditions to investigate the solutions. Different choices for these factors correspond to different assumptions about the biological system, and it is possible to simulate different ecological situations by varying these parameters.[7]

Suppose we make the particular choice[8]

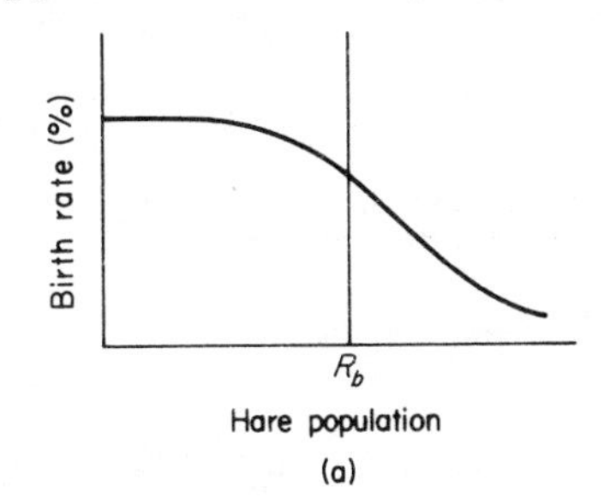

FIG. 7-3.

[7] C. W. Bell and R. L. Linebarg, Applications of computer modeling and simulation to science education, *Simulation*, pp. 185–190, April (1970).

[8] Choosing $x(0) = y(0) = 2$ does not necessarily mean that we start with the condition prevailing at the end of the Flood. The units are not specified and this could equally well represent the presence of 2000 of each type.

$$\frac{dx}{dt} = 2(x - xy), \qquad x(0) = 2$$

$$\frac{dy}{dt} = (xy - y), \qquad y(0) = 2$$

These conditions lead to periodic solutions for x and y (not every set of choices does), but it turns out to be a nontrivial matter to obtain the correct solution.

When differential equations are solved numerically by computer, a number of choices have to be made. For example, the derivative is represented by the finite difference approximation

$$\frac{dx}{dt} = \frac{x(t + h) - x(t)}{h}$$

and this requires a choice for h, the time increment. At each step of the solution some integration formula will have to be used to advance the solution one time increment, and different choices for the integration formula give us the different methods for solving systems of differential equations. Euler's method, a method based on the trapezoidal rule for integration, and the Runge–Kutta class of methods are all well-known examples. The accuracy of a solution to a differential equation depends on the roundoff error due to the finite word size, the truncation error introduced by h, the method of solution chosen, and the particular system of equations; there is no best method for all cases. Table 7-2 shows the solutions for $x(t)$ to the above equation obtained by using (1) three values of h with Euler's method, (2) three values of h with a midpoint integration rule, and (3) an accurate Runge–Kutta routine available in

TABLE 7-2
SOLUTION FOR NUMBER OF HARES IN HARE-LYNX SYSTEM

	Euler h			Midpoint integration rule h			
t	0.1	0.01	0.001	0.1	0.01	0.001	Accurate Runge-Kutta
0	2.00000	2.00000	2.00000	2.00000	2.00000	2.00000	2.00000
5	4.58493	2.00463	1.88139	1.81463	1.86853	1.86905	1.86906
10	−0.03807	2.26822	1.78250	1.63346	1.73892	1.73995	1.73996
15	0.00000	2.86305	1.70413	1.46083	1.61283	1.61431	1.61433
20	−0.00002	3.55993	1.64636	1.29987	1.49157	1.49346	1.49348
25	−1.91256	3.49788	1.60910	1.15256	1.37619	1.37843	1.37845

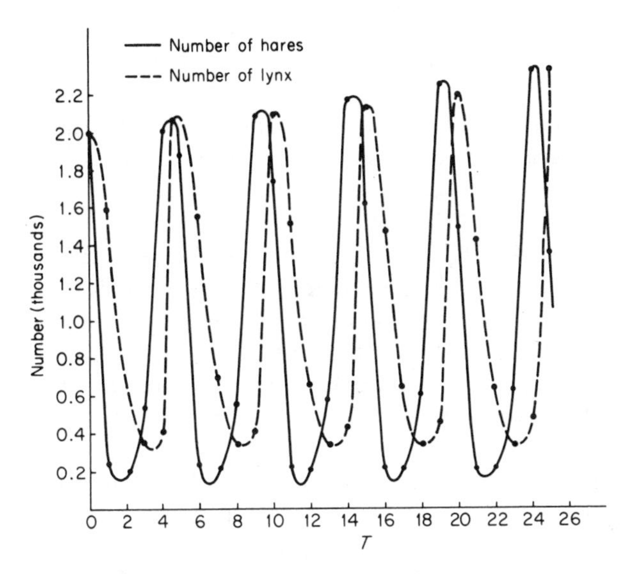

FIG. 7-4. *Solution of hare–lynx system.*

the library of the computer on which the runs were made. It will be noted that Euler's method failed to give acceptable results at all and that for $h = 0.1$ we get meaningless negative values for x. For the midpoint method h must not be greater than 0.01. Graphs for $x(t)$ and $y(t)$, illustrating the periodicity, are shown in Fig. 7-4.

The accuracy of the solution to the differential equation is a technical question in the domain of numerical analysis. The question of whether the mathematical model is a good representation of the real situation is a more difficult one, which must be answered by comparing the mathematical solution with observations on the real system. In this case, the fact that the mathematical solution possesses the essential periodicity in x and y makes us feel that the model mirrors the real situation. Of course in the real system the amplitudes of x and y are not constant, as they are (approximately) in the mathematical solution, but we are inclined to accept that if the limiting factors mentioned previously were to be taken into account, it would be possible to obtain solutions which correspond more closely to the observations. It would not be difficult to find solutions based on the more realistic birth rate and death rate curves, but uncertainty in the observations would soon bring us to the point where it would not be possible to choose between alternative mathematical models, so that there is a point beyond which it does not pay to make the model more complex.

7.5. Discrete Event Simulation

Because discrete event simulations are so basic to the study of systems, it is important to understand them better, and we shall present a general framework for describing them.

We first distinguish between the components and the dynamic behavior of the system. The components are the physical entities of the system. For example, when simulating the performance of an elevator both the elevator and the people using it are components. Associated with each component is a list of attributes. The attributes of an elevator might be its total capacity, its current position and direction, its current occupancy, and so on; the attributes of a passenger might include the floor number for the beginning and end of his trip. Note that some attributes are permanent and others change as the system functions. Note also that some components are permanent parts of the system while other components, for example, the passengers, are transient.

The *state* of the system at a given time is a specification (e.g., a list) of all the components and their attributes. We describe the dynamic behavior of the system as a sequence of events, each of which is a change from one state to another. Events may be triggered by previous events, and they in turn trigger new events, or events may occur because of random processes. In the example above an event may be the stopping of an elevator at a floor or the arrival of a passenger. One event may give rise to several other events and to changes in several of the components; thus the stopping of the elevator will be associated with several exits and entrances of passengers and with a change in occupancy of the elevator.

The system can be *time-driven,* that is, time is simulated by assuming that there is a simulation clock which marks off equal intervals and that events can occur only at the beginning of a clock pulse. The event itself is assumed to occur instantaneously. Alternatively, the model may be *event-driven,* in which case there are equations or rules for calculating the time intervals between events. Here also, the events are instantaneous. In our elevator example using the simulation clock corresponds to taking a motion picture of the elevator and observing the system at each time frame; the event-driven model corresponds to taking a snapshot of the system at given events, for example, each time the elevator doors close. Although in the time-driven model care must be taken to ensure that the period of the simulation clock is appropriate to the timings between events, in essence the methods are equivalent.

The question arises as to whether systems which are continuous physically can be properly represented by discrete state systems. The answer depends on what are regarded as the essential characteristics and whether they are preserved in the idealization. Certainly if the interval of the simulation clock is short enough, the model will be valid; but if it is too short, a great deal of effort can be spent in observing the system when no changes have occurred. In the example discussed above, too fine an interval would correspond to the elevator being photographed with a high-speed camera, resulting in long runs of film of no interest.

A system where each state can have only one possible successor state is said to be *deterministic.* A deterministic system, when it is set to its initial position, will sequence through its possible states until it comes to a halt. It behaves like a clockwork mechanism which is wound up, started, and carries out its movements until it stops. A well-behaved computer program is a deterministic system.

In the real-life systems for which models are built, a given state may be followed by several states, and there will be a probability distribution which specifies which state actually occurs. These systems are said to be nondeterministic, probabilistic, or *stochastic.* It is a philosophical (or perhaps a theological) question whether physical systems, or systems involving human components, are really deterministic or probabilistic. But we do regard many systems and events as being probabilistic, and we introduce various kinds of random probability distributions to describe the occurrence of events. For example, the arrivals and departures of people in the elevator or of cars in a parking lot are stochastic.

7.6. A Stochastic Discrete Event Simulation

We illustrate the ideas we have just presented by simulating the short-term parking lot at Toronto International Airport. Although it is a very small scale system, a number of simplifying assumptions have to be made to carry out the simulation. Cars enter and leave the lot through single-lane ramps. The lot contains 37 parking spaces, arranged in two rows, one on each side of the double-lane road which goes from the entrance to the exit. The parking spaces have meters which allow up to one hour parking, 25 cents entitling one to half an hour. The lot is very heavily used and there is much congestion and activity in it, so that in practice it is not possible to back up (except when leaving a parking space).

A driver wishing to park may find that the ramp is filled with waiting cars (there may be up to four) in which case he has no alternative but to go on to the more distant long-term parking lot, or circle around the airport and come back again in a few minutes. If the ramp is not blocked and there is a parking space, he occupies it; if there is no space, he must wait in position in the ramp until one is freed. It is clearly useful to have some strategy in mind when entering the lot. In particular it is desirable to know whether to enter the ramp at all, given that one can see the number of cars waiting (zero to four). To help decide this our simulation will determine the expected waiting times for the cars entering the ramp in positions 1, 2, 3, and 4.

To carry out the simulation, a number of parameters have to be identified and assigned specific values, and some assumptions, additional to those already mentioned, have to be made. The simulation results to be presented are based on the following[9]:

1. The arrival of cars is determined by an exponential distribution, with mean interarrival time λ.
2. The time spent in a parking space is a normal distribution with mean μ and standard deviation σ.
3. A car takes one minute to vacate a parking spot and one minute to park, assuming there is no obstruction (e.g., another vacating car).

Clearly the behavior of the system will essentially be determined by the average parking duration μ and the mean interarrival time λ. To study the system it is necessary to carry out a number of simulation runs in which these parameters take on different values. Table 7-3 shows excerpts from the computer runs when the average parking time $\mu = 20$ minutes (with a standard deviation of ten minutes), and the interarrival time is varied between 0.10 minutes and 0.70 minutes.

How valid are the results? Even accepting all the assumptions, the accuracy of the numbers obtained from the simulation very much depends on the number and duration of the computer runs. From the data shown in the table, when a car comes to the parking lot it can expect to wait between 0.02 and 1.95 minutes, depending on the "busyness" of the traffic, that is, the interarrival time. For an interarrival time of 0.10 minutes the waiting time as determined by the simulation varied between 0 and 5.42 minutes; the average was 1.95 minutes and the standard deviation 0.98 minutes. To obtain these results it is necessary to run the model to the steady state—for if the simulation is started with no cars in the lot, the waiting time will increase until there is some balance between the number of arrivals and number of departures. The balance will depend, of course, on μ and λ. Presumably by carrying out enough

[9] The model as described here is simple enough so that a mathematical solution could be formed; for our purpose, however, it is better to consider a computer simulation.

TABLE 7-3
PARKING SIMULATION[a]

Interarrival time (minutes)		Waiting time to park (all cars)(minutes)			Average waiting time				Percentage of cars that leave without parking because ramps are full
λ	Observed in simulation	Average	s.d.	Maximum	1	2	3	4	
0.10	0.09	1.95	0.98	5.42	0.59	1.15	1.54	2.07	81
0.20	0.20	1.88	1.19	6.61	0.13	1.09	1.56	2.26	66
0.30	0.30	1.56	1.18	6.67	0.24	1.08	1.59	2.20	45
0.40	0.40	1.07	1.04	4.68	0.15	1.18	1.58	1.94	25
0.50	0.48	0.66	1.06	6.43	0.10	0.97	1.65	2.45	13
0.60	0.61	0.16	0.45	3.07	0.03	0.93	1.33	1.77	2
0.70	0.67	0.02	0.17	1.63	0.00	0.99	1.29	1.07	0

[a] Average parking time = 20 minutes; 37 parking spaces; four waiting spaces (s.d. = 10 minutes).

computer runs acceptable accuracy could be obtained for a given set of assumptions and parameters.

Still another question is whether exponential and normal are reasonable assumptions for the arrival and waiting-time distributions, and what values the parameters in these distributions should have. It would require actual observation of these events to determine whether these were the correct distributions but presumably this could be done. Even if no equation for one of the standard distributions could be fitted, it would not be difficult to incorporate an observed distribution into the model. All of these concern technical and mathematical questions, but one is inclined, as in the example of the lynx–hare model, to accept that the model could be adjusted to deal with these in a satisfactory manner.

Much more difficult are the questions which arise when we ask whether the simulation represents the actual situation faithfully, and especially whether the behavior of people, as car drivers, has been represented correctly. Are the interarrival times and the mean parking duration really independent? Will a driver wait at the head of the ramp, or will he move into the parking area and wait double-parked? Is there any simple way to describe if and when a car will exit if the driver fails to find a parking spot? Observation can give some answers to these questions, but it is very difficult to induce rules for the behavior from observation; behavior is probably not consistent enough. The consequence is that the parking model, though interesting, has limited use for determining parking strategy. Just how limited has to be determined by observation.

In spite of this, the model should be useful for other purposes. The short-term parking lot is one component of a larger system which includes the long-term parking lot, the employees' parking lot, and the approaches. From the point of view of this large system the main feature of the short-term subsystem might be the average number of cars parked and the average duration of their stay. These averages may be quite insensitive to such parameters as the mean arrival rate, and certainly the parking strategy will have only a minor effect. The usefulness of the model depends therefore on the detail which is required of it. But when human behavior is involved even a relatively simple system can be difficult to model, and the validities of all the assumptions, techniques, and results have to be examined and qualified before acceptance.

7.7. Social Systems

The examples we have just studied show that mathematical and computer models can provide insight into the workings of simple systems, that is, those whose structure can be discerned, even when behavioral factors are present. But more and more the problems confronting society are in the management and planning of large systems where there is a complex interplay of economic, social, and political forces. In many countries serious studies of such systems are being undertaken, and since they are too complex for mathematical analysis, they are being simulated by computer models. Typical are studies of urban systems (for which there may be subsystems for land use, transportation, budget allocation, etc.), econometric systems, ecological systems, and even systems for modeling the whole world where attempts are made to focus attention on factors important to human life.[10] Since the problems which beset cities, countries, and the world are so major and so ubiquitous, it is important to be able to assess the validity of any solutions offered through the use of computer modeling. To understand the assumptions on which the solutions are based and the limitations of the methods, we examine two simulations in more detail, first that for an urban transportation system, and second a world simulation.

Urban Transportation

The goal of these studies is to evaluate alternative transportation network configurations. To do this the urban area under study is divided into traffic zones, each with a set of attributes, for example, land use, employment, population densities, and so on. Certain assumptions and uncertainties are immediately apparent, since to estimate the attribute values it is necessary to extrapolate existing activities from past data, from known public and private plans, from zoning bylaws, and from intuitive judgments. Next, calculations are made to determine how many trips made by individuals originate from a zone, given a knowledge of the land use and population of the zone. Trips are for different purposes: home-to-work, work-to-shopping, home-to-recreation, and other errands. From them origin–destination pairs are calculated, showing how many trips originate from each zone to each of the others. It is then necessary

[10] For urban systems see Forrester (1969); I. S. Lowery, "Seven Models of Urban Development: A Structural Comparison," P-3673. Rand Corp., Santa Monica, California, 1967. For a review of transportation systems see E. N. Dodson, Cost effectiveness in urban transportation, *Operations Res.*, pp. 374–394, May–June (1969). For an example of budgeting simulation see J. P. Crecine, "Governmental Problem Solving: A Computer Simulation of Municipal Budgeting." Rand McNally, Chicago, Illinois, 1969. For examples of econometric systems and ecological systems see G. Fromm and P. Taubman, "Policy Simulations with an Econometric Model," Brookings Inst., Washington, D. C., 1968; L. W. Ross, Simulation of the dynamics of air and water pollution, *AFIPS Conf. Proc.*, pp. 105–113, November (1971). The periodical *Simulation* is devoted to description and reports of computer simulations.

to distribute the trips among the different modes of transport,[11] and from this distribution important quantities of the transportation system components are computed, for example, the load, the average travel time, the revenue. These quantities are combined with other factors such as estimates of the cost for construction and maintenance of the different transportation modes to determine the overall effectiveness of the system and the relative effectiveness of alternative components. Computers are essential to the calculations since realistic models contain hundreds of zones, thousands of origin–destination pairs, and many alternatives.

It was after conducting such studies that the Metropolitan Toronto Planning Board recommended the construction of a highway, called the Spadina Expressway, from the suburbs into the core of the city. The expressway was to have a subway line running through its center, and the subway was generally accepted as being highly desirable. After the expressway was started there was mounting opposition because of the large area which would have to be devoted to it and its interchanges, and the consequent major disruption all along its route.

The Metro Toronto Planning Board issued a report describing the computer model used to evaluate alternative transportation systems.[12] While justifying the costs of their models and simulations, the Planning Board clearly avoided any mysterious claim to computer infallibility. It did, however, specifically state that their simulation had substantially increased the probability that decisions based on their predictions would be correct. In describing the simulation the Planning Board listed the following limitations of their procedure.

1. The statistics used to describe the average travel behavior were based on actual surveys and subjected to series of tests. However, it has been assumed that the basic travel characteristics of the survey year (1956) would be the same for the projection year (1980).

2. It is recognized that changes in the transportation system may generate changes in land use. However, in the models studied, land use was kept constant.

3. Because of the many factors involved, it was difficult to predict values for many variables. Values were assumed for variables such as car

[11] A common technique is to use the so-called gravity model, which is based on the assumption that all trips starting from a zone are attracted by so-called traffic generators, and that the number of trips is proportional to the attractiveness of a generator and inversely proportional to the separation between the zones. See Toronto Area Regional Model Studies, "Modal Split." Ontario Dept. of Transportation and Commerce, Toronto, December, 1970 (also "Trip Generation." July, 1971).

[12] Report on The Metropolitan Toronto Transportation Plan, Metropolitan Toronto Planning Board, Toronto, December, 1964.

ownership and distribution, transit fares, the supply and cost of parking, and the distribution of per capita income.

4. In order to make the model economically feasible, many components of the system were aggregated. For example, the distribution of population, employment, dwellings, and so on, was described in a relatively coarse array of zones of various sizes. Similarly, the transportation system was generally described by a system of links of various capacities and operating conditions rather than specifying the individual roads, highways, transit lines.

The main criteria used to evaluate the alternative transportation systems were the following.

1. Minimize total traveling time.
2. Maximize average traveling speed.
3. Minimize points of congestion.
4. Equalize accessibility within the urban areas, and in particular maximize accessibility to the central area.
5. Maximize the use of public transportation, in particular, rapid transit.
6. Maximize the use of expressways.

The criteria were not offered in any particular order of importance.

The construction of the expressway was challenged by citizens' groups in a series of hearings, which culminated in a decision of the Provincial Government, taken in June 1971, not to contribute toward the cost, thereby causing a termination of the plan. It is of some interest to consider the role that the computer played in the controversy. The main arguments of the expressway critics were based on the contention that the computer studies were too narrowly based, and that they did not take into account the social, human, and aesthetic factors which have to be considered in making any major decision involving a large number of people. Is this necessarily true of computer studies? Certainly by the Planning Board's own admission there were questionable assumptions in formulating their model, components were substantially aggregated, and the survey data were inadequate. Moreover, only a limited number of alternative transportation systems were considered. Yet, if we accept their assumptions as reasonable, it is fair to grant their claim that the simulation results improved the probability of making correct decisions. Certainly the model could be (and in fact was) improved. But whether or not the probability was improved to the extent that one would want to base a major decision on it is another question. *The real problem is that there is no agreement on the values which are to be optimized with respect to urban transportation.* Thus the major criticisms against the recommendations of the Planning Board were not primarily directed against the model itself, but rather at the limited choice of alternative systems and at the criteria of values by which the alternatives were assessed.

As an attempt to widen the criteria, consider another study and computer simulation of urban transportation systems, sponsored by the U. S. Department of Housing and Urban Development.[13] In conducting a cost–benefit analysis of systems which could be available in a 3- to 15-year period, the objective function was given as "improvement in the quality of urban living." That is, effectiveness of a system must eventually be evaluated relative to this rather all-encompassing, vague, yet universally desirable goal, "quality of life."

The evaluation was divided into four categories:

1. Dollar costs of investment and operation.

2. User benefits and costs (other than dollar outlays). This category includes the usual measures of total travel time, average speed, and so forth, and moreover includes measures of inconvenience (including factors such as congestion time, outside trip time subject to weather, wait, and transfer times), exertion (including average walking distance and driving, as distinct from riding), passenger accommodation (i.e., percent of passengers seated), privacy (ratio of vehicles to travelers), and reliability.

3. Social costs and benefits capable of quantitative description: (a) Safety hazards (accidents). (b) Air pollution. (c) Measures based on accessibility.

i. Accessibility for special groups. Here it is recognized that at least one-third of an urban population (the young, the aged, the poor) have identifiable transportation needs which cannot be met by cars.

ii. Accessibility to special zones (businesses, shopping, hospitals, airports).

(d) Physical intrusion of transportation systems within the city. The space for rights of way and various structures is calculated for various regions in the city. (e) Costs of dislocation of residents. (f) Choice of modes of travel to various zones.

4. Social costs and benefits not amenable to quantitative description. Included in this category are factors such as sociological integration due to mobility, prestige, community spirit, and aesthetics.

[13] W. F. Hamilton and D. K. Nance, Systems analysis of urban transportation, *Sci. Amer.* **221** (1), 19–27 (1960).

Here the costs and benefits have been specified in a more detailed manner. Moreover, components in the system are relatively disaggregated. Different groups of people are identified and the varying costs and benefits are measured for each group. Also, data and evaluating are disaggregated with respect to time (peak period versus off-peak hours), regions (central, urban, suburban), and by modes of travel.

The approach then is that the parts be made explicit before they are combined in a single measure. To choose a particular system from among the alternatives, all the parameters and specific factors must be weighted and resolved eventually. But it seems imperative that in decisions where there is not a consensus about the relative importance of the various costs and benefits, that the individual factors must be made explicit and the ultimate resolution and compromises be acknowledged as human subjective decisions.

Conclusions drawn from cost–effectiveness studies of several U. S. urban areas using this model do not favor further expressway development (for any of the cities studies) when the quantitative elements of alternative systems were modeled and observed via a detailed simulation program. Since this second model was not actually used in Toronto it is not possible to say whether its use would have led to a different conclusion than that reached by the Toronto Metropolitan Planning Board, who recommended the construction of the Spadina expressway as a result of its own studies. It is not even possible to insist that the second model is more valid than the one used by the Planning Board. What is different about the second model is that it considered other values and goals, and only when there is agreement about these and about how to measure the achievement of the goals is it possible to reach a consensus about the inferences which can be drawn from the computer simulations.

Global Simulations

The controversies and reservations we have just outlined about transportation systems also apply to computer models of urban systems.[14] It is nevertheless possible to argue that some insights into transportation and urban systems are emerging, and that simulations can help formulate good decisions. But there are current attempts to model systems which are far larger and far more complex than transportation systems. At the extreme end of the scale there are attempts to conceive our planet as one huge social and ecological system, and to model this on a computer.

[14] See G. D. Brewer, "Evaluation and Innovation in Urban Research," P-4446. Rand Corp., Santa Monica, California, August, 1970; J. P. Crecine, "Computer Simulation in Urban Research," P-3734. Rand Corp., Santa Monica, California, 1967.

There are many modeling projects of this kind, and a listing published in April, 1970[15] shows at least five which might be regarded as world simulations, along with many other simulations of large-scale systems. One of the best known world simulations is that of the Club of Rome.[16]

The Club of Rome is an informal, multinational, and nonpartisan group of individuals who have organized to develop an action-oriented program on the "Predicament of Mankind." The predicament is that "we can perceive the individual symptoms and the components of profound social problems, but we are stymied in our effort to comprehend the total situation and develop global solutions." The root of the problem, as perceived by the members of the Club, is that population and technological growth are increasing so rapidly that the social and ecological systems of the planet cannot adapt. Since the planet is finite, growth must eventually be replaced by a global ecological equilibrium. The aim of the Club is to provide direction for an enlightened, international effort which will bring about a desirable equilibrium (rather than an equilibrium characterized by overcrowding, pollution, and food shortages).

While certain individuals and groups grapple with particular problems, the Club wishes to bring all aspects of the problems confronting human society under one conceptual framework and then to evaluate policy options available to mankind. The conceptual framework chosen is the view of global dynamics as a single large growth and decay system, analogous to the hare–lynx system we have studied previously. Having established this viewpoint, the Club then begins to develop a model using standard techniques of systems analysis, namely, to identify the important components of the system and the interrelations among these components.

The approach taken by the Club of Rome and the results attained so far are illustrated by Forrester (1971). In the model five major subsystems are identified, those for world population, capital investment (or industrial development), natural resources, pollution, and food production. As in the hare–lynx system, the dynamic behavior and interrelations of the systems are modeled by describing how the rate of change for the level of each component depends on present levels of the given and related components. Among the rates considered important in understanding global equilibrium are the birth rate, death rate, pollution generation rate, capital investment rate, and resource depletion rate.

[15] Surveying the simulation scene: Ongoing public problems projects, *Simulation*, pp. 176–179, April (1970). See also Summary and status, *Simulation*, p. 296, June (1970).

[16] "The Club of Rome: Project on the Predicament of Mankind, Phase I: The Dynamics of Global Equilibrium." Alfred P. Sloan, School of Management, MIT Press, Cambridge, Massachusetts, 1970.

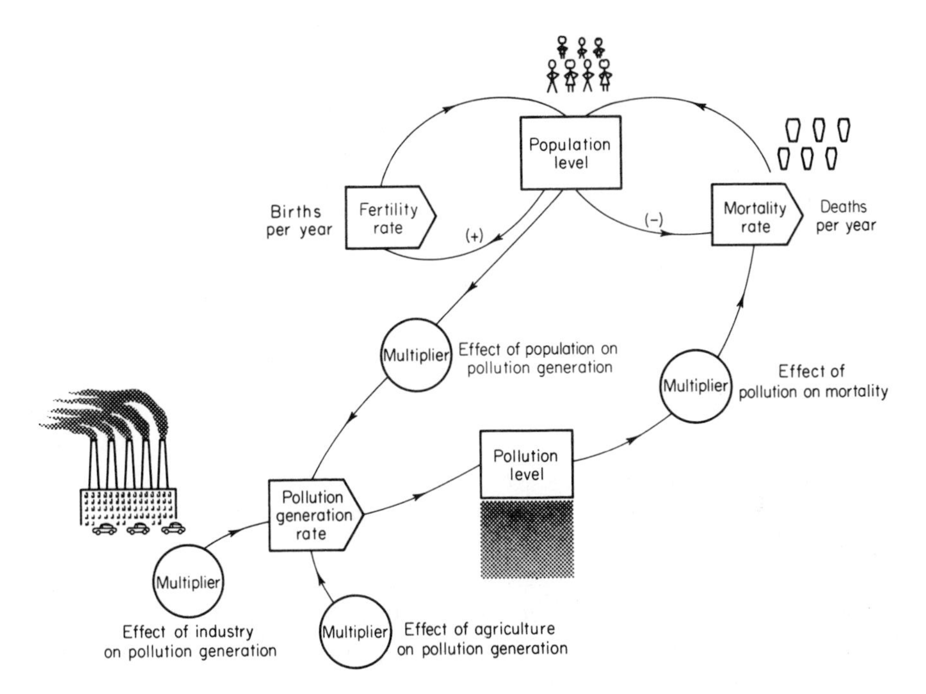

FIG. 7-5. *Population–pollution feedback loop.*

Figure 7-5 illustrates pollution feedback loop in the population subsystem. By taking different values for the parameters which describe the initial levels, rates, and feedback ratios in the various subsystems, it is possible to solve the large set of interconnected differential equations and obtain families of curves which show how the quantities of interest change with time as a result of the assumptions.

Figure 7-6 is typical of the resulting curves.[17] Although the calculations are regarded as preliminary, a number of observations are made from them.

• Assuming a gradual depletion of natural resources, an increasing population, and a buildup in capital investment, all of the curves show decreasing population and sharply increased pollution starting at about the year 2020, accompanied by a steady erosion in the quality of life.

• Curves derived by assuming a slower depletion rate of natural resources and a greater rate of capital investment show a very sharp rise in pollution and a catastrophic fall in population. This illustrates a point raised by Forrester that many of the measures which are being consid-

[17] J. W. Forrester, Counterintuitive behavior of social systems, *Simulation,* pp. 61–76, February (1971).

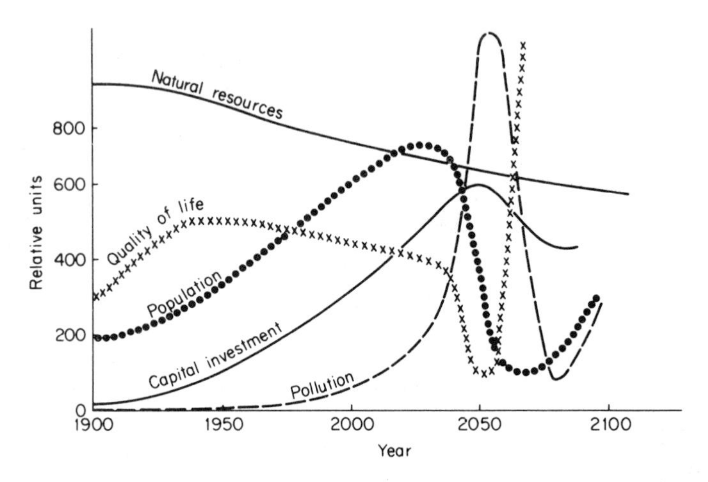

FIG. 7-6. *World projection. [Sample set of curves as illustrated in J. W. Forrester, Counterinteractive behavior of social systems, Simulation, February, 61–76 (1971).]*

ered to combat social problems are counterintuitive in the sense that they aggravate the ills even though they seem to be sensible.

- The only curves which produce stability are based on the simultaneous adoption of a number of conservation policies, for example, a 40% reduction in capital accumulation (and hence industrialization), a 50% reduction in the birth rate, and a 50% decrease in pollution generation.

The calculations (predictions?) are disturbing and one cannot escape asking how seriously they are to be taken. Is it assumed that political and social measures to combat poverty and improve the quality of life should only be undertaken by those who understand simulation and modeling? How much credibility should be attached to the calculations? In simulations of urban growth and decay carried out by methods very similar to the world simulation of the Club of Rome, Kadanoff challenges the counterintuitive behavior observed by Forrester. Whereas Forrester (1969) concludes from his study that there should be less low-cost housing in the central run-down core of a city and that this is counterintuitive, and certainly counter to current housing rehabilitation programs, Kadanoff sees this conclusion as a natural consequence of the assumptions made on the desirability of having less unskilled labor in the city core.[18] It can be similarly argued that all of the results of the world

[18] L. Kadanoff, An examination of Forrester's 'Urban dynamics,' *Simulation*, pp. 261–268, June (1971).

simulations are obvious consequences of the exponential population increase and resource depletion, and that no additional insights or results quantitatively useful are provided by the calculations themselves. *It is impossible to argue with the conclusion that exponential growth cannot be continued.* In the last 100 years there have been basic additions to energy supplies, foodstuffs, and material resources, and dramatic changes can still be expected. But these are finite limits to materials and resources.

Nevertheless there are some doubts which come to mind about the conclusions reached by systems planning when applied to social systems. The Club of Rome admits that their initial model is just a beginning and states "candidly" that their preliminary computer-simulated experiments are to be viewed primarily as illustrations of the approach, not predictions of outcomes which could be expected if the policy changes were actually implemented. But if previous experience on the results of modeling is any guide, such warnings become less and less emphatic and eventually disappear, and the model predictions become more and more directives for action,[19] this in spite of the fact that an examination of the approach clearly reveals how simplistic it is. It is simplistic among other reasons because it implies that complex attitudes and values such as quality of life can be estimated by a few numbers; because it leaves out the enormous influences of emotion, tradition and culture, and religion on the human condition; and because what cannot be quantified tends to be ignored. Behavioral models involving conflict situations are very much a research subject, and there is very little experience on how to apply the results of such research to the kind of direct action at the political and planning level which the Club insists must be initiated immediately if wild catastrophes are to be avoided.[20]

[19] For example, I. R. Hoos, When California system-analyzed the welfare problem, *in* "Information Technology in a Democracy" (A. F. Westin, ed.), pp. 409–418. Harvard Univ. Press, Cambridge, Massachusetts, 1971. Later world simulations, as illustrated in "The Limits To Growth" (D. H. Meadows *et al.*, 1972), show much more detail and include curves for specific subsystems such as nuclear wastes, carbon dioxide in the atmosphere, heat generation in the Los Angeles basin, copper and steel consumption, and so on. The curves are still considered to be preliminary, but the authors state that "after the assumptions have been scrutinized, discussed, and revised to agree with our best current knowledge, their implications for the future behavior of the world system can be traced *without error by a computer, no matter how complicated they become*" (p. 22, our emphasis).

[20] Neglecting conflict results in the conclusion that the quality of life was at a peak during the 1940s, a proposition hardly likely to be accepted by the millions who were living under Nazi domination during those years. It may be noted that quality of life no longer appears in "The Limits to Growth."

An extensive assessment of the application of modeling and other techniques to social planning can be found in Sackman (1971). Sackman emphasizes both the need for normative planning and the need to democratize the planning effort, and predicts that mass information utilities will result in wide participation, making it possible to achieve consensus about goals (see Section 11.3). He argues forcefully that planning must be evolutionary, constantly changing to reflect a better understanding of the system; models and plans must continue to pass the ultimate test of verification in the real world. In particular, our understanding of social systems must be tested in the real world, and not just under the laboratory conditions of an abstract computer model.

There are several reservations that must be raised about Sackman's vision of a planning science and its application to social systems. While "experimental realism" and evolutionary planning are highly desirable, the cost of real-world experiment in a social system is often unacceptable. Once a highway is built, it remains built for some time; or to take a more extreme example, the real test of a defense system is a war. While one must accept the need for normative and participatory planning, the "creative search techniques" suggested by Sackman (including Delphi experiments and other methods of brainstorming, gaming models, and techniques derived from psychological theories of group expectation) should only be viewed as aids in the process of making decisions. There is no evidence that these techniques have been successful in achieving consensus in a complex setting, and it is too much to expect that they will revolutionize the ability to resolve basic value conflicts.

What is the answer then? Is it wrong to attempt to build models of our basic social and economic systems? Of course it is not. We must welcome the fact that scientists and engineers are finally becoming directly involved with the problems of society, and have come to recognize that technology is a major factor both in bringing about these problems and in learning to cope with them. But while such concern is a prerequisite for the improvement of our society, it is misleading to suggest that it can be immediately translated into a quantified prescription for cures. Confidence has to be built up in using computer models on small socioeconomic systems in such a way that goals and values are not lost. During this phase, which is likely to take decades, global simulations are interesting and probably worthwhile. But the application of systems planning to social problems has not yielded enough successes to offer the technique as a definite answer to the more difficult problems of society. Systems analysis and modeling are planning and forecasting methods. As emphasized in Section 6.2 and also in our discussion of transportation systems, it is essential to reach agreement on goals and values before the results of using these techniques can be accepted.

Bibliography

Assoc. for Comput. Machinery (1969). *Annu. Symp. Appl. Comput. Probl. Urban Soc.*, New York.

Churchman, C. W. (1968). "The Systems Approach." Dell Publ., New York.

Forrester, J. W. (1969). "Urban Dynamics." MIT Press, Cambridge, Massachusetts.

Forrester, J. W. (1971). "World Dynamics." Wright-Allen Press, Cambridge, Massachusetts.

Meadows, D. H., Meadows, D. L., Randers, J., and Behrens, W. W. (1972). "The Limits to Growth." Universe Books, New York.

Metropolitan Toronto Planning Board (1964). Report on The Metropolitan Toronto Transportation Plan, December.

Sackman, H. (1971). "Mass Information Utilities and Social Excellence." Auerbach Publ., Princeton, New Jersey.

Simulation (monthly). Simulation Councils Inc., La Jolla, California.

Problems and Further Work

1. Write the mathematical iteration which defines the minimum time and the critical path through a PERT network. Apply this to the network of Fig. 7-1.

2. Identify the five system aspects (objectives, environment, components, resources, management) for (a) a motor vehicle, (b) a cat, (c) the steel industry, (d) a computer operating system, (e) a set of political parties.

3. Look up how the pair of differential equations representing the hare–lynx system can be solved on an analog computer. What are the advantages of such a model? The disadvantages?

4. Give a mathematical formulation for the population–pollution feedback loop in Fig. 7-5.

5. Write a computer program for the parking lot simulation and compare your answers with those given in the text. Does the difference between the average parking time for your simulation and that given in the text fall within the 5% confidence level? Instead of a normal distribution for the parking duration assume a uniform distribution. Are the results significantly different?

6. List (at least ten) system objectives which you regard as most important for measuring the "quality of life" when developing an urban or world model. Compare your set of objectives with those set by others.

7. The fare structure is a key element in a transportation system. Suggest surveys which would help determine the dollar value people attach to (1) reduced travel time, (2) elimination of a transfer point, (3) reduction in the distance they have to walk. What kind of operating statistics about transportation should be maintained to help obtain such data? What arguments can be advanced for free public transportation?

8. Models of the electorate are commonly constructed to predict voting trends. The models may be based on previous voting patterns (cf. the computer predictions made as returns come in) or they may be sociometric models constructed demographically to test public response to particular questions. Discuss the issues involved in using such models. See

G. H. Orcutt, M. Greenberger, J. Korbel, and A. M. Rivlin, "Microanalysis of Socioeconomic Systems: A Simulation Study," Harper, New York, 1961. Also, I. de Sola Pool, R. Abelson, and S. Pophen, "Candidates, Issues and Strategies." MIT Press, Cambridge, Massachusetts, 1964.

9. Models have been constructed to simulate the judges in a court, based on the records of their previous decisions. Discuss possible uses and objections to this type of modeling. See

R. N. Freed, "Materials and Cases on Computers and Law," 2nd ed., Sect. II-L. Boston Univ. Book Store, Boston, Massachusetts, 1969.

10. There is an extensive literature on games, simulations, and mathematical theories which describe international relations, conflict management, war, and disarmament, all of which is, in turn, part of the literature of peace research. Look up the Prisoner's Dilemma, the basic game for illustrating the difficulty of achieving cooperation when there is mutual distrust. Sketch the essential components of a computer game to simulate international relations. Compare your game with one which has actually been constructed. Can the prisoner's dilemma be worked into the game? See

H. B. Thorelli and R. L. Graves, "International Operations Simulation." Free Press of Glencoe, Glencoe, Illinois, 1964; and the following articles in *Peace Res. Rev.*, Canad. Peace Res. Inst., Oakville, Ontario; A. Rapoport, "Games Which Simulate Deterrence and Disarmament," 1 (4) (1967); P. Smoker, "International Relations Simulation," 3 (6) (1970); A. Narden, "Theories of Conflict Management," 4 (2) (1971). Also *Internat. Peace Res. Newsletter,* Internat. Peace Res. Assoc., Oslo, Norway.

Chapter

8

COMPUTER CAPABILITIES AND LIMITATIONS

Many of the issues and fears about computers stem from the question: What will computers do that is now being done by men? We can break the question down into parts: What can *now* be done with computers? What can we expect them to be able to do? What can we trust to computers and what must we insist that men do? To answer these questions we start by examining what is meant by thought, intelligence, and creativity.

8.1. Artificial Intelligence

The expression "artificial intelligence" brings together two terms which might be regarded as irreconcilable, and it already suggests the controversy which surrounds this subject. To what extent can an inanimate object, a machine, possess intelligence and think? Alan Turing, in a provocative article published in 1950,[1] suggested a game which might be

[1] A. M. Turing, Computing machinery and intelligence, *Mind* **59**, 433–460 (1950).

used to decide whether a machine could think. The game consists of a machine *A*, a human *B*, and a human interrogator *C*. *C* is to determine whether *A* or *B* is the human by a series of questions and answers. *A* tries to deceive the interrogator, whereas *B* attempts to convince *C* of his true identity. The game is arranged so that *C* can only make his decision on the basis of the answers to the questions (he cannot observe *A* and *B* directly). The "intelligence" of the machine is determined by its success in deceiving the interrogator. Turing speculated that by the year 2000 a machine could be made to think by this definition.

While this is an interesting definition of intelligence, it is of course a highly subjective one. Others have proposed that we might accept that a machine can think if we could make it carry out tasks which most people agree require thought on the part of humans. Examples of such tasks are game playing and problem solving, especially if the games and problems require planning and the application of mathematical reasoning. This identification of intelligence with mathematics may occur because most of the workers in artificial intelligence bring a mathematical background to it, or it may represent a view that while some thought is to be associated with emotions and instincts, these are to be found in the animal world as well as the human, but intelligence is logical and hence mathematical. As illustrations of intelligent behavior we look at game playing, exemplified by checkers and chess, at problem solving, exemplified by theorem proving, and at question–answering systems which are somewhat less ambitious than that proposed by Turing.

The earliest work in artificial intelligence involved games in which rules could be defined with complete precision. Checkers and chess are perhaps the most popular two-player games. These games illustrate the complexity of producing successful strategies. It is easy enough to represent the board and the players in a two-dimensional array; moves can be input and output, and a relatively simple program can be devised to check whether a move is legal; the difficulty lies in choosing a sequence of moves which leads to a winning game.

One way to conceptualize a game is as a *tree* in which each node or vertex represents a position and the edges represent moves from one position to a succeeding one (Fig. 8-1).

The task of finding a winning (or at least a nonlosing) strategy is then equivalent to searching the game tree for acceptable paths from the initial to the final positions. The problem is that making an exhaustive search for the game of checkers would require investigating approximately 10^{40} move choices (the estimate for chess is 10^{120} move choices). We shall avoid the temptation to try to explain how astronomically large these numbers are; it is enough to say that exhaustive searches are im-

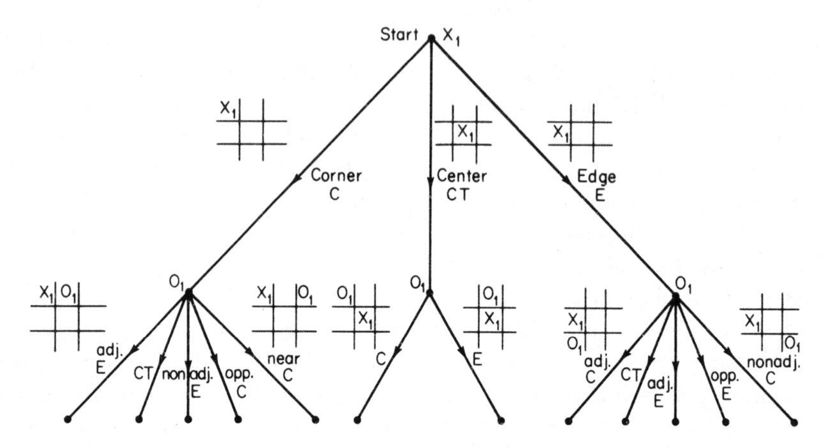

FIG. 8-1. *A game tree for Tic-Tac-Toe.*

possible. It is possible to reduce some of the search effort by analysis (e.g., by recognizing symmetries and forcing win positions). But a complete analysis does not appear feasible and any games of interest require significant amounts of searching. Methods of "pruning" the tree must be found, that is, avoiding the investigation of unpromising moves, and for this heuristics are developed.

A *heuristic* is a method or rule for improving the efficiency of a problem-solving system. Humans appear to develop heuristics naturally in game playing. In order to reduce the search effort, we can program the machine to investigate only a limited number of moves for any one position and to look ahead only in certain directions. There is good evidence that even experts do not look ahead more than five or six moves in most positions, although special situations are explored to much greater depth. Samuel's[2] (1959) checkers program and the Greenblatt chess program[3] (1967) are reasonably successful programs that rely heavily on heuristics for their games. Positions are evaluated according to criteria such as piece count, mobility, advancement, center control, and so on. Moves are evaluated on predictions of position improvement, and there are special heuristics for recognizable special situations in the game (for example, checking moves to which there are the fewest replies receive first attention).

In some games programs based on heuristics can match the play

[2] A. L. Samuel, Some studies in machine learning using the game of checkers, *IBM J. Res. Develop.*, Part I, 3 (3), 211–223 (1959); Part II, 11 (6), 601–617 (1967).

[3] R. D. Greenblatt, D. E. Eastlake, III, and S. D. Crocker, The Greenblatt chess program, *AFIPS Conf. Proc.* 31, 801–810 (1967).

of better-than-average human opponents. But contrary to predictions made in the late 1950s, machine programs can not yet match expert players. One might think that once a program is defeated it can then always be defeated by repeating the same performance. However, one of the underlying themes of artificial intelligence is to try to imbue programs with learning capabilities, that is, have the programs use and generalize upon past experience. In computer programs this learning capability is usually limited to simple success or failure reinforcement schemes. Thus, if a particular choice of moves appears to be more (less) fruitful than expected, the property functions of a board position, or other parameters associated with the choice of moves, are modified so as to effect a positive (negative) tendency to make such moves in the future. This one aspect of the learning mechanism was one of the outstanding and novel features of the Samuel checker program. As a result the program will always modify a losing strategy.

Although it is tempting to credit the program with a learning capability, the limitations and simplicity of the approach are more significant than the boldness of the attempt. Even in the structured environment of a well-defined game, it is necessary to devise an explicit means for distributing credit or success of a complex strategy among the many decisions that comprise the strategy. One of the significant negative results of game-learning programs is that they eventually reach a stage beyond which there is no improvement in play.

Another substantial effort of artificial intelligence in a well-defined environment is the application of computerized mechanical theorem proving. The logic theory program of Newell, Shaw, and Simon[4] was an imaginative attempt to program a machine to prove theorems in propositional logic (for example, given NOT *B* and *A* IMPLIES *B;* prove NOT *A*). The basic inference ability has considerable practical importance. Here also this problem is completely solvable in the sense that given any statement in this logic, one can test for a theorem by a truth table for the variables and the statement. The truth table of Table 8-1 indicates that whenever both NOT *B* and *A* IMPLIES *B* are true then NOT *A* is true. However, if the number of variables is N, the number of rows in the truth table is 2^N, and when N is large, exhaustive listing becomes impractical.

The logic theory program attempted to produce an efficient theorem prover. The authors' interest in how humans do mathematics led them to examine heuristics and so-called training sequences, how to establish

[4] A. Newell, J. C. Shaw, and H. Simon, Empirical explanations of the logic theory machine. *Proc. Western Joint Comput. Conf.* **15**, 218–239 (1957).

TABLE 8-1
TRUTH TABLE[a]

A	*B*	Not *B*	*A* implies *B*	Not *A*
T	T	F	T	F
T	F	T	F	F
F	T	F	T	T
F	F	T	T	T

[a] T = true, F = false.

goals and subgoals, when to give up on a line of attack, and when to make and reserve assumptions.

As a theorem prover, this program must be considered a failure. H. Wang[5] and later Davis and Putnam[6] showed how to produce nonheuristic theorem provers for the propositional logic which were far more efficient than the logic theory program and which always worked. The system of logic required to do most mathematics is more complicated than the propositional logic (for example, statements should contain quantifiers such as THERE EXISTS and FOR ALL). Much of the effort of the 1960s in mechanical theorem proving centered on nonheuristic procedures for proving theorems in this more difficult setting. While the results have been theoretically interesting, mechanical theorem proving has not been successful in any practical sense, and the work is more and more removed from human thought processes.

Marvin Minsky, one of the most optimistic believers in artificial intelligence, is probably right when he argues that any program to solve real mathematical problems will have to combine mathematical *and* heuristic sophistication.[7] Moreover, the indications are that the best chance for success is to restrict attention to a particular field of mathematics and to use special heuristics rather than attempt to develop a general-purpose problem solver. Hopes and claims for a general-purpose problem solver, which were entertained for some years, have to be abandoned for the foreseeable future.

Another example of making computers carry out tasks which require human intelligence is the attempt to have them translate natural languages. Programs to do this were suggested early in the development of machines. Once again, a simple solution suggests itself: translate word for word; that is, transliterate. The defect in this approach is simply

[5] H. Wang, Toward mechanical mathematics, *IBM J. Res. Develop.* 4, 2–22 (1960).

[6] M. Davis and H. Putnam, A computing procedure for quantification theory, *J. ACM* 7 (3), 201–215 (1960).

[7] See the Introduction in Minsky (1968, p. 15).

that it does not produce a reasonable translation. One reason is that we do not presently know how to describe enough of the syntax (word formation and sentence construction) of a natural language to recognize the rich variety of valid ways to express ourselves. But a more fundamental reason is that good translation depends on the ability to sense the *meaning* of the ideas being communicated by the language. This cannot be done without introducing the context in which the idea occurs. Thus one is forced to consider the more central question: How can we make machines learn and understand natural language.

Attempts to understand language have proceeded along many different lines. From a computational point of view, we mention two. One is represented by the school of the linguist N. Chomsky which tries to develop formal grammars which will account for both the so-called surface and deep structures of constructs such as the sentence. It seems fair to say that the impact of this work has been mostly of a mathematical nature; it has important applications to programming languages but as yet negligible practical value for natural language. Most linguists feel that the separation of syntax and semantics, which is characteristic of the formal language approach, limits the usefulness.

A distinctly different approach has been pursued by others: not to produce a general model, but rather to develop heuristic and semantic techniques to permit discourse for one particular topic. An example of an early attempt was D. Bobrow's STUDENT[8] algebra program. This program was capable of handling some simple high school algebra problems when expressed in a highly structured form of English. (If John is three years older than Tom and Tom is five, then how old is John?) Efforts in this direction are continuing, and experience is showing that a limited but not necessarily artificial discourse is possible if the context is severely restricted.[9] The range of discourse has to be very much narrower than that which Turing envisaged in his classic paper, so much so that one wonders whether this line of investigation corresponds to a study of intelligence.

It has been suggested that the ability to learn natural language is the distinguishing characteristic of human intelligence, from which other abilities follow. Everyone who has used a computer knows how artificial the input–output mechanisms are compared to natural language. While man–machine interface is being improved greatly in some ways, for

[8] D. C. Bobrow, Natural Language Input for a Computer Problem-Solving System, in Minsky (1968, pp. 135–215).

[9] See T. Winograd, Procedures as a representation for data in a computer program for understanding natural language, Project MAC TR-84, Ph.D. Thesis, Massachusetts Inst. Tech., Cambridge (1971).

example, by graphic facilities, the inability to communicate in natural language is still the most obvious inadequacy in dealing with present-day computers. The subtleties and ambiguities in natural language, the variety and complexity of structural forms, the declarative capabilities, the finer forms of literary expression (e.g., sarcasm, irony) make human discourse richly expressive and illustrate why it is so difficult to model language capability well. Most serious of all is the limited ability of a computer to be aware of the context of a discourse in a way which allows it to attach semantic significance to terms it encounters.

8.2. Thought Processes

The fact that present-day computers have limited capabilities for playing games, solving problems, and dealing with languages is not in itself a guide to predicting their eventual capabilities. In attempting to understand and improve on the performance in what might be called the macro-activities, it is natural to study the more basic processes which underlie thought and intelligent behavior, for example, concept formation, pattern recognition, memorization, and perception. There is the hope that by building computer models which imitate the brain in these functions, we might both understand mental processes better and build more intelligent machines.

Concept formation has been a subject of speculation and study for centuries by philosophers and psychologists such as Kant and William James, by child psychologists, by neurologists, and more recently by mathematicians and computer scientists.[10] The end achievement of abstraction must undoubtedly be preceded by stages in which different things are recognized as being similar. In his book on statistics, "Knowing and Guessing," Watanabe (1969) distinguishes between *cognition*, grouping objects with perceived properties into classes according to the intensity of their intermember relationships and *recognition*, assigning an object to a class after a number of samples or paradigms have been presented along with a statement of the class to which each belongs. One of the promising ways of modeling cognition is through the statistical technique of cluster analysis. Watanabe identifies three phases in cluster analysis: (1) selecting predicates and weighting variables—that is, choosing attributes which will be sought in the objects under study and deciding their relative importance; (2) determining the intensity of similarity and of other interobject relationships; (3) placing the objects

[10] See E. B. Hunt, "Concept Learning." Wiley, New York, 1962.

in classes. He proves that the general problem of clustering is unsolvable because of necessary arbitrariness in the notion of similarity and in the assignment of weights to variables. Even after decisions are made for the first two phases there are enormous difficulties in the third. There are questions such as: Should an object belong to one class? How many classes should there be? Should there be classes which contain almost all or almost none of the objects? Should the classes be fixed *a priori* or should there be provision for defining new classes? The number of strategies in choosing a method of clustering is unlimited, and good ones impose severe requirements on computer memory and speed.

Pattern recognition has probably received more attention than any other topic in artificial intelligence (see, for example, Uhr, 1966; Bonzard, 1970). The optical recognition of printed and handwritten characters has obvious commercial applications to document reading and mail sorting, for example. Also the classification of photographs is an essential stage in scientific experiments such as the analysis of bubble chamber data from high-energy accelerators and weather pictures taken from satellites. We can define a pattern as a set of objects which can be usefully aggregated. One pattern might be the set of all handprinted letters A, another might be the set of all triangles, and a more complex pattern might be the set of all immovable objects in a room. As in our previous examples, a simplistic approach first suggests itself for the problem of recognizing patterns by computer.

We can try simple matches of a given object (which is an instance of some pattern) against prototypes or templates for the known patterns. If the distortions are not too significant and if the object can be normalized (placed in some reference position), then such template matching can often produce acceptable results. But as one would expect, this approach is too limited to be of use for the numerous perceptions we make every day. A somewhat more powerful method is to associate a list of properties with each pattern. Besides using the mathematical technique of cluster analysis, heuristic procedures can also be devised to determine which pattern best describes an object. While this method does afford more descriptive power, it does not say how to develop new properties or combine existing properties to produce a more sophisticated recognition system when needed. In addition, more complex descriptors are required when we attempt to recognize patterns consisting of several objects which are related in some specified way. The analogy questions that appear on intelligence tests are a test of the ability to recognize relations either among geometric objects or word objects.

As an example of a program which works successfully in the environment of a limited number of primitive objects and relations between them, Evans[11] has written a geometric analogy program which is said to perform at the high school level. In the robot programs at Stanford[12] and MIT,[13] we have results in pattern recognition in a much more complicated and interesting setting. To understand the motivation behind these programs, consider the perceptual functioning required for a small child to walk into a room and correctly identify a toy contained in a box. Note that even a three year old can easily perform this task "even though the amount of light reflected from the toy, its shape, its color, etc., are all different from what he has experienced before. In fact, the child can recognize the toy when only part of it is visible. And if the toy moves, the child can usually track it, and considers that it is the same toy despite the perceptual changes that took place."[14]

Robots can not yet perform at this level. Shakey, the Stanford Research Institute robot, was programmed to explore a limited environment such as a large room. It could make some distinctions between movable and immovable objects and be instructed to navigate around the room or move a given object. The MIT robot is a stationary device which can be instructed to observe a pattern consisting of a few rectangular solids, and then, using one artificial hand, reproduce that pattern identically. Perhaps this copier best demonstrates the successes and limitations of the present state of heuristic pattern recognition. This project was first envisioned as a summer project but it took five years to complete. The program can handle only a small number of blocks, and there has not yet been an attempt to use a variety of shapes nor has there been an attempt to produce two-hand coordination (which is certainly required to permit balancing). Yet this limited project represents a tremendously sophisticated planning and programming effort, resulting in 80,000 characters of program in core and a total of 1,200,000 characters of program.

Attempts to build computer models of human memory and learning have likewise proven how far we are from possessing a mechanism which can account for the enormous and often confused body of experimental results which psychologists have been accumulating over the last few

[11] T. G. Evans, "A Program for the Solution of a Class of Geometric Analogy Intelligence Test Questions," in Minsky (1968, pp. 271–353).

[12] For a report on Shakey see N. Nilsson, "A Mobile Automaton," in Walker and Norton (1969). For a report on robot activity in Japan, see M. Ejiri *et al.*, An intelligent robot with cognition and decision making ability, in Brit. Computer Soc. (1971).

[13] Project MAC Progr. Rep. VI pp. 13–33 (1968–1969), Massachusetts Inst. of Tech., Cambridge.

[14] This example appears in an article entitled "The Psychology of Robots" by H. Block and H. Ginsburg, in Pylyshyn (1970, pp. 246–255).

decades. When computers were first developed they were commonly referred to as "giant brains"; the term "memory" for storage is a reminder of the extent to which computers were identified with brains. The attention given to the perceptron,[15] a device which was regarded as a model of the process for adaptive learning, shows how hard it has been to give up the belief that computers and computer processes are close approximations to the brain and its functioning. The current view, still highly tentative,[16] is that human memory has three distinct components:

1. a very short term visual memory, called the sensory register,
2. a short-term so-called primary memory, with perhaps a 15-second decay time, in which verbal and auditory sensations are stored,
3. a long-term store, to which impressions, sounds, and images are transferred eventually.

In addition, it has long been accepted that human memory is, in part at least, associative or content-addressed since recall can occur along a chain of interconnected ideas. Nevertheless there must also be some kind of addressing mechanism of the type present in computer storage; for our ability to know, apparently without a search, that "mantiness' is not a word in the English language must imply that we recognize its absence in that region of our memory where similar words are to be found (Norman, 1969).

In spite of the converging efforts by scientists from many disciplines, it is turning out to be enormously difficult to understand how memory, learning, recognition, and conceptualization take place in the brain. But the more that is learned, the more clear it becomes that present-day computers and computer programs are far too simple to be accepted as representations for these complex mechanisms and processes. In a systematic analysis of the limitations of computers Dreyfus (1972) reasons that the failure of computers to achieve intelligence is the inevitable consequence of mistaken assumptions implicit in all work on cognitive simulation and artificial intelligence. The assumption which cannot be avoided is that computers treat observations as data which are represented in memory as a fixed structure, and which are operated on by an essentially fixed program. But humans interpret observations in the total context of a situation. They have a sense of "Gestalt," derived from human experience, which enables them to interpret observations as dif-

[15] F. Rosenblatt, "Principles of Neurodynamics." Spartan Books, Washington, D. C., 1962.

[16] See R. M. Shiffrin, Memory search, *in* "Models of Human Memory" (D. A. Norman, ed.), pp. 375–447. Academic Press, New York, 1970; and also Norman (1969).

ferent concepts under different conditions. Any attempt to program context into computers requires a higher order program which can recognize contexts as data, and this then leads to an infinite regression. The conclusion is that in general situations machines will never behave like people.

8.3. Computer-Assisted Instruction

As an example of a situation where the capabilities of computers have become an issue we look at computers in education. In using computers as administrative aids for scheduling classes, processing student records, or maintaining personnel files, we encounter only the same technical and economic problems found in other administrative applications. Also, when students program solutions to problems to be run in a batched or a time-shared computer environment as part of their course work, we are on familiar ground, for there the computer is clearly a calculating device similar to a desk calculator and to laboratory equipment. The issue arises in computer-assisted instruction (CAI) where students use terminals in conversational mode to learn subjects taught in school. In these circumstances the computer is playing, in part at least, the role of the teacher. This use of computers opens up not only difficult questions of cost–effectiveness but also questions on the larger issues of the effects on the skills, motivation, and values imparted to students, when machines are substituted for teachers, and in general of the effects on the goals of education.

CAI is a subsequent development to programmed instruction, the training technique advanced by B. F. Skinner, based on presenting students with subject matter divided into small segments (frames), testing immediately for comprehension, and applying rewards (in the form of an advance to new material) when the frame has been learned. With CAI the linear sequence of presentation common in programmed books and teaching machines is not followed. Instead CAI takes advantage of the flexibility of computers to make use of branched programs, whereby students who make mistakes are directed to remedial exercises before they go on to new material.[17] There are three types of CAI programs:

[17] There are debates on the relative merits of linear and branched programs. It has been argued that the constructed (word) response of a linear program is preferable to the multiple-choice answers which are employed in a branched program, and that allowing students to make errors as happens in branched programs is not good educational practice. However, branched programs do provide for a wider range of answers to each question, and this provision allows CAI to deal with greater variations in the student's knowledge.

drill and review, tutorial, and dialogue.[18] The most common is drill and review in which students reply, on their terminals, to a sequence of short exercises on a lesson taught by the teacher and the computer scores the results and produces class lists and summaries. In tutorial and dialogue systems the computer presents lessons and concepts as well as exercises, although there are usually supplementary classes conducted by human instructors. CAI tutorial programs can consist of many lessons, each with branched subprograms in which the same material is presented in different formats and at different rates to match the learning rate of the student. Some make use of complex terminals capable of accepting typewriter and light-pen input and of presenting material visually on a cathode-ray tube screen or a slide projector, or in audio form through tapes. As with other high technology devices, educational television, and computers themselves, CAI utilization is limited by the availability of software, that is, prepared material to be used with the hardware equipment; but the rate of software production is growing appreciably, and a catalog prepared in 1971 lists 1272 CAI instructional programs.[19]

Of all the advantages claimed for CAI, the most important is that it enables each student to learn at his own pace instead of being forced to stay locked in step with classmates whose knowledge and learning rates are irreconcilably different. Individualized instruction has long been a goal in education,[20] available until now only for the very rich, but computers suggest this may be a realistic possibility for all. The principal beneficiaries of CAI, under these circumstances, are the very bright students and those who have learning difficulties, for both these groups are at a disadvantage in being forced to learn at the average rate set when a class is taught together.

Papert emphasizes the versatility of CAI and the exciting opportunities it offers for teaching concepts and techniques in mathematics, problem solving, biology, and mechanics, even to elementary school students.[21] The potentialities are demonstrated in the LOGO project at MIT where a number of simple devices such as a "turtle" which can move and turn and a box which can emit a note are attached to a computer. Students

[18] P. Suppes and M. Morningstar, Four programs in computer-assisted instruction, *in* "Computer-Assisted Instruction, Testing and Guidance" (W. H. Holtzmann, ed.), pp. 233–265. Harper, New York, 1970. Actual programs may, of course, be a mixture of types.

[19] H. A. Lekan (ed.), "Index to Computer-Assisted Instruction," 3rd ed. Harcourt, New York, 1971.

[20] R. A. Weisgerber, "Perspectives in Individualized Learning." Peacock, Itasca, Illinois, 1971.

[21] S. Papert, Teaching children thinking, *in* "World Conference on Computer Education 1970" (B. Scheepmaker and K. L. Zinn, eds.). Science Associates, New York, 1971.

manipulate these under program control and soon learn to write simple algorithms which make the turtle move in prescribed ways, draw pictures, or which make the music box play tunes. They become creatively involved in exploring the possibilities of the devices, and learning is natural and effective.

Other advantages claimed for CAI are the ability to correct work immediately, the opportunity for a continuous audit of learning progress, better retention because of a more effective presentation, and a more relaxed approach to learning which some students at least experience by receiving automatic encouragement for their efforts, and not having to work under the watchful supervision of a teacher. There are secondary advantages: The computer relieves the teacher of the administrative chores of taking attendance, grading, and class scheduling, and presents the opportunity to learn more about how learning takes place.[22]

A most serious objection to CAI is cost, especially as related to effectiveness and alternative ways of achieving better teaching. Cost estimates for CAI (and also for other instructional modes) are so dependent on assumptions about the size of population being served and the components which should be included, and show so much variation that it is necessary to accept any brief summary on them with caution. With this caveat, Table 8-2 shows estimates for the cost of CAI in $/student-hour, as well as comparable costs for traditionally administered instruction (TAI) and instructional television (ITV).[23] In spite of the uncertainties, the figures speak for themselves. For ITV the most important component of the cost arises from the preparation of the material, which can range from $50 to $500,000 per hour, with $6000 per hour a reasonable average. An estimate of 100 hours is generally taken for the time required to prepare one hour of CAI instructional material. This results in a cost of

[22] Empirical evidence on the effectiveness of CAI relative to other teaching methods is scarce and difficult to evaluate. See F. Kopstein and R. J. Seidel, Computer-administered instruction versus traditionally administered instruction *in* "Economics in Computer Assisted Instruction" (R. C. Atkinson and H. A. Wilson, eds.), p. 345 et seq. Academic Press, New York, 1966.

[23] In addition to the sources quoted in the table see also: E. Hartmann, The cost of computer assisted instruction. *Educ. Technol.* pp. 59–60, December (1971).

The report of the Carnegie Commission on Higher Education ("The Fourth Revolution: Instructional Technology in Higher Education." McGraw-Hill, New York, 1972) cites, in an Appendix, the cost figures of J. G. Miller [Deciding whether and how to use educational technology in the light of cost-effectiveness evaluation, *in* "To Improve Learning: An Evaluation of Instructional Technology" (S. G. Tickton, ed.), vol. 2, pp. 1007–1027. Bowker, New York, 1971]. Miller shows such broad ranges for the costs of the various educational modes (with ratios which vary from 12 to 500) that it is difficult to make comparisons, but the estimates of Table 8-2 lie within the ranges he gives.

TABLE 8-2
INSTRUCTIONAL COSTS

Instructional mode	Estimated cost $/student-hour	Notes	Source[a]
TAI—elementary and secondary schools (traditionally administered instruction)	0.38	Average U. S. cost for 1970–1971 based on projections from estimates for period 1956–1966	1
TAI—high education	1.40	Cost for 1970–1971 based on projections from estimates for 1956–1964	1
CAI—drill and review	1.81	Assuming a population of 100,000 students who use the equipment 1 hr/day	2
CAI—tutorial	4.79	Assuming a population of 100,000 students using the equipment 1 hr/day	2
CAI—elementary and secondary schools	3.73	Estimated costs 1967	3
CAI—higher education	2.76	Estimated costs 1967	3
ITV (instructional television)	0.35–0.06	Variation depends on population density	3

[a] (1) K. A. Simon and M. G. Fulham "Projections of Educational Statistics to 1974–75," Circular 790 (OE-10030-65) Office of Education, U. S. Dept. of Health, Education and Welfare, 1965; (2) C. N. Carter and M. J. Walker, "Costs of Installing and Operating Instructional Television and Computer-Assisted Instructions in the Public Schools," Booz, Allen and, Hamilton, Chicago, 1968; (3) F. F. Kopstein and R. J. Seidel Computer-administered instruction versus traditionally administered instruction *in* "Economics in Computer-Assisted Instruction" (R. C. Atkinson and H. A. Wilson, eds.) pp. 327–362. Academic Press, New York, 1969.

from $2000 to $10,000 per hour for prepared material, but assuming a lifetime of three years, this contributes only a few percent to the CAI costs, the major components coming from the hardware.

The objections to CAI are not only based on costs. Oettinger[24] is very critical of CAI because the claims made for it are in such contrast to the realities. Individualized instruction, he points out, can only be achieved to a degree, for one reason because students with different abilities soon arrive at quite different points of a course, and limitations of the computer store make it impractical to provide the full range of material which is really needed at a class session. The content of CAI lessons is

[24] A. G. Oettinger, "Run, Computer, Run." Harvard Univ. Press, Cambridge, Massachusetts, 1969.

characterized as rigid and unimaginative because the questions must be of multiple-choice types and the machine is unable to deal with variants in spelling and word order. Oettinger also points to major problems in the lack of reliability of the equipment, difficulties of scheduling use, and of convincing teachers, administrators, and school boards to make any changes at all in the educational system. Others have expressed concern about the depersonalizing effect of education in reducing the role of the teacher, and the discouraging effect on teacher recruitment which a widespread use of CAI could bring about.

The whole question of the possibility and desirability of replacing teachers, relevant to our discussion on the potentialities of computers, is surrounded with a high degree of ambivalence. There are assurances that computers must be regarded as aids to teachers, and their inability to carry out such tasks as counseling or conduct a discourse with students in natural language make it clear that they cannot be considered as replacements. While some claim that CAI finally makes individualized instruction possible, others maintain that its effectiveness in this regard is limited, and moreover that individualized instruction is not necessarily to be regarded as an unqualified blessing. One of the aims of education is to develop individuality; another is to teach young people how to play a cooperative role in society. And although there are advantages to the impersonal and impartial (depersonalized?) aspect that a computer-teacher presents to a student, most CAI programs make use of simple devices such as responding to a student by name, offering words of encouragement, and imitating a human teacher as far as possible.

Since CAI is so expensive it is impossible to see how it could be adopted on a large scale, adding to education costs which already constitute a large fraction of municipal taxes in many jurisdictions, unless there are some compensating savings in labor.

What would happen if the cost of CAI were to come down to a fifth or a tenth of the present cost? One of the most continuous investigations of CAI has been conducted at the University of Illinois in the successful PLATO programs, which started in 1959. Although the costs for the current PLATO III are estimated to range between $2 and $3 per student-contact hour, in line with those shown in Table 8-2, Bitzer suggests that for PLATO IV the operational costs will be in the range of $0.34 to $0.68 per contact hour.[25] It is believed that this very low figure will be achieved for a number of reasons.

[25] D. Alpert and D. L. Bitzer, Advances in computer-based education, *Science* **167**, 1582–1590 (1970). Also in the MIT LOGO project, Papert estimates that the computer costs would be about 75 cents per student-hour if several hundred students are involved.

1. The system will be very large with consequent economies of scale (the computer is to be a 6000 CDC series); there will be 4096 stations with an annual use of 8.2 million student-hours.

2. A totally new, inexpensive student console has been invented; this contains a key set, a plasma display panel, and a low-cost random access image projector capable of displaying any image on a microform card on which textural and photographic lesson materials are stored.[26]

3. It will be possible to locate student consoles at remote stations through the use of cable TV and telephone communication links.

If CAI costs were to approach those cited, there can be no doubt that there would be a very great rise in the volume of CAI instruction. No matter where one stands on the debate about the merits of CAI instruction compared with TAI, there are certainly types of learning for which it is useful. The view is that computers are far from being able to replace teachers now and in the foreseeable future, but they could come to be important if, as is considered desirable, schools become more decentralized and the educational process is extended over longer periods into adult life. Teachers could then concentrate on what machines cannot do; suggest reading and projects which match the special interests and capabilities of the student; stimulate the desire for knowledge, learning, and scholarship; encourage originality and creativity; and in general work with students in all those ways which make learning and teaching rich experiences.

It cannot be said as yet that the cost objectives of PLATO IV will be met. But in view of the history of computer technology it cannot be said that they will *never* be met. Moreover other innovations are being tried in education besides CAI and educational TV—the use of cassette videotapes, team-teaching methods, and open schools to name a few. The computer is only the latest candidate in a long line of technological devices that were supposed to revolutionize education.[27] In 1841 it was blackboards, in the 1920s it was radio, in the 1930s it was films, in the 1950s it was language laboratories, and in the 1960s it was programmed learning. The forces for change are today so strong, and the means for achieving it so many, that teaching and learning will undoubtedly undergo technological change. Citing the successes of Britain's Open University and Japan's University of the Air, the Carnegie Commission

[26] D. L. Bitzer and D. Skaperdas, Plato IV. An economically viable large scale computer-based education system, *Proc. Nat. Electron. Conf.* **24**, 351–356, 1968.

[27] M. Rubinoff, Planning for the effective utilization of technology in educations systems, *in* "World Conference on Computer Education 1970" (B. Scheepmaker and K. L. Zinn, eds.), pp. III/20–III/30. Science Associates, New York, 1971.

on Higher Education predicts that by the year 1990 instructional technology will reduce (on the average) a professor's time per course by at least 15%.[28] But the human contribution to teaching is likely to remain large, and the time is remote, if it ever comes, when teachers' salaries cease to be the major component of the operating costs in education.[29]

8.4. Machine Limitations

If the performance of computers now falls so short of human performance, and computer mechanisms and computer programs are so primitive compared to the human brain and human thought processes, a question immediately arises: Why are there so many forecasts that in the not too distant future computers will be carrying out many tasks for which we now need people, even tasks requiring judgment and intelligence? There are several reasons for such predictions.

Over the last century those who have predicted what would *not* be possible have come to look foolish time and time again. There are few tasks which, one can be sure, will remain unaffected by computers during the next 25 years. For this reason the futurists try to be daring. An examination of predictions shows that although people tend to be overly optimistic about what will be accomplished in any field in the short run, say in five years, they tend to underestimate what will be achieved over a longer period.

Another argument for optimism is that it is not necessary for computers to imitate people to achieve high-level performance in some tasks. Where the task is primarily computational, the computer can find solutions using techniques such as mathematical programming to arrive at solutions which a human would fail to find altogether.

But there is a more important reason for not placing bounds on the ways in which computers will eventually be used. Although speculation on what computers can be made to do and how closely they can be programmed to imitate human behavior is philosophically interesting, it is not really relevant to knowing what computers will be used for or how widespread computers will become. The answers to these latter questions, which are the crucial ones with regard to the social effects of com-

[28] See "The Fourth Revolution" (footnote 23). The Commission observes that instructional technology may be best suited to teaching skills (rather than for general education) and as such will be a central component of mass-oriented extramural education.

[29] If student living costs were to be added into the costs of education (as they are for some educational programs and in some countries), this statement would have to be qualified.

puters, depend on what man, using a computer to help him, will be able to do, and how the capabilities of a few men, enhanced by computers, will affect the type and quantity of work most men do. In seeking answers to these questions there is already clear evidence that the effects are significant to society. There have been noticeable changes in the numbers of people doing certain kinds of work and in the nature of their work, particularly for those who are engaged in routine clerical tasks. The extent and implications of these changes are examined more closely in the next chapter. People will be able to use computers to do jobs which require intelligence, imagination, and even creativity better than they can now.

To go back to our chess example, although it is not possible to say when a computer program will win the world chess championship or even qualify for master status, one can assert with confidence that a chess master who had the services of a computer at his disposal would have a decisive advantage over one who did not, if only because the computer would in effect slow down his clock by enabling him to explore certain lines of play very quickly and thoroughly. A computer may never be used in this way because it would be too expensive or because it is contrary to the spirit of chess tournaments where players may not use aids, but the extension of man's chess performance is definitely there. A similar situation exists with respect to the use of computers in the creative arts, but here we can already see a strong tendency to put computers to actual use in the process.

The power of a computer as a data processor makes it obviously useful for certain tasks such as cataloging, information retrieval, and stylistic analysis in many areas, for example, literature, music, and architecture. But it is more interesting to see how computers enter into the creation of artistic works, and here the greatest efforts and the most noteworthy results have been achieved in music and art. Musical composition with computers dates back to 1956, and there is already a substantial body of works which have been produced in this way.[30] It is not necessary for our purpose to judge whether the products are good or even interesting musically. What is relevant is to note that there is a general acceptance that it is perfectly in order to undertake musical composition with computers. Undoubtedly this acceptance stems from the long history of musical experimentation, both in composition (where certain recognized composers have at times used mathematical techniques) and in the de-

[30] L. Hiller, Music composed with computers—A historical survey, *in* "The Computer and Music" (H. B. Lincoln, ed.), pp. 42–96. Cornell Univ. Press, Ithaca, New York, 1970. See also J. S. Moorer, Music and computer composition, *Comm. ACM* **15** (2), 104–113 (1972).

velopment of new instruments. To date the computer works have been generated by programs and then selected and arranged by the composer, but there are new techniques in which the composer uses the computer in a much more dynamic and interactive way, through a keyboard, to obtain at will instrumental and melodic transposition, polyphonic arrangements, variations, special effects, and so on.

In the graphic arts, the entry of computers has been even more noteworthy. Computer art has been taken up by a growing group of artists and designers who have collaborated with computer scientists to produce a great variety of charts, sketches, designs, paintings, and even sculptures. These are exhibited regularly at computer conferences and, increasingly, in general exhibitions.[31] Here again many modern artists are engaged in a deliberate exploration of new techniques, materials, surfaces, and forms of expression, and it is most natural that some of them should seize upon the possibilities offered through computers. In art it is possible to state that some of the computer products are "interesting" (see Fig. 8-2); at the very least they show a range, variety, and complexity which makes it impossible to distinguish computer art from the works of human artists which art judges have found worthy of display.

In industry computer-aided design has been slow to spread, although there were enthusiastic predictions for it when graphic input to computers, by means of a light pen, was first demonstrated. The difficulties seem to be very similar to some of those inhibiting the widespread utilization of computer-assisted instruction—doubts about the cost–effectiveness, the need for special equipment, the lack of software, and so on. But even those who feel that there is no further value in research on artificial intelligence agree that there is great promise in investigating how man can use computers to extend his capabilities.[32] Man–machine symbiosis simply means man using a tool, and it has been happening since man threw a stone or used a stick for a poker. By this token using a computer for any of the applications we have considered earlier is man–machine symbiosis. But as we use computers more and more for mental and creative processes, a deeper significance is being given to the term. We can expect both the economic and the practical difficulties in using computers to diminish, and the range of jobs in which computers find application to grow. In particular we can expect computers to be used more in the design processes, as well as in the administrative and production processes where they are mostly used now. In this sense man–machine symbiosis is increasing. There are those who regard this increase, and any increase in

[31] J. Reichardt (ed.), "Cybernetics, Art and Ideas." Studio Vista, London, 1971.
[32] For example, Dreyfus (1972, Chapter 10).

FIG. 8-2. *An example of computer-assisted art. Reprinted with the permission of L. Mezei.*

the dependence of man on technology, as a harmful development. We shall examine these objections in Chapter 13.

In review, we have arrived at the following position. For problem solving and pattern recognition where intelligence, judgment, and comprehensive knowledge are required, the results of even the best computer programs are far inferior to those achieved by humans (excepting cases where the task is a well-defined mathematical computation). Further, the differences between the mode of operation of computers and the modes in which humans operate (insofar as we can understand these latter) seem to be so great that for many tasks there is little or no prospect of achieving human performance within the foreseeable future. Nevertheless, it is not possible to place bounds on how computers can be used even in the short term, because we must expect that the normal use of computers will be as a *component* of a man–machine combination.

This does not mean that there are *no* limitations on the use of computers, or even that we should refuse to consider ways in which computer use should be deliberately restricted. Aside from reasons of cost, there may be other factors which would lead to restrictions in the extent or manner of use. In certain situations computers might, for example, cause unacceptable levels of unemployment. There may be desirable restrictions on the data to be stored in computers or one might wish to assure equality of access to different groups of people. In Chapter 12 we examine questions of ethics relating to the use of computers, and these could lead to restrictions in use. In medicine it might be argued that computers should not be used for automatic medical diagnosis because this must remain the prerogative and the responsibility of the doctor. While it is true that computers are far from being able to perform diagnosis now, they can already be of help, and will undoubtedly come to be used more and more; the question arises of how much reliance it is proper to place on computers.

Whatever the shortcomings of computers now and in the future, we cannot take refuge in their limitations in potential. We must ask what we want to do with them and whether the purposes are socially desirable. Because once goals are agreed upon, the potentialities of men using computers, though not unlimited, cannot be bounded in any way we can see now.

Bibliography

Arbib, M. A. (1964). "Brains, Machines, and Mathematics." McGraw-Hill, New York.

Bonzard, M. (1970). "Pattern Recognition." Spartan Books, Washington, D. C.

Brickman, W. W., and Lehner, S. (1966). "Automation, Education and Human Values." School and Society Books, New York.

Brit. Computer Soc. (1971). *Proc. Advance Papers Internat. Joint Conf. Artificial Intelligence, 2nd.* London.

Dreyfus, H. (1972). "What Computers Can't Do: A Critique of Artificial Reason." Harper, New York.

Feigenbaum, E. A., and Feldman, J. eds. (1963). "Computers and Thought." McGraw-Hill, New York.

Knezevich, S. J., and Eye, G. G., eds. (1970). "Instructional Technology and the School Administrator." Amer. Assoc. of School Admininstrators, Washington, D. C.

Minsky, M., ed. (1968). "Semantic Information Processing." MIT Press, Cambridge, Massachusetts.

Norman, D. A. (1969). "Memory and Attention." Wiley, New York.

Pylyshyn, Z., ed. (1970). "Prospectives on the Computer Revolution." Prentice-Hall, Englewood Cliffs, New Jersey.
Uhr, L., ed. (1966). "Pattern Recognition." Wiley, New York.
Walker, D. E., and Norton, L. M., eds. (1969). *Proc. Internat. Joint Conf. Artificial Intelligence, 1st.* Washington, D. C.
Watanabe, S. (1969). "Knowing and Guessing." Wiley, New York.

Problems and Further Work

1. Computer games have been widely used as educational and training tools in business, management, military studies, political science, and so on. Familiarize yourself with one of these games, if possible by participating in it, and write a critique of it as an educational aid. Draw up a list of advantages and difficulties in using games. What is involved in constructing a game? What type of computer system is useful for game playing? See

R. C. Harshaw and J. R. Jackson, "The Executive Game." Irwin, Homewood, Illinois, 1968; H. B. Thorelli and R. L. Graves, "International Operation Simulations." Free Press of Glencoe, Glencoe, Illinois, 1964.

2. Complete the center branch of the game tree of Fig. 8-1 for naughts and crosses. Approximately what reduction in the number of paths is achieved by taking advantage of symmetries? What implications does this have for computer game-playing programs?

3. The term *content analysis* is used to describe methods of examining texts in order to determine and measure an author's attitudes, sources, and influences. Suggest how such measures might be attempted and look up some examples of content analysis on literary textual materials. What are the limitations of the methods? To what extent are they successful in overcoming the difficulties in having computers understand the semantic content of language? See

Nat. Conf. Content Anal., Annenberg School of Comm., Univ. of Pennsylvania, Philadelphia, 1967; R. A. Fairthorn, Content analysis, specification and control, *Annu. Rev. Informat. Sci. Technol.* 4, chapter 3. (1969).

For an example see

J. D. Smith, A computational analysis of imagery in James Joyce's 'A Portrait of the Artist as a Young Man,' *Proc. IFIP Congr.* 2, 1443–1447 (1971).

4. In addition to the difficulty of making computers responsive to natural languages, another limitation which is often mentioned is their inability to observe obvious relationships between data. Give some examples of this from your own experience. Is this an inherent weakness or are there methods of overcoming it?

5. A "turtle" is a computer-controlled device which can move forward or backward a unit distance, rotate a degree, and raise and lower a writing pen. Describe a project which would use a turtle to motivate and describe concepts in elementary geometry (e.g., convexity). See

LOGO Memos 1–5, MIT Artificial Intelligence Lab., Massachusetts Inst. of Technol., Cambridge, Massachusetts.

6. Survey predictions made in the computer field. Have they been overly optimistic in the short run? What examples can be cited where predictions have underestimated achievements? See

Dreyfus (1972, Part I).

7. Discuss the present state of artificial intelligence according to the following definition of intelligence: "Intelligence is the ability to cope in a new environment." Do humans still possess this ability?

8. Recognition of paradigms seems to be one of the basic ways by which humans learn to identify situations and contexts. What else is involved in learning to recognize context? What are the difficulties in attempting to construct a computer program which would learn to recognize context in the way that a human does?

9. What is the evidence for believing that speech is essentially related to human intelligence? (Take into considerations data available from experiments in which animals, e.g., chimpanzees, have been brought up as humans, and from experiences of deaf-mutes.)

10. Obtain access to a CAI course and after working through a number of lessons, write a critique based on your experience. Look for the following features:

- the mechanism for restarting the lesson after some error or failure
- the ability to bypass a section of the lesson
- the variability permitted in the answers

- how the program deals with a response which it fails to recognize as a change from the answer just given
- the pace at which the subject matter is presented (is it too slow or too fast?)
- any aspects which are particularly satisfying (irritating)

Which of the shortcomings do you regard as specific to the lesson and which inherent in the mode of instruction?

Chapter

9

COMPUTERS AND EMPLOYMENT[1]

The relationship of computers and automation to employment is part of the more general relation of technological change to employment. The most obvious effect is that increases in productivity due to technology can eliminate jobs. Technology affects the individual worker both in his attitudes toward work and in the nature and amount of the work he does. Furthermore, the structure of the entire economy as well as the organizational structure of individual firms are affected by such changes. Because of the central importance of these effects, the impact of technology has been the subject of extensive study by economists, sociologists, political scientists, and psychologists. Even within a single discipline, studies are often contradictory and conclusions are colored by political overtones. We wish to delineate some of the issues, and present arguments given to support different viewpoints.

9.1. Technology, Productivity, and the Labor Force

The twentieth century has witnessed major changes in productivity and in the composition of the labor force, coincident with, and in large part attributable to, technological change. The commonly accepted index of technological change is productivity or output per man-hour, measured in terms of some unit product or service (see Section 6.2). Substantial changes in productivity, in conjunction with demands for new products and services, bring about significant changes in the composition of the work force. The most striking example of this is the steady decline, over decades, in the number of farm workers in North America, Western Europe, and other industrial nations at a time when technological change made it possible for output to increase. In the United States from 1947 to 1965, total farm employment and the number of farms decreased by 50% while net production increased by about 40%. This phenomenon can be accounted for by the dramatic 285% rise in farm output per man-hour, contrasted with the substantial (but far less dramatic) rise of 82% in non-farm productivity during the same period. Figure 9-1 shows the increases in the output per man-hour for agriculture and for the non-farm sector in the United States for the period 1910 to 1961.

Let us define *service-producing* industries to include trade, government, finance, insurance, real estate, transportation, health services, education, and miscellaneous (hotels, laundries, domestic) services. Economists

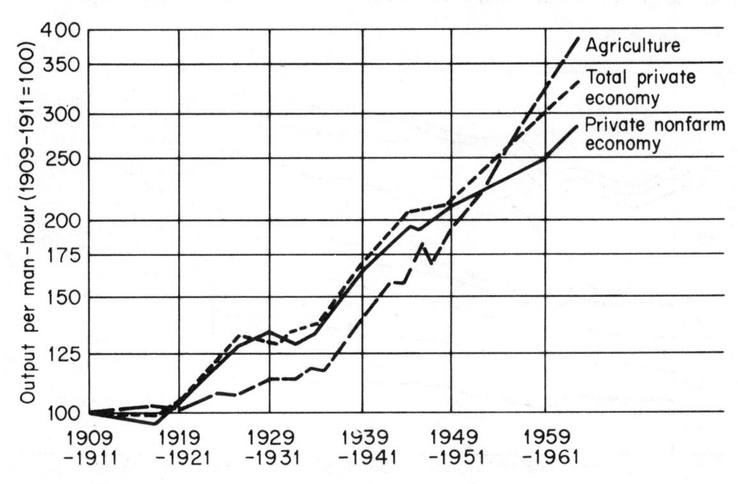

FIG. 9-1. *Indexes of output per man-hour, total private, farm, and private non-farm economy, 1909–1965, based on three-year moving average. [From "Technology and the American Economy" (Nat. Comm. on Technol., Automation, and Econ. Prog. Rep., 1966).]*

---

[1] Parts of this chapter are reprinted, by permission, from C. C. Gotlieb and A. Borodin, Computers and employment, *Comm. ACM* **15**, 695–702 (1972). Copyright 1972 by the Assoc. for Comput. Machinery.

commonly call these *tertiary* industries. *Primary* industries are those which produce basic items (food, clothing, etc.) while *secondary* industries are those which manufacture other products. These last two are goods-producing industries. The development of an industrialized economy is characterized first by the shift from producing basics to the production of manufactured goods, and then by a shift to the provision of various services (culminating in what is often called the *postindustrial society*). Figure 9-2 indicates this continuing shift in the United States. Note the substantial increase in government, wholesaling, retailing, and service occupations.[1a]

Of course not all changes are directly related to technology. Interrelated factors such as education, social and political attitudes, and the readiness to accept women in senior levels of employment affect the numbers of teachers, athletes, waiters, stockbrokers, and so on. It is difficult to distinguish between those trends which are direct effects of technology and those which are coincident with technological development. In any event, we continue to witness the growth of those industries which employ mostly white collar, professional, and technical workers. In the period from 1947 to 1971, we find (see Fig. 9-3) increases in professional and technical workers from 6.6 to 14.6% of the employed labor

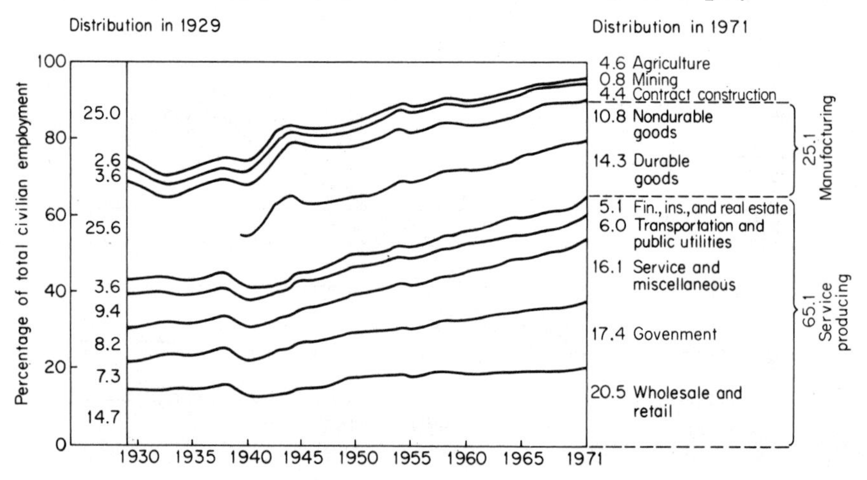

FIG. 9.2. *Distribution of employment by major industrial sector, 1929–1971. Note: Total civilian employment equals the total employment on payrolls of nonagricultural establishments (excluding self-employed and unpaid family workers) plus agricultural employment (including self-employed and unpaid family workers). [From: 1929–1964 (Nat. Comm. on Technol., Automation, and Econ. Prog. Rep., 1966, Fig. 8); 1965–1971 (U. S. Dept. of Labor, 1972, Tables A-1 and C-1).]*

[1a] For a detailed analysis of the structural makeup of the U. S. economy, including both technological factors and labor aspects, see Carter (1970).

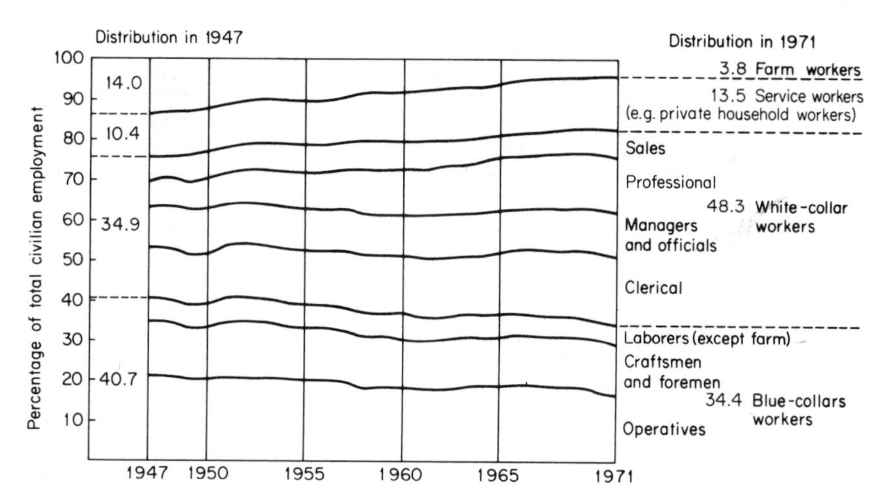

FIG. 9-3. *Change in distribution of employment by major occupation group. Note: Statistics for 1947–1964 and 1964–1971 are based on somewhat different sets of occupational data (e.g., changes in the lower age limit for inclusion into the labor force). Similarly, the statistics for 1971 are not strictly comparable with earlier years. However, the changes do not significantly affect Fig. 9-3. For 1964, the discrepancy was approximately 0.3 in the major classifications (e.g., white collar, etc.) and the two sets of statistics were averaged for Fig. 9-3. [From: 1947–1964 (Nat. Comm. on Technol., Automation, and Econ. Prog. Rep., 1966, Fig. 10); 1964–1971 (U. S. Dept. of Labor, 1972, Table A-11).]*

force, and in white collar workers from 34.9 to 48.3%. During this interval the percentage of blue collar workers decreased from 40.7 to 36% by the early 1960s, rose to 37% in the mid-1960s, but by 1971 had decreased to 34.4%.

In spite of the high rate of technological change in the twentieth century and the resulting gains in productivity, the total labor force (of the industrialized nations) has increased throughout the period. The reason is, of course, that the demand for products and services (only partly due to increased population) has increased even more rapidly than productivity, so that more workers are needed. As is sometimes painfully obvious, there are severe fluctuations in the demand for labor. However, the data[2] from the admittedly incomplete measure of unemployment rates suggest that high rates of technological change and increasing productivity do not, by themselves, sufficiently account for unemployment. As an example of this evidence, consider the period from 1953 to 1961. The unemployment in the United States was relatively high (at

[2] Unemployment rates only indicate those who are known to be seeking employment (e.g., by registering for unemployment insurance). It is much harder to gauge the true extent of involuntary unemployment and part-time subemployment.

TABLE 9-1
AVERAGE ANNUAL PERCENTAGE INCREASE IN OUTPUT PER WORKER[a,b]

Country	Percentage increase
Japan	6.4
East and Southeast Asia (excluding Japan)	5.2
European Economic Community	4.6
Latin America	4.2
Europe	3.6
United States	3.0

[a] Mining, manufacturing, electricity, and gas.
[b] From data in United Nations "The Growth of World Industry, 1938–1961, International Analyses and Tables," SN64.XVII.8. New York.

an official level of 6%), although the increase in the output per worker was the lowest of the countries listed in Table 9-1. In the countries of the European Economic Community there was relatively little unemployment, and in Asia (excluding Japan) and Latin America there was consistently higher unemployment.

To illustrate the relation between demand, productivity, and employment, consider the following simplified model:

Let

Y = output of goods and services (assumed to be equal to the demand)
P = productivity (goods per worker per year)
L = labor force
H = average hours worked per worker per year
A = available labor force
U = unemployed labor force

We then have

$$U = A - L \quad \text{and} \quad U/L \text{ is unemployment rate}$$
$$Y = P \cdot L \cdot H \quad \text{or} \quad L = Y \cdot P/H$$

Letting Δ represent "change/year," it follows that

$$\Delta U = \Delta A - \Delta L = \Delta A + L \cdot \Delta P/P - \Delta Y/P \cdot H + L \cdot \Delta H/H$$

If we regard the change in hours worked as minor (i.e., ΔH is close to zero), then the change in absolute unemployment is determined by the growth in the available labor force ΔA, the increase in the productivity ΔP, less the growth of total demand for goods and services, ΔY.

This model is not adequate for explaining the effects of technological change since it unrealistically assumes that labor supply and demand operate in a highly simplified system; that is, all workers are equally available for each job. During the 1960s two opposing schools of thought emerged concerning automation and the underlying reasons for prolonged unemployment. One is that of the "structuralists," who believe that insufficient skill and education levels and other structural factors (age, sex, race, mobility) are the main obstacles to full employment. On the other hand, proponents of the demand theory believe that while structural factors exist to some extent, insufficient demand is the main barrier to full employment. Between these opposing viewpoints there are all shades of opinion.[3]

We may note that the assumption concerning the constancy of the hours worked is not too unrealistic. Although there has been a decline in hours per worker per year throughout the twentieth century, the average workweek has only been decreasing at the rate of about 3.5 hours/week per decade. The consequences of increased leisure are discussed in Chapter 13.

Some final comments are in order before proceeding to specific studies of automation and computing. If one believes that significant productivity increases will continue, then either demand must continue to increase, the labor force must shrink (at least relative to the population), and/or the hours worked must be reduced. There are many who believe that as our society matures and as its material needs are satisfied, demand will begin to level. Unfortunately (or fortunately, depending on the viewpoint), there is little evidence to support this view. In light of environmental factors, a leveling in the demand for those goods which require a large consumption of resources is necessary for continued survival. But demand does not necessarily mean a search for more and more gadgets and a glut of superfluous services. It is conceivable that we will direct our demand toward better housing, better transportation, and better health, education, and recreational services. In addition to these possibilities, recycling of materials may necessitate a significant labor component.

[3] For some opinions on the "structuralists–insufficient demand debate" see E. Gilpatrick, On the classification of unemployment: A view of the structural-inadequate demand debate, *Ind. Labor Relations Rev.* **19**, 201–212 (1966); V. Stoikov, Increasing structural unemployment reexamined, *Ind. Labor Relations Rev.* **19**, 368–376 (1966); Silberman (1966); and for a summary of these positions see Jaffe and Froomkin (1968, Chapter 5). There is actually a third major factor in unemployment, namely, the frictional unemployment rate for a given economy which is supposed to reflect the normal percentage of unemployment in a fluid labor market. Thus full employment is achieved when the percentage of unemployment equals the frictional rate. Of course, one may argue that a high frictional rate is symptomatic of structural unemployment.

9.2. Productivity and Automation: Mitigating Factors

Today, technological change primarily means automation, and automation in the office means computers. Automation should be distinguished from mechanization[4] in that it also implies automatic control and integration of a process. For example, a card sorter is a form of mechanization (where a machine replaces a human skill), as distinct from an airline reservation system which regulates the entire reservation process.

The advent of modern computers and of automatic process control in the factory understandably has caused a great deal of anxiety regarding the future of human employment. As early as in 1950, Norbert Wiener (1950) saw the possible end to full employment and the obsolescence of all but a small fraction of the work force because of computers. The argument is logical enough: If entire processes can be fully automated, then increases in productivity will be so great and so rapid, that only a few individuals will be needed to monitor and repair equipment. Fortunately, the predictions have not materialized. Figures 9-4 and 9-5 show that the growth of productivity in the last two decades has been somewhat (but not drastically) faster than the growth throughout the twentieth century.

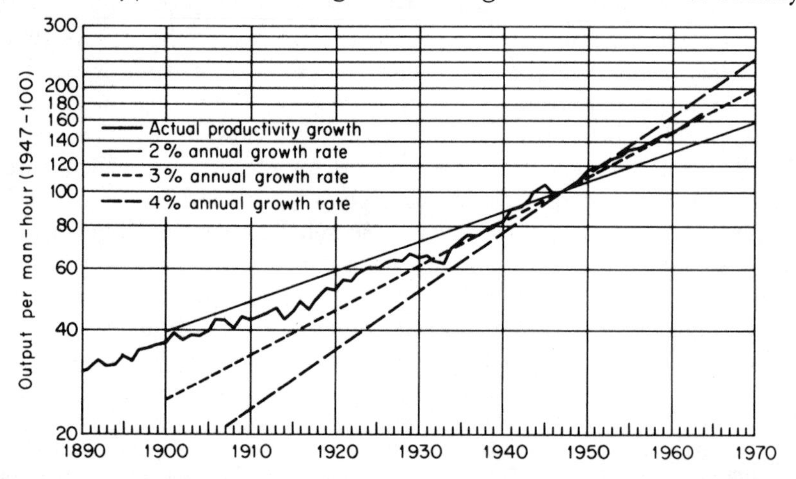

FIG. 9-4. *Long-term productivity growth in the private economy. (Reprinted with the permission of Fortune Magazine from C. Silberman, "The Myths of Automation." Harper, New York, 1965. Copyright: Alexander Semenoick, Fortune Magazine, © 1965 by Time, Inc.)*

[4] Mechanization is often called Detroit Automation, defined as the integration of machines or linking together by means of automatic transfer, devices of machine production. See J. Diebold, The nature of computers and automation, *in* "The New Technology and Human Values" (J. Burke, ed.), pp. 109–118. Wadsworth Publ., Belmont, California, 1966.

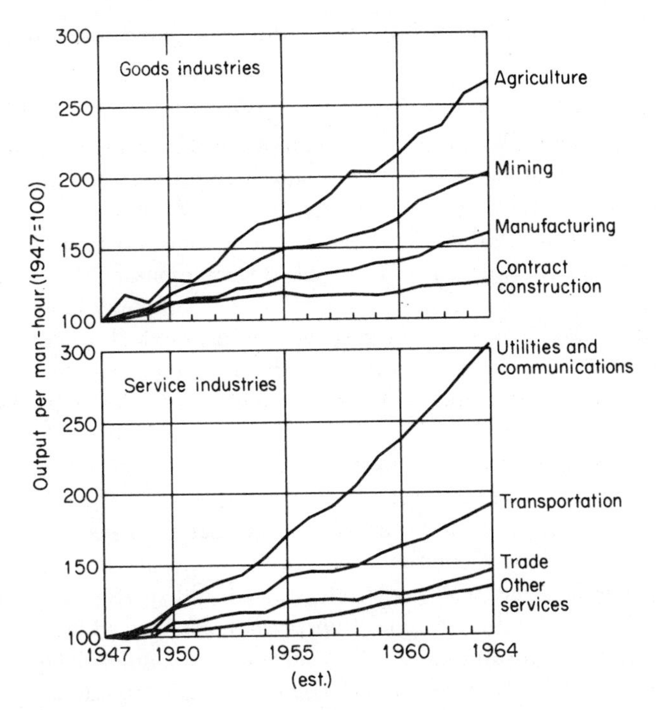

Fig. 9-5. *Postwar productivity growth by industry. Talk of the overall rates often tends to blur the widely divergent trends from one industry to another. For all the talk about automation, output per man-hour has increased more slowly in manufacturing than in the economy as a whole since 1947—that is, by 2.9% a year versus 3.4% for the economy. These recent gains in manufacturing are barely half as large as those realized during the 1920s, when a real revolution in manufacturing technology was taking place. (Reprinted with the permission of Fortune Magazine from C. Silberman, "The Myths of Automation." Harper, New York, 1965. Copyright: Alexander Semenoick, Fortune Magazine, © 1965 by Time, Inc.)*

This is not to deny that automation and computing have caused serious displacements in particular circumstances. Some studies[5] have revealed that there were reductions in staff (even during periods of business growth) directly attributed to the introduction of computers, but this has distinctly not been the usual case. Automation and computing are having measurable effects on productivity and the labor force, but thus far the overall reduction in employment due to productivity growth seems to be still within manageable limits.[6]

[5] For example, see R. Helfgott, EDP and the office work force, *Ind. Lab. Relations Rev.* **19**, 509 (1966); I. Hoos, When the computer takes over the office, Harvard *Business Rev.* no. 38 (1960).

[6] See Jaffe and Froomkin (1968) for a comprehensive assessment as of 1965.

What are some of the factors that appear to have mitigated the impact of automation?

1. There are few manufacturing plants which have proceeded to full automation; essentially, control has remained in human hands. In general, most processes still need careful human monitoring and adjustment of parameters at several stages.

2. As we emphasized in Chapter 8, the replacement of sensory and manipulative operations as well as of decision-making by machine is often beyond the present state of technology. Moreover, there is still a significant lag between scientific discovery and practical implementation.[7]

3. Office work in service-producing industries requires interfacing with human customers. Recalling Chapter 8 again, we may note that there are no immediate possibilities of having machines conduct the discourse required for normal customer inquiries.

4. In offices, typing and secretarial positions have been largely unaffected by computers. In both office and factory, decreases in direct labor may be partially compensated for by increases of indirect labor. *Direct labor* is that whose withdrawal would cause an immediate cessation of the work being done. *Indirect labor* is that whose withdrawal would result in a substantially rapid (but not immediate) delay in process performance. This includes maintenance, support functions (i.e., keypunching), and first-line supervision but excludes research and higher management. Many plants maintain a number of workers mainly as insurance against system failure.

5. Computers and automated process control are sometimes selected not for a reduction in labor but rather for improved accuracy or resource utilization. Also, only small gains can be expected when automation is applied to processes which are already highly sophisticated and have small labor requirements.

6. Years of planning and implementation are required for the installation of automatic equipment, especially in service-producing industries which cannot disrupt service for installation. (Recall the implementation schedule for the airline reservation system.) This delay allows time for manpower planning and training.

7. There are some companies which have deliberately slowed the introduction so as to avoid large-scale displacements. Sometimes this has occurred at the insistence of unions or to counter the threat of unionization. But many companies are simply aware of the dangerous effect on workers' attitudes and performance if a reasonably smooth transition is not achieved.

[7] This lag, although decreasing, has been estimated at about 15 years.

Of the studies relating to the effects of computers in office employment,[8] the results of a study in Great Britain are typical.[9] It shows that up to 1964, in spite of the introduction of over 600 computers in offices, there was an 8% increase in the aggregate number of staff employed; it is estimated that there would have been a 13% increase if computing equipment had not been installed. The report also predicted that there would be no dramatic change in office employment over the next five years (a prediction subsequently confirmed) and, because of the time required to plan and organize a computing installation, there would be adequate opportunities to redeploy staff. For the 1970s, because of the growing requirements for office work and only a slow rise in the working population, the report predicted that computers would have to be used extensively to cope with the work load.

In the final summary of a series of reports on labor and automation published by the International Labour Office,[10] an earlier conclusion concerning automation is repeated: "For various reasons, the introduction of automation in offices has thus far not brought about any significant dismissal of personnel nor resulted in a decline in the general level of employment for office workers."

In spite of the reassuring conclusions about aggregate employment to date, there are still serious concerns about the future. Early computers have now been replaced by much faster and larger machines. Input–output interfaces are undergoing major improvements; marked sense cards and remote terminals may spell the end of keypunching. Some processes are now fully automated. In one chemical industry a computer controls all the process variables for air liquefaction and separation. Some specialized jobs, such as typesetting, are being eliminated. We could go on but these are enough examples to warn against complacency.

Moreover, as suggested before, aggregate unemployment is not the whole story. Specific occupational groups (e.g., non-farm laborers) are affected disproportionately. In the United States it is well known that

[8] Impact of office automation in a government service (USA), *in* "Technical Change and Manpower Planning" (S. Barkin, ed.), pp. 257–268. OECD, Paris, 1967; also J. Urvoy, A tentative interpretation of a number of case-studies of firms and industries using office computers and J. Kruse, Comparative manning practices in data processing installations, *in Manpower Aspects Automation Technolog. Change,* Eur. Conf. (1966), supplement to the final report. *OECD publ.,* Paris, 1966; "Impact of Office Automation in the Insurance Industry," Bull. no. 1468. U.S. Govt. Printing Office, Washington, D. C.

[9] Computers in Offices, Manpower Stud. No. 4, Ministry of Labour, Great Britain, HM Stationery Office, London, 1965.

[10] "Labour and Automation," Bull. 1–7, Internat. Labour Office, Geneva, 1964–1968.

the unemployment rate for blacks and young workers is considerably higher than that for whites and for those over 25. Technology has obviously had an effect on the makeup of the labor force, but to what extent can we say that new skill levels are a major cause of structural differences? In contrast to the United States, the youth unemployment rate in Great Britain is only 1.3 times that for adults, which suggests that social barriers rather than technological factors are the main obstacles to employment opportunities.

9.3. Automation and Skill Levels

The complexity of the relation between employment and the technological change brought about by computers can be illustrated by the following question: Do computers bring about an increase or a decrease in the skills required for jobs? The impact of automation on skill levels is another facet of the relation between technology and jobs which has received considerable attention. Among the difficulties in attempting to carry out studies are the following.

1. The need to devise methods for measuring the skills required for a job. Here we must be careful to differentiate requirements from formal qualifications imposed as screening devices. Rising educational levels do not necessarily represent required skill levels.
2. The need to carry out experiments with good statistical controls—for instance, on comparable plants, one of which has been automated and the other has not.
3. The need to estimate the effects of other variables: changes in the economy, differences in attitudes, training, management, and the effect of unions.
4. The tendency to overestimate the difficulty of a new job. In initial studies exaggerations about the difficulty of doing jobs related to computers resulted in inflated reports of job upgrading. On the other hand, the occupational content can change significantly while the title remains the same.
5. The need to estimate the contribution of indirect labor.
6. The problem in distinguishing between skill and other aspects of a job, such as accuracy and responsibility, which are related but which are generally regarded as different.

Although many of the early studies on automation seemed to indicate a marked general upgrading of the skills required, after more than a decade of study the consensus is that skill levels are both increased and decreased, and that the nature of the process has a greater effect than the technological change itself. For example, experience with numerically controlled machine tools has shown that the requirements for worker skill are often decreased with the advent of automatic control. A man tending an automatic machine may have a more routine job, with less opportunity to exercise control than he would have on the same process nonautomated. The worker may be given more training so that he can better understand what he is doing, but how much of this training is required for carrying out the job effectively?

One thorough study, indicative of the many complex factors, can be found in the research of Crossman, Laner, and their associates (Crossman and Laner, 1969). They examined 18 cases of the application of digital computers or analog automatic control in six different process types. The processes were check processing and account posting in banking; annealing, galvanizing, and tinplating steel; machining aircraft parts; electric power generation; hydrocarbon cracking, and air liquefaction and separation; and an airline passenger reservation system. Tables 9-2 and 9-3 summarize the changes in direct and indirect skill requirements for each of the processes.

The conclusions are as follows.

1. Direct labor productivity increased in 13 of the 18 cases, and was unchanged in the remaining 5. In the eight cases where indirect labor could be assessed, four cases actually showed a small decrease in overall productivity. However, if one could measure product value, then the gains in the other four cases would probably indicate an overall increase in productivity due to automation.

2. In a majority of the cases, technological change increased the direct skill requirements and decreased the indirect skill requirements.

3. In only two of the six process types (demand deposit accounting and airline reservation systems) did the overall increase in mean skill level exceed 5%. In computer-controlled electricity generation and in air separation, there was a small but distinct decrease in overall skill level. (However, all percentages for the fully automated air separation must be qualified because of the extremely small labor requirement.) A perceptible (but not major) upward drift in aggregate mean skill level is indicated.

4. There were little changes in the man-hour requirements for skilled labor (operators and craftsmen) and some decreases in the requirements for semiskilled and unskilled labor. The overall tendency toward skill upgrading is largely accounted for by reductions at the semiskilled levels,

TABLE 9-2
RELATIVE CHANGES IN SKILL LEVEL DUE TO AUTOMATION[a,b]

Technological change	Sample process	Industry	Product unit	Direct labor change	Overall (direct plus indirect) change
Machine-aided manual to computerized	Demand deposit accounting	Banking	1000 items processed	+9.8% +15.8%	+26.0%
Batch to continuous process	Annealing strip	Steel	10 tons	+23.3% +8.8%	+4.7%
	Coating strip (galvanizing and tinplating)		10 tons 100 base boxes	+50.0% −3.0%	
Conventional to numerically controlled machinery	Machining aircraft parts	Aerospace	1 part	−2.5% −10.0%	

Decentralized to centralized control	Power generation	Electric utility	1 plant operating hr	+43.8% +95.5%	−6.3%
Conventional analog to digital computer process control					
Monitoring and performance calculations	Power generation	Electric utility	1 plant operating hr	0.0% 0.0%	−5.0%
Partially closed loop	Hydrocarbon cracking	Oil	1000 barrels	0.0% 0.0% 0.0%	
Fully closed loop	Air liquefaction and separation	Chemical	10 tons	0.0%	−11.6%
Semiautomatic to computerized random demand real time service	Airline passenger reservation systems	Air transportation	100 passengers boarded	+18.5% +5.0%	

[a] From Crossman and Laner (1969).
[b] Plus sign indicates a higher skill requirement for the new technology.

TABLE 9-3
CHANGES IN LABOR INPUT (DIRECT AND INDIRECT) DUE TO AUTOMATION[a]

Technological change	Sample process	Industry	Product unit	Change in man-hours per unit product (new tech.–old tech.)		
				Lower skill levels	Medium skill levels	Higher skill levels
Machine-aided manual to computerized	Demand deposit accounting	Banking	1000 items processed	+0.7	−17.4	−0.4
Batch to continuous process	Annealing strip Coating strip (galvanizing and tinplating)	Steel	10 tons 10 tons 100 base boxes	0.0	−0.6	+0.3
Conventional to numerically controlled machinery	Machining aircraft parts	Aerospace	1 part			
Decentralized to centralized control	Power generation	Electric utility	1 plant operating hr	−2.8	−2.5	−2.6
Conventional analog to digital computer process control						
Monitoring and performance calculations	Power generation	Electric utility	1 plant operating hr	+0.6	+0.2	+0.3
Partially closed loop	Hydrocarbon cracking	Oil	1000 barrels	0.0 0.0 0.0	0.0 0.0 0.0	+0.2 +0.1 +0.4
Fully closed loop	Air liquefaction and separation	Chemical	10 tons	0.0	0.0	−0.2

[a] From Crossman and Laner (1969).

and somewhat at the unskilled levels, with little contribution by increases in skill at higher levels.

5. New processes generally require a slightly better educated work force, but once again the general nature of the process has more effect than the technological change.

The Crossman–Laner study, with its careful attempt to differentiate process types and to assess job categories and skill ratings, clarifies some of the apparently contradictory findings of earlier studies. For example, Helfgott[11] found significant upgrading in the composite skill level in the introduction of data processing to banking and insurance, and suggested that increased productivity due to computing might have been responsible for the low growth rate of clerical positions in the early 1960s. On the other hand, Bright[12] observed a decline in skill requirements with the introduction of automation to metalworking industries.

Some comments on the structural versus demand theory debate on unemployment are relevant here. Although there has not been an explosive impact on skill levels, many questions remain. Will a continuing shift to service-producing industries increase the importance of the rising skill levels observed in banking and insurance? Will there be a continuing rise in the number of professionals? What are the job prospects for domestics, attendants, waiters, deliverymen, and other relatively unskilled service workers? Will the unskilled components of office work tend to disappear? What if automatic control proves so dependable that there will be more risk than insurance in human monitoring?

The change to automation in certain processes, while not significantly affecting the immediate labor requirement, has made the process more *labor static*. That is, once the marginal operating requirements are met, an increasing demand for the resulting product does not require a proportional increase in the labor component. It follows that demand directed at labor static industries will not alleviate unemployment. Even more disturbing, it is possible that with advancing technology, processes which are labor elastic become labor static, and thus perhaps require zero or near-zero labor increases once they are launched. If it is mainly the higher skilled social and personal service industries which are more elastic, then cutbacks in the less skilled segments of the economy will present serious structural problems which will be very difficult to overcome by conventional job retraining.

[11] R. B. Helfgott, EDP and the office work force, *Ind. Labor Relations Rev.* **19**, 509 (1966).

[12] J. R. Bright, The impact of automation in the work force *in* "Automation and Management," Chapter 12, pp. 170–188. Graduate School of Business Administration, Harvard Univ., Cambridge, Massachusetts, 1958.

9.4. Automation and Attitudes

What differences in worker attitudes are brought about by introducing automation, and in particular, computers? To answer this we must ask to what extent is one's work interesting? How do we measure alienation? Attempting to assess attitudes is even harder than analyzing skill levels; in particular, the problems of performing statistically controlled experiments arise again.

Yet the importance of this question has been recognized from the beginning of industrialization. Karl Marx was one of the first to proclaim productive and satisfying labor as a necessity of life. It is not surprising that every study of technological impact returns to questions of attitudes and job satisfaction. Management reports on introducing computers into companies repeatedly emphasize the need to prepare employes long in advance of the computer's arrival. There is a deep-rooted fear of being displaced by computers, and this fear necessarily influences attitudes. A number of recent books have been entirely devoted to the question of the impact of automation on the nature of work and the resulting attitudes.

In the study by Shepard (1971) (which is strongly influenced by the research of Blauner and Faunce[13]), alienation among factory workers is compared with similar attitudes of office workers; in particular, the attitude of factory workers in an auto plant and in an oil refinery are compared with those of clerical workers, operators, and programmers within EDP installations in insurance companies and banks. Shepard makes a clear distinction between craft production systems (where the worker is basically an "artisan" using a tool), mechanized production systems (where the worker operates a machine which performs a specific function, i.e., the assembly-line worker), and automated production systems (where a large process is being automatically controlled, and the worker performs monitoring or design functions). Given these definitions, the conclusion can be anticipated: Automation reverses the historical trend (observed during mechanization) toward increasing alienation for both office and factory workers.

Among the aspects of work alienation identified by Shepard are *powerlessness* (the lack of control over the process, the work content, and schedule), *meaninglessness* (the inability to identify the purpose of one's work with respect to the process and the society), and *normlessness*

[13] R. Blauner, "Alienation and Freedom." Univ. of Chicago Press, Chicago, Illinois, 1964; W. A. Faunce, Automation and the division of labor, *Social Probl.* **13**, 149–160 (1965).

(the lack of confidence in proper recognition and fair rewards). The given definition of automation implies a greater emphasis on the entire process, more centralization, and better integration within the system. This in turn usually results in a less specialized division of labor, job enlargement, and a great degree of interdependence between jobs. It is not surprising then that those in automated production and craft production jobs score better (i.e., lower) with respect to the meaninglessness scale than those in mechanized jobs.[14] Meaninglessness is the aspect of alienation most clearly related to functional specialization. It is also reasonable that craft workers suffer least from powerlessness while mechanized workers suffer most. Of course, these broad job categories do not tell the complete story. Computer operators contrasted with programmers feel significantly more impotent because they are tied to the machine. In fact, except for programmers and systems analysts, the work pace in automated production appears to be as uniform as in mechanized production.

Finally, with regard to normlessness, automated workers scored best in this respect, and again the mechanized worker is least confident of fair recognition. A number of studies have found that most workers in automation-related jobs perceive greater responsibilities, more deadlines, and a greater need for accuracy in their work. To the same extent then, the worker will feel that his performance is more easily judged, and given a fair employer, that good performance will be recognized. On the other hand, several studies have found that clerical workers associated with automation often feel that promotion chances have been decreased. They feel that the middle steps in the promotional ladder (jobs involving coordination of specific functions, and some supervisory positions) are disappearing. Moreover, promotion into higher level jobs for computing is based on training and aptitude, and not experience in lower levels. So while workers may tend to believe that the system is fair, they may simultaneously be resigned to limited upward mobility, and hence experience a higher level of normlessness.

The work of Elizur (1970) on attitudes is particularly interesting because of its in-depth survey. A series of detailed questionnaires was given to 450 employees of two organizations in the Netherlands. One organization was responsible for payroll administration in the government, the other was a bank in the public sector. Both organizations have com-

[14] Wilensky also finds evidence that job enlargement (and job rotation) can reduce discontent and lead to improved job performance. See H. L. Wilensky, Work, careers, and leisure styles, *summary in* "Harvard University Program on Technology and Society, Final Review," pp. 140–144. Harvard Information Office, Cambridge, Massachusetts, 1972.

puterized and noncomputerized departments, so that a comparative study of the attitudes of employees directly involved with computers, and those who were not involved (but might be later) could be carried out. Even though the work force differs in important ways from comparable workers in North America (men form the majority of clerical workers, and there is a high rate of stability for such positions in the Netherlands), the observations are quite similar to North American studies. Some of the observations were as follows.

Initially:

1. There was appreciable resistance to the introduction of the computer from supervisors and middle management as well as from rank and file.
2. Many expressed anxiety about the future of their work, about the possibility of dismissal or transfer, about their difficulties, and about their concern that the work would be less interesting.

After the computers were introduced:

3. The majority liked the presence of the computer, more so in the computerized departments than in the noncomputerized departments.
4. Substantial changes were reported in the computerized departments; most felt that their work demanded more knowledge, accuracy, regulations, and an increased work load.
5. Most felt that the work was more varied, interesting, responsible, and productive.
6. The majority were satisfied with job security, social relations with their colleagues, the work, and the organization. Attitudes were more pessimistic, however, in the noncomputerized departments.
7. Many disliked how the change was introduced; in retrospect, it appears that little information or training about the new systems was given, even to those in the computerized departments.
8. The majority were concerned about opportunities for promotion and felt that upward mobility had been decreased. There were divided opinions on opportunities to show ability and exert influence.

An attempt was made to develop a theory of attitudes and behavior, distinguishing between different facets of behavior, referents to whom the behavior is ascribed, and the object toward which the behavior is directed. For example, the behavioral facet is defined by three elements: emotion (characterized by likes, dislikes, satisfaction, etc.), cognition (characterized by evaluations of good, bad, useful, necessary, etc.), and action (characterized by overt action for or against the object). All combinations (cross-products) of the facet elements are studied to produce a more complete behavioral description. The study illustrates how difficult it is to report attitudes and attempts to display them as quantitative measures, but it also shows that there are gains to be made in attempting a structured approach to such problems, an approach where there is an attempt to examine (and statistically validate) causes and display relations in an explicit manner.

Although the conclusions about computers, automation, and attitudes expressed by Elizur are plausible and generally supported by other studies, it must be emphasized that quite different results can occur in particular situations. The organizational structure, the quality of supervision and management, and the manner in which changes are introduced exert a strong influence on attitudes. The conclusions about the variety and interest of work are not as generally accepted as those concerning increased responsibility, accuracy, and amount of work. As an extreme example, Gruenfeld and Folman[15] report on the rejection of an EDP system by employees to the extent that unreliable information was supplied by supervisors, eventually resulting in the system being withdrawn.

A number of disturbing questions persist. While automation may introduce factors which reverse the trend of alienation invoked by mechanization, as the novelty and prestige wear off, will attitudes approach those associated with mechanization? To what extent can we say that work is and will remain a significant part of our lives? In the past, work and everyday living were much more closely related; Japan is often cited as a country where this continues to be true through strong company–employee attachments. The large companies are very paternalistic and they exercise considerable influence on the employees' social, educational, and personal affairs. But this closeness is counter to the trend in Western societies. Wilensky[16] identifies three major approaches in attempting to deal with the boredom and alienation associated with mechanized work: (1) develop compensating leisure activities, (2) provide increased benefits, (3) redesign technology and work environments to offer job enlargement and variability. The first of these approaches is discussed in Chapter 13, and the second in the next section. While there is promise in the third approach, it is unfortunately one which encounters considerable resistance. To many employers, the economic benefits do not seem commensurate with the difficulties and costs, and the alternative of greater specialization appears more attractive. Nevertheless the report "Work in America" (Secretary of Health, Education, and Welfare, 1973) insists

[15] L. W. Gruenfeld, and F. F. Folman, Relationship among supervisors' integration, satisfaction, and acceptance of a technological change, *J. Appl. Psychol.* **51** (1), 74–77 (1967).

[16] See "Work, Careers, and Leisure Styles" (footnote 14).

that both clerical and production-line jobs must be redesigned to meet the rising expectations of today's younger, more mobile, and better educated work force.

9.5. Some Specific Considerations

Statistical and aggregate studies do not convey the full impact of automation on employment; technological displacement is a continuing and often harsh occurrence. Unions attempt to protect their members from the negative effects of technological innovation and often come into conflict with management over such issues. Many engineers and other professionals who are not unionized face a different type of displacement—the job remains, but the older engineer may become less capable of performing it satisfactorily. Whereas highly industrialized and affluent nations may be able to compensate for technological displacement, unemployment and displacement in a developing nation are a much more critical issue.

Displacement and Compensating Policies

Industrial and construction workers have suffered the threats of periodic layoffs since the beginning of industrialization. In their efforts to attain good working conditions, unions have always tried to promote job security. No union can guarantee complete security, for if the demand for a product decreases sufficiently, a company may be forced to cut its staff or go bankrupt. But unions can be expected to fight for jobs and/or compensation when technological innovation is viewed primarily (by the workers) as a means to achieve greater profits by lowering labor costs. Today, industrial and office innovation usually mean automation and computing. While lower cost is not the only reason for such innovation, it is a primary one (see Section 3.2).

Mansfield[17] and Weber[18] assess the effects of technological displacement on union, industry, and government policies in the United States. Union–management actions and responses take place against a background of the general economy, the labor supply, and labor laws. Specific policies are determined by three factors: the nature of the innovation, the nature of the industry or firm, and the nature of the union.

If a new technique does not reduce employment throughout the com-

[17] E. Mansfield, Automation, Labor Displacement, and Adjustment Problems, *in* "The Economics of Technological Change," Chapter 5. Norton, New York, 1968.

[18] A. Weber, Collective bargaining and the challenge of technological change, *in* "Industrial Relations: Challenges and Responses" (J. Crispo, ed.). Univ. of Toronto Press, Toronto, Canada, 1966; also in Walker (1968).

pany so that affected workers can be transferred to new positions within the same plant and the same union, then there will usually be few difficulties. If the technology causes location transfers, requires substantially new skills and working conditions, or brings about changes in union representation, there will be some resistance, but not nearly as strong as when employment is endangered. When competition and other market factors genuinely necessitate new efficiencies, then the options available to both management and labor are restricted. A company's normal attrition rate and its ability to withstand a strike will also influence policy. And obviously the strength of a union (its support from members, financial assets, percentage of representation in the industry) and its traditional approaches to change will influence any actions taken. Depending on such factors, unions will embark on various policies, ranging from willing acceptance to total opposition to technological change.

Recognizing some significant exceptions, Mansfield and Weber agree that most innovations are accepted by the unions. The usual response is to try and ensure that the union has a say, if not the controlling voice, in how the innovations are introduced and who will be affected. It may be that at the same time, management has shown proper consideration for problems of transition and unions have recognized the need for change, or it may be just a sense of ultimate futility, but in any case few unions have tried to resist technological innovation overtly. One of the strongest reactions to change that a union can take is the introduction of "make work" rules into contracts. Such practices have occurred in the case of longshoremen, railroad workers, and newspaper guilds. Inevitably these practices are usually abandoned in return for momentary compensation.

There are two general directions along which responses to innovation can proceed: redistribution and retraining of manpower, and various forms of monetary compensation for displacement. When there is a sizable attrition rate, workers affected by a change can often be retrained on the job for positions that become available. Recall that for many industries, the average skill level required is not increased with the introduction of automation. Some companies (e.g., Armour and Kaiser Steel) have formalized interplant transfer and retraining programs so that the widest range of employment opportunities is made available. When displacement seems inevitable, unions and management can cooperate in providing individualized counseling, job referral, and training. It is well accepted that such programs are dependent on adequate notice. In computing applications, there is often a substantial transition period which provides more than sufficient time to formulate constructive policies. Shultz and Weber[19] argue that work performance does not suffer appreciably when employees are given advance notice of displacement. Another approach to distributing employment opportunities is to encourage early retirement or extended vacations.

Monetary compensation can be obtained in two basic ways. First, the industry may provide severance pay to the individual workers involved and/or compensation to a union pension fund. These payments can be made in a lump sum or over a period of years. The effect is to soften the effects of displacement by providing some wage security. The 1961 agreement between the West Coast Longshoremen and the Pacific Maritime Association is a prime example of this approach, with the union receiving a 29 million dollar compensation to finance early retirement and annual wage guarantees. If the union can force a high enough compensation, then this may act as a partial deterrent to rapid innovation. The other form of compensation is profit-sharing. Here innovation is made attractive, or at least palatable, by the economic benefits it can bring. Note the basic distinction in the two forms of compensation: in the former, benefits are aimed at those displaced, threatened with layoffs, or forced into early retirement; in the latter, it is the remaining full-time workers who are the principal beneficiaries. John L. Lewis championed this type of compensation, preferring an industry in which a few coal miners received high wages, over one in which many were paid marginally.

Profit-sharing as compensation is acceptable when total employment is high. But full-time employment in the bituminous coal industry shrank from 450,000 in 1946 to 110,000 in 1965. It is not surprising that wildcat strikes have occurred throughout this period, reflecting a demand for more security. Some see profit-sharing as inevitably setting protected older workers against younger workers. Displacement causes disproportionate hardship for older workers. For this reason, unions often insist on seniority protections. But once displaced, the older worker will be at a disadvantage for a number of reasons: relatively high salaries, obsolete skills, the cost of pension programs, lack of mobility, and so forth.

When a plant is totally shut down, or when an industry or region suffers a serious depression, the effects of displacement are beyond the powers of the private sector. There is now a consensus that local and federal governments have responsibilities in these situations. First and foremost, the federal government is expected to provide the "climate" for a sound economy. In economically depressed areas particularly, it is expected to help failing industries or encourage the establishment of

[19] G. Shultz and A. Weber, "Strategies for the Displaced Worker." Harper, New York, 1966.

new ones. Also, we now increasingly look to governments for a general planning of manpower needs and resources. In cooperation with educational authorities they are expected to develop broad-based education and training programs to achieve a flexible work force, leaving specific vocational skills to be produced by on-the-job training.

One final question must be raised: Are automation and concurrent shifts in the labor force endangering the strength and bargaining power of unions? Postindustrialization implies a shift to services and white collar employment, sectors of labor which are often traditionally opposed to unionization. The proportion of unionized non-agricultural labor has been decreasing in the United States since 1950 (from about 34% to 28%), whereas in Canada it has fluctuated around 32%.[20] The decrease in the United States is directly attributable to the fact that white collar unionization (including professional, technical, clerical, and sales workers) has stayed near 11%, while white collar labor has increased from 38% in 1950 to 48% in 1971.[21] But the trend is not uniform. Services such as transportation and education are effectively unionized, and government employee unions have become widespread. Strikes in the public sector have recently caused many to question whether unions might have too much power. Though only a relatively small percentage of white collar workers in the private sector are unionized in the United States, the threat of unionization may be partially responsible for the careful introduction of automation and computing into the office.

Another aspect of the question of unions and their future role is whether automation will effectively eliminate the strike potential and thereby weaken labor's power in collective bargaining. Raskin[22] and Weber[23] emphasize this possibility and claim that some industries (e.g., Bell Telephone, electric and gas utilities, oil refining) have become virtually strikeproof. It is easy to overestimate the extent of fully automated industries and underestimate the importance of indirect labor. Most industries such as steel, construction, transportation, as well as education, recreation, and other services are still strongly dependent on direct labor. And many relatively automated industries, while able to withstand a strike of short duration, may not be able to continue operating profitably or safely for an extended period when strikebound. Thus while automa-

[20] E. Kassalow, Canadian and U. S. white collar union increases, *Mon. Labour Rev.* **91**, 41–45 (1968).

[21] See Manpower Rep. (U. S. Dept. of Labor, 1971); and also A. Blum, The office employee, *in* "White Collar Workers," (A. Blum, M. Estey, J. W. Kuhn, W. A. Wildman, and L. Trooy, eds.). Random House, New York, 1971.

[22] A. H. Raskin, Making strikes obsolete, *Amer. Mon.*, pp. 47–52, June (1966).

[23] See Weber (footnote 18).

tion may weaken the effectiveness of strikes, it is certainly premature to sense an end to them.

Information processing has had an operational effect on the collective bargaining process. Specifically, computers have been used to evaluate the costs of proposed demands, particularly those for pension programs and health and welfare funds, and to analyze a company's economic outlook. They have also been used to administer complex wage and scheduling agreements and to coordinate the processing of grievances. Some principals in the bargaining process[24] have expressed a cautious optimism for the potential of computer-based information systems to help diminish industrial conflict. Two reasons are offered: The bargaining parties are apt to be more knowledgeable about each other's needs and capabilities, and personal administration will be improved in such matters as vacation scheduling, crew scheduling, and the handling of transfers.

Technological change has definitely altered the meaning of collective bargaining. The issues now extend far beyond wages and salaries to job security and working conditions. Satisfactory resolution cannot be expected in last minute, intensive negotiations.

Obsolescence

Just as a low unemployment rate does not preclude displacement because of technology, the constancy of average skill levels does not preclude people becoming *obsolete*. Through what Armer[25] calls the "Paul Principle" (in allusion to the "Peter Principle"), "individuals often become, over time, uneducated and therefore incompetent at a level at which they once performed quite adequately." Older workers are particularly vulnerable when there is a need for new skills, and this facet of technological displacement receives special attention.[26] The people Armer has in mind are those in the "knowledge profession," especially scientists, engineers, and management in technologically oriented industries. In 1970, there were already 1.6 million scientists and engineers in the United States and this class continues to grow.

There is some evidence that the Paul Principle is having its effect. Dalton and Thompson[27] have studied the performance of 2500 engineers

[24] See A. J. Siegel (ed.), "The Impact of Computers on Collective Bargaining." MIT Press, Cambridge, Massachusetts, 1969.

[25] P. Armer, The individual: His privacy, self-image and obsolescence, *Proc. Meeting Panel Sci. Technol., 11th* "Science and Astronautics," p. 129. U. S. House of Representatives, U. S. Govt. Printing Office, Washington, 1970.

[26] For example, the monograph series "Employment of Older Workers," Org. for Economic Cooperation and Develop., Paris, 1964–1968; and the journal *Industrial Geratology.*

in six organizations (performance as perceived by both management and the engineers). Because of management practices and constant changes in the "state of the art," the years of high performance are starting and ending sooner for many engineers. And the same holds true for the computing professions. Industry views those under 40, and especially those in their early thirties, as being the most valuable. This viewpoint is reflected in performance ratings, challenging work assignments, and salary increases. The engineers themselves agree, although they tend to think one's peak occurs in the late thirties.

It is hard to judge how much of this phenomenon is induced by management practices, as differentiated from the continual increase in knowledge. Engineering firms have long been known to give the best raises to the younger employees who are most apt to change jobs. Locked-in pension plans coupled with the usual decrease in mobility leave the older worker more dependent on the firm, which then responds with decreasing salary incentives. Once job adaptation is discouraged, even small changes in skill requirements can produce obsolescence. The problem becomes critical in the rapidly changing fields of computing, electronics, and aerospace where up-to-date information can be more important than experience.

How can the talents of older and more experienced workers be fully utilized? Many of the psychological aspects of the problem might be alleviated by improved management practices. In Canada and the United States, the universities have transferable pension programs and, although they are more costly, such programs could be instituted in all industries. Salary practices must be restructured in order not to discriminate automatically against older workers. And new projects must be distributed as much as possible among all age groups.

With respect to the knowledge and skills required for a job, continuing education in a variety of forms is a necessity. In the occupations most affected by rapidly changing technologies, part-time reeducation is not enough. Many engineers are dismayed by the prospect of spending one or two nights at classes every week for the rest of their careers. Companies will have to contribute time if they are seriously committed to maintaining performance and enthusiasm. There is a growing feeling that periodic retraining sabbaticals ranging from six months to two years may sometimes be necessary. Presently, only a few select companies can afford to look beyond immediate competitive demands and institute more concentrated educational programs. As Armer sees it, the solutions are

---

[27] G. Dalton and P. Thompson, Accelerating obsolence of older engineers, *Harvard Business Rev.*, November (1970).

so costly that substantial support from the federal government is a prerequisite. Estimating a one-year educational stipend of $8000 for 5% of the United States work force, Armer derives a $30 billion per year cost figure. Moreover, Armer cautions that such a program might even be self-defeating in that it would further accelerate a knowledge explosion.

At this time, most segments of the work force are not in occupational need of educational sabbaticals, and Armer's estimate of 5% of the total labor force (approximately 3.5 million people per year) in occupational need of educational sabbaticals appears as an exaggeration to emphasize a point. But on the other hand, the provision of such programs is consistent with the need to distribute employment opportunities evenly and maintain a flexible work force. For the immediate future, however, programs which enable an employee to spend one work day per week in either university or company courses can be effective and perhaps acceptable to industry.

Computers and Employment in Developing Countries

The experience of industrialized countries with regard to automation and employment cannot be applied without modification to developing countries because of differences in educational opportunities, mobility, job security, and other socioeconomic factors.[28] In the developing countries, much of the labor force is engaged in agriculture and basic process industries. A rapid, large-scale introduction of automation almost always leads to a massive displacement of the labor force. The economic, social, and personal costs of unemployment and retraining in developing countries are critical factors in any decision to introduce computers. Each country must formulate general policies for dealing with technological innovation. In some cases, economic and trade considerations may require the adoption of new processing techniques available only with computers; in others, the introduction of computers may have to be deferred because of employment considerations.

The complexities of the situation can be illustrated by some of the problems confronting India. In the State of Bengal computers have been forbidden entry because of the loss of jobs accompanying their use. But India, with one of the lowest per capita use of computers in the world (see Table 2-2) recognizes the need to apply them in sectors of the economy where their use is justified. These are not easy to determine.

[28] This viewpoint is taken from United Nations, "The Application of Comput. Technol. for Develop." Dept. of Economic and Social Affairs, E/4800, New York, 1971.

For example, airline reservation systems, a common application in other countries, does not warrant a high priority. The advantages of an automated system, in assuring that all seats are sold, can be achieved instead by applying a penalty cost for canceling a reservation without adequate notice. This alternative is adopted for internal flights, but for international flights Air India must be competitive and be able to offer automatic reservations. Clearly the policies regarding computer use require very careful adaptation to the prevailing conditions.

SUMMARY

In industrialized countries, the present evidence indicates that computing has not had the unsettling effect on employment forecast by many. The conclusion of the previous sections is that the effects have been similar to those accompanying other technological innovations. The nature of the work force does change, and productivity continues to increase, but at a gradual rate. Thus far, increased consumer demands have kept pace with productivity increases, and employment in the aggregate sense has stayed relatively stable. When indirect labor is considered, the skill levels required within various industries have both increased and decreased. And while alienation is still present, the introduction of automation and computing may have improved work attitudes when compared to the effects of earlier mechanization. But it is not possible to be complacent about the effects of computers and automation on employment. Even if changes continue to be gradual, we must expect that the accumulated effects will come to have a profound impact on the nature and meaning of work.

Bibliography

Carter, A. P. (1970). "Structural Change in the American Economy." Harvard Univ. Press, Cambridge, Massachusetts, 1970.

Crossman, E. R. F. W., and Laner, S. (1969). "The Impact of Technological Change on Manpower and Skill Demand: Case-Study and Policy Implications." Dept. of Ind. Eng. and Operations Res., Univ. of California, Berkeley, California.

Elizur, D. (1970). "Adapting to Innovation." Jerusalem Acad. Press, Jerusalem, 1970.

Jaffe, A. G., and Froomkin, G. (1968). "Technology and Jobs: Automation in Perspective." Praeger, New York, 1968.

Mansfield, E. (1968). "The Economics of Technological Change." Norton, New York.

Nat. Comm. on Technol., Automation, and Econ. Progr. Rep. (1966). "Technology and the American Economy," vol. 1. U. S. Govt. Printing Office, Washington, D. C.

Secretary of Health, Education, and Welfare (1973). "Work in America," Report of a Special Task Force, MIT Press, Cambridge, Massachusetts.
Shepard, J. M. (1971). "Automation and Alienation; A Study of Office and Factory Workers." MIT Press, Cambridge, Massachusetts.
Siegel, A. J. (1969). "The Impact of Computers on Collective Bargaining." MIT Press, Cambridge, Massachusetts.
Silberman, C. (1966). "The Myths of Automation." Harper, New York.
Simon, H. A. (1965). "The Shape of Automation." Harper, New York.
U. S. Dept. of Labor (1971, 1972). Manpower Report of the President (April, 1971; March, 1972).
Wiener, N. (1950). "The Human Use of Human Beings." Houghton, Boston, Massachusetts.

Problems and Further Work

1. In "The Myths of Automation," Silberman (1966) called attention to the comeback of the blue collar worker. There was good statistical evidence that the need for blue collar workers had stabilized after a decade of decrease. Silberman conjectured that early automation had eliminated the most routine jobs, but now the more skilled jobs would still require human manipulative skills. What explanation might there be for recent (since 1969) decrease in the percentage of blue collar workers? What evidence might be gathered to support your explanation?

2. Design a questionnaire for studying worker attitudes to a work environment where automation has been recently introduced.

3. What types of employment are now considered labor elastic? Which of these will tend to become more labor static in the near future?

4. Try to establish a methodology for assessing the skill level associated with a job. Apply your concepts to a specific setting, for example, a branch of a large bank, before and after automation. Consider the following jobs: teller, accountant, auditor, manager.

5. Are the communications and computer industries secondary, tertiary, or a mixture? (Justify your answer.) There have been suggestions that the postindustrial society is characterized by the emergence of "quaternary" industries. What might these be?

6. Look up reports of recent strikes and ascertain whether automation has been a contentious issue in them. Where it has, how do labor and management seek to retain control of the ways new technology is brought in? Are any patterns emerging in the settlements?

Chapter

10

THE DISTRIBUTION OF COMPUTER PRODUCTS AND SERVICES

The computing industry, as we saw in Chapter 2, is increasingly complex, and there are many aspects to the production and distribution of computer hardware and software. Governments, recognizing the potential of the technology and the influence it has on other industries, have sought policies which would ensure the effective use of computers at the national level, and have often sought to encourage production and marketing capabilities. Although these policies and measures are primarily economic, the importance of the computer industry is such (see Chapter 11) that interest transcends economic considerations. In this chapter we focus attention on four aspects of the distribution of computer products and services: antitrust regulation, the relation between computers and communication systems, the protection of software, and the adoption of standards. All are complicated by technical, legal, and historical backgrounds, and it is only possible to outline the main points here. As in the case of privacy, legal considerations mean that actual solutions to any problem must be framed nationally. But in all four topics the issues which arise are very much alike in different countries, and guidelines and policies which eventually emerge in one country are often adopted in another.

10.1. Antitrust Actions

Many Western countries have followed the lead of the United States in enacting antitrust legislation to prohibit large companies from engaging in activities which unfairly prevent competition, on the basis that the public interest is best served when there is free competition for markets. In the computer industry, as we saw in Chapter 2, the dominant position of IBM creates a near-monopoly situation, and some of the consequences of this dominance were noted there. In spite of the fact that giant companies such as General Electric and Radio Corporation of America have been unable to sustain themselves in the market for general-purpose computers, there is evidence that there has been effective competition in some sectors of the industry and resultant benefits to customers. At the extreme ends of the equipment range, the Control Data Corporation has consistently designed and sold the very largest scientific computers (as well as a full line of intermediate machines) and the Digital Equipment Corporation has established and maintained the major share of the market for minicomputers. Companies making special equipment such as disks, core memories, and input–output devices, as well as those offering specialized time-sharing, software, and computer leasing services, continue to compete successfully with IBM.

Nevertheless the history of the computer industry in the United States is one of almost continuous antitrust action involving IBM, actions which have been prosecuted mainly by the United States government, but more recently by IBM's competitors as well. It is significant that many of the opportunities for entry into the market for computer products were created only as a result of earlier antitrust suits. In 1932 (before the era of computers) IBM was enjoined from requiring that only its own punched cards be used with tabulating machines. In 1956 IBM consented to a decree which required it to operate its computing (as distinct from its manufacturing) facilities as a separate subsidiary, and which further required it to offer its equipment for sale as well as for rent. The first provision has led to the growth of independent computing bureaus (including those for time-sharing services) and the second to computer-leasing firms which specialize in purchasing IBM equipment and renting them to customers at rates lower than those offered by IBM.[1] Both of these are substantial industries in their own right.

[1] These leasing companies operate under the IBM umbrella mentioned in Section 2.5. The rental rates quoted by IBM are such that effectively the equipment is

Successful outcomes of the suits currently being prosecuted against IBM by some of IBM's competitors (Control Data, Greyhound Leasing, Applied Data Research, etc.) and, more importantly, by the United States Justice Department, could result in IBM's having to divest itself of certain divisions of its operation, and even in an overall reorganization of the company. This would certainly have major effects on the computer industry. Critics (and competitors) of IBM argue that such action is necessary if the technology is to advance in the best way. They maintain that competition exists on IBM's sufferance, and that IBM's vested interests make it impossible to bring about changes in design, computer languages, and operating systems which would result in greatly improved and much less expensive systems.[2] But the issues are exceedingly complex. It is not certain that the emergence of a number of companies, each having a larger share of the computer market, would automatically lead to better systems and standards or lower prices. One likely result, disadvantageous to the United States but beneficial to other countries, would be that companies outside the United States would gain a more secure position.

The effects on social issues involving computers are even less clear. IBM's size and ubiquity have undoubtedly contributed an element to the resentments sometimes expressed against computers—certainly IBM is the butt of many computer jokes. But it is difficult to know how much weight should be attached to such attitudes, and in any case, even if IBM's share of the market were to be diminished significantly, it would take a very long time for the public to cease identifying computers with IBM. IBM's technical and marketing positions on such matters as the adoption of hardware and language standards, data security, software protection, warranties, educational discounts, and nonstandard systems are almost decisive in that competitors have to accommodate themselves to IBM. There is certainly legal debate whether decisions on these matters in effect constitute monopolistic practice and restraint of trade. The important secondary effects of the decisions on employment, privacy (as distinct from data security), centralization of government operations,

---

amortized in a period of five to six years. The profits of the leasing companies depend on their ability to use the equipment longer, moving it from one customer to another, as necessary.

[2] See, for example, statements by: H. R. Grosch, *Computerworld*, p. 52, May 19 (1971); W. Bauer, *Computerworld*, p. 33, Oct. 28 (1970); J. Guzy, *Datamation*, p. 80, Feb. (1972); Editorial, *Computerworld*, Oct. 13 (1971). Not everyone agrees that IBM should be broken up. See, for example, the statement of I. Auerbach reported in *Canad. Information Processing Mag.*, p. 5, July (1972). See also *Computerworld*, Oct. 15 (1972).

or on other large questions in the public interest have hardly been examined at all.

Clearly more study is required, most importantly in trying to clarify the public interest with respect to computers. This need for study is advanced by Gilchrist and Wessel (1972) in "Government Regulation of the Computer Industry," who suggest that government should attempt to delineate the public interest, that there should be more discussions of such matters in the conferences of professional societies, and more attention to them in the research and reports undertaken by universities and foundations.[3] So great are the sensitivities which surround these questions that advocating this view of needs has been criticized, presumably on the grounds that officials of the professional computer societies should not be involved in legal, nontechnical issues, nor should they be giving weight to arguments in favor of government intervention.[4] Such criticism opens up questions of ethics and responsibility which we discuss further in Chapter 12.

10.2. Communications

Certain industries, where the advantages of scale are particularly important, are regarded as natural monopolies, and they are not subjected to the restrictions placed on monopolies. Instead they are usually subject to regulations which require them to offer service to everyone willing to pay for it, which limit the rates for services (and the profits), and which prevent the company from using its monopoly as a competitive advantage in other situations. The communications industry is a natural monopoly; there are obvious advantages in size, and the consumer benefits if the range of services is extended to as large a population as possible. In many countries communications are operated by the state; in others, a few companies, the common carriers, are given monopolies or near-monopolies, often so as to allow each to provide specialized services: telephone, telegraph, radio broadcasting, television transmission, and so on. The issues which interest us arise out of the interactions between the highly regulated communications industry and the, by comparison, unregulated computer industry. Many if not most of the conflicts arise because of the potential for profit which is created when permission to provide certain types of services is granted or denied to a company.

[3] See Gilchrist and Wessel (1972) where there is a more complete survey of antitrust regulation (Chapter 7) along with references to and excerpts from some of the principal documents.

[4] See *Datamation*, p. 8, June (1972).

Some examples are discussed briefly here, and further details are available in Mathison and Walker (1970).

When some common carriers formed subsidiaries to carry on service bureaus and time-sharing operations, existing service bureaus objected that this practice goes beyond the carriers' needs; because it enables them to offer better communications to their own service bureau subsidiaries, it is discriminatory. But the carriers in some sense have always engaged in data processing, since the data transmission which they normally perform involves signal translation and data compression. The rulings which have emerged from the U. S. Federal Communications Commission have had the effect that carriers are allowed to form service bureaus with appropriate safeguards to ensure that they keep those companies separate (so that they will not be subsidized by communications) and that they offer, generally, the same capabilities they provide for their subsidiaries.[5]

The carriers have also been criticized by companies wishing to provide services which the carriers have claimed as their prerogative. Computer manufacturers and other companies have contested the carriers' sole right to supply certain devices and marketing arrangements. As an example, computers interface with communication channels through modems (modulator–demodulators) which convert the computer signals into a form acceptable by the line. The carriers for a time insisted that only they supply these, by virtue of their authority to prohibit foreign attachments which might degrade the quality of their lines. Their opponents argued (successfully) that it was only necessary to insist that the modems meet defined specifications. As an even more important example of other companies wishing to compete with the carriers, communications costs and rate structures are such that very large economies are to be had by sharing lines. This can be done by time-sharing, in which different customers use the line at different times, or capacity sharing, in which high-capacity lines (with data transfer rates of 50,000 bits/sec and more) are subdivided into many low-speed lines, of the 1200-bits/sec type used in voice grade channels. The carriers have resisted the attempts of computer utilities to market equipment which concentrates the low-speed lines of terminals for line-sharing purposes. Still other companies which offer subscription time-sharing services (for credit reporting, stockmarket quotations, and legal research) have found that these impinge on the telephone, teletype, and telegraph message serv-

[5] We may also note that the Association of Data Processing Service Organizations (ADAPSO) challenged the right of banks to offer computer services other than banking (inventory maintenance, payroll). See Freed (1969, section I-AE), and Gilchrist and Wessel (1972, Chapter 6).

ices operated by the carriers, especially when the services are carried by the public lines of the toll system as well as by private lines dedicated to them. The division of the market is still at issue.

Aside from the many specific arguments about rates, the general criticism has been raised that the whole communications system is not appropriate for *data* communications. Computers place different requirements on communications than do voice and message switching. Because they operate in bursts, they need high-capacity channels for short times, and it is suggested that it would be fairer if they were charged for the volume of data transmitted rather than for the time required to hold a line, as is the case now. Other demands have been for lower error rates and more rapid connect and disconnect times. Another aspect of present-day communications facilities which has been questioned is whether they offer sufficient protection for privacy, but as we have seen in Chapter 5, it is almost certain that technical safeguards for this can be incorporated into the computer systems. In reply to these arguments, the carriers point out that the traffic volume for data is only about 1% of that for voice, that the accumulated investment in communications facilities is very high, and that installed systems must change slowly.[6]

In fact, however, the communications industry is changing as rapidly as the computer industry. Satellite transmitters operated by multinational agencies are making it necessary to renegotiate jurisdictional rights with regard to transmission and broadcasting, nationally as well as internationally. As exemplified by the ARPA (Advanced Research Project Agency) network,[7] a beginning has been made on the development of computer systems which enable two or more computers, far apart from one another, to cooperate on a single calculation. In the ARPA network no single processor has a commanding role; instead the processing centers

[6] See The President's Task Force on Communications Policy, Final Report, 1969, U. S. Government Printing Office, Washington, D. C., for a discussion of the effects of competitive issues, and so forth, and also "Instant World" (Information Canada, 1971). The literature on this whole subject is voluminous. See L. Kestenbaum, "The Regulatory Context of Information Utilities," in Sackman and Nie (1970), for a concise statement of the complexities, and Mathison and Walker (1970) for a comprehensive bibliography of the United States literature.

[7] Such a system was first proposed by P. Baran (see "On Distributed Communication Networks," Rand Corp. Paper, P-2626, September 1962). In 1966 ARPA began to implement a store-and-forward message-switching system (using existing communication channels) which came into operation during 1971. (See L. G. Roberts, "A Forward Look," NIC Document 7542. Advanced Research Projects Agency, Washington, D. C., June 1971.) The ARPA network interconnects over 25 computers, made by many different manufacturers, located in government laboratories or university installations. Although it is not a public network, it is being expanded in scope and geographical coverage.

are distributed throughout the system. Communication takes place through transmission of "message packets" which are forwarded through intermediate nodes of the network, along the most appropriate route, until they reach their destination. There have also been proposals for "store and hold" systems which would have the capability of holding packets at intermediate nodes, and for communications systems based on transmission of digital signals rather than on modulation of the continuous frequencies, as takes place now. Construction of such networks, particularly the latter, would require major reorganization of the whole communications system.

But the most immediate, and perhaps the most far-reaching interaction between computers and communications is through CATV, cable TV, or community antenna television. High-frequency board-band coaxial cable makes it possible to bring many more communications channels directly into the home than are now available through broadcasting. This opens up the possibility of providing many special services since it is no longer necessary to insist on large audiences for each channel. If one envisages a system which allows data to be *sent* from the home (as well as being received there) and which allows the data to be switched to many receiving centers, we have a system like the existing telephone system, but one capable of dealing with a very much greater variety of information streams. Among the services which have been suggested are the following:

- entertainment
- educational television (conventional broadcast)
- computer assisted instruction
- telephone, picture 'phone, and message recording
- facsimile reproduction of newspapers, magazines, and documents
- information retrieval, reference and library services
- mail delivery
- home shopping, banking, and travel arrangements
- meter reading
- alarm systems (burglar, power failure, fire, emergency)
- voting and participation in surveys, debates, and conferences
- advertising

The term "wired-city" has been used to characterize an urban society in which such services would be prevalent. It is obvious that many of these would depend on computers and on expansion of the information and time-sharing utilities we have discussed earlier.

So far even in those metropolitan areas in the United States and Canada where cable TV has become common there has been no extension of services—not even the provision of new commercial or educational programs beyond those already available through the broadcast network. As an example, the market for special entertainment (current movies which the consumer pays to see) has been slow to materialize. Although for several years governments have been attempting to define policies which will be in the best public interest, to date the cable companies have been governed by the regulations which apply to commercial broadcasting. Experience with radio and TV makes it obvious that special steps will be needed to ensure that commercial values and entertainment services do not prevail above all other considerations, but it is not at all clear precisely what measures should be taken. Should a separation be maintained between companies which provide the cable equipment and those which provide the services? Should there be many cable companies or is this another case of a natural monopoly? What services should the computer companies and information utilities be encouraged to render?

In view of the difficulties of predicting the costs, benefits, and policies which should be pursued with respect to community information utilities there have been suggestions that a Prototype Community Information Utility (PCIU) should be designed and built.[8] This might take the form of a two-way system, serving a community of 80,000 to 100,000 people, based on television receivers fed by cable, and a low-speed input device. Assuming that appropriate monitoring devices were incorporated, invaluable experience would be gained in the technical development of the software, data bases, and switching computers necessary for such a system and in determining the usefulness and acceptability of the different services. Even more important would be the experience gained in managing the system and the results to be obtained from observing how the community was affected socially, economically, and culturally. Problems are to be expected. For example, it could be difficult to assure that there was access to poor users, to those whose knowledge of English was limited, and in general to those who might presently be regarded as "information poor." Problems of confidentiality and privacy would arise. And of course there would be the basic problems of finding funds to design and build the system and of developing a rate structure which

[8] Planning community information utilities (summary of a conference session), *AFIPS Conf. Proc.* **39**, 669–673 (1971).

would be fair to the users, manufacturers, purveyors of services, and the general public. Although no one use would likely be important enough to justify a community information utility, the totality of uses—education, information retrieval, entertainment, shopping, and so forth—may eventually make the system economically feasible. There is a general sense that the potentialities of community information utilities are enormous. If they come to be even partly realized, there may well be a new major technological force for change in society. Some of the possibilities are considered in the next chapter.

10.3. Protection of Software

Another area where law, new technology, and computers intersect is in the protection of software. These issues originated in the 1960s when it became apparent that software is as important to a successful computer operation as hardware, and when expenditures on software, both by manufacturers and customers, began to approach those for hardware. They came to the fore in 1970 with IBM's decision to "unbundle," that is, to charge separately for its hardware and software products. This decision (resulting in part from pressures exerted by the United States government and by customers) for IBM to allow greater competition in certain aspects of the computer market was followed by the adoption of similar policies on the part of other (but not all) computer manufacturers in the United States and elsewhere. Even before the unbundling there were strong arguments from software companies that a diversified, strong software industry would require legal protection for software products through patents, copyrights, or some other format, and since then the arguments have been advanced even more vigorously. Our interest in this topic, as before, concerns the implications it has for the decentralization of computer services.

Patents are exclusive rights granted to inventors which govern the use and manufacture of products or processes. Copyrights are protection granted to authors and composers, and govern the copying or performance of works they have created. Both patents and copyrights are valid for a fixed period. The conditions under which patents are awarded vary from country to country; there are differences in duration and in requirements for originality, registration, and disclosure. The World Intellectual Property Organization[9] (WIPO) provides the secretariat for the admin-

[9] This is the successor to an earlier organization, the United International Bureaus for the Protection of Intellectual Property (BIRPI).

istration of international conventions and multilateral treaties on copyrights and patents.

The arguments for protecting software follow those generally advanced for granting proprietary rights to inventions, namely that:

1. Scientific advances will be stimulated by providing incentives for innovation.
2. Public disclosure will be encouraged since the need for trade secrets to maintain a competitive position will be reduced.
3. Costs will be reduced since licenses will not have to include charges for the risk of unauthorized use.
4. A basis is provided for new entries into the industry.[10]

There are counterarguments:

1. Proprietary rights inhibit the spread of knowledge, and so impose a social cost.
2. They create monopoly positions which are strengthened by cross-licensing and sustained after the right expires.
3. The whole protection system has become so institutionalized that most of the gain accrues to large corporations and not to individuals.
4. Adequate advantage can be had from the lead time gained by prior knowledge; process inventions (as distinct from product inventions) can be kept secret and the legal protections are not needed.

Those who feel that protection is needed have strongly divergent views on the form it should take. Although copyrights are obtained promptly and inexpensively, and programs have already been copyrighted in some countries, this form of protection has deficiencies. The duration is unnecessarily long, and more important, there is usually no protection against use (as distinct from copying) or against translation from one computer language to another. Those who favor patents argue that this is the right way to recognize that a computer with its program is really a piece of equipment for realizing a process, and that this is the only adequate protection against the modifications which can easily be made to a program. Others propose new types of registration systems in which programs would be deposited but not made public (until their five- or ten-year term had expired), along with definitions and remedies for in-

[10] These are essentially the points made in arguing that the patent system promotes the transfer of technology to developing countries [see "The Role of Patents in the Transfer of Technology to Developing Countries," United Nations (1964)]. There are reservations in accepting them, however, on the part of the developing countries, who feel that royalty and licensing fees impose an unfair burden on them.

fringement. Still others have argued that the rules governing trade secrets and the laws of contract presently in effect in most countries are adequate until evidence to the contrary is presented.

With so many conflicting opinions it is not surprising that most countries are adopting a cautious attitude with respect to legal protection of software. In part this is because other new developments such as Xerox copies and videotape recordings are necessitating review of copyright and patent laws.[11] International agreements through WIPO will have to follow the formulation of national policies in key countries.[12] Since unbundling, software as a distinct industry has developed only slowly, but there is no evidence whether the absence of copyright or patent protection has been a factor. Nondisclosure agreements are usual and they seem to be effective.[13] With time-sharing no *new* situations arise because it is sufficient to provide a customer with the ability to use a program rather than the program itself. It may be, however, that as computer networks evolve, problems will arise. It is already difficult to agree on the extent of use for a company which has branches and subsidiaries or for a state university system, and this type of difficulty is likely to be compounded; whether or not new forms of program protection are defined, it will be necessary to define the rules for program exchange and dissemination much more carefully. The practices recommended in Chapter 5 for privacy and confidentiality of data will be of considerable help in making these rules effective.

[11] Among the changes which have been suggested for patent laws are provisional granting of patents with examination delayed (so as to eliminate the search for applications which do not turn out to be important), lump awards, and compulsory licensing.

[12] In 1969 France adopted a patent law which regarded computer programs as industrial inventions capable of being patented. In the United States, the situation is confused. There have been contradictory actions and statements on the part of the U. S. Patent Office; both copyrights and patents have been awarded. In November 1972, the U. S. Supreme Court ruled against one specific patent application but a general ruling on software patents has not yet been established. For reviews see E. W. Galbi, Software and patents: A status report, *Comm. ACM* **14**, 274–280 (1971); also M. A. Duggan, Patents and programs: The ACM's position, *Comm. ACM* **14**, 278–280 (1971); and D. Goldberg, Legal protection of EPP software, *Datamation,* pp. 66–70 (1972). For the position in the United Kingdom, see British Computer Soc. "Software Protection." London, 1970. On the international level, see "Report on Meeting of the Advisory Group of Governmental Experts on the Problem of Computer Programs," AGCP/6, World Intellectual Property Organization, Geneva, March 1971.

[13] In effect software houses employ trade secrets when they distribute their programs in the form of object decks and instructions without explaining how the program works.

10.4. Standards

Here we come once again to the need for reconciling conflicts. Briefly:

• The existence of standards is an advantage to the customer for it enables him to compare alternative products and interchange components when making purchases.

• If standards are adopted too early, progress may be inhibited because of the inability to accept valuable innovations which do not conform to existing practices.

• Companies seeking to enter a market benefit from the existence of standards for they can manufacture a recognized product; those possessing a large share of the market will find it a disadvantage if their customers can change to compatible products made by their competitors. In the electrical and electronic industries there are large companies with vested interests in many countries, including the United States, Germany, Japan, and the United Kingdom. A great deal may be at stake for a company or a country when a particular standard is approved or rejected, and the advocacy can be partisan and fierce.

An example of the debate which so often surrounds standards development can be seen in the stormy history of the CODASYL task group which has been responsible for the specification of the COBOL programming language. Although vested interests of the many participating companies have played some part, the debates have largely hinged on differences of opinions about technical matters. The proponents of COBOL point to the advantages of having a rigorously defined language with narrative English formats; the result is that COBOL compilers exist for the computers of every major manufacturer, and (it is claimed) 80% of all commercial programmers in the United States use COBOL, making interchangeable jobs and systems a reality. Throughout the history (since 1959) of COBOL development there have been several variants of the language ("required" COBOL, "elective" COBOL, "extended" COBOL) which have differed in the way they handle sorting, writing, and processing mass storage files, diagnostic messages, graphical display devices, communication facilities, string data, and so on. Nevertheless COBOL and CODASYL critics have argued that the concentration of commercial programs in COBOL is a mistake because the language was frozen before major features such as block structure and recursion could be incorporated into it, and without being able to take advantage of modern multiprogrammed and time-shared operating systems. Whatever the merits of the arguments, COBOL has achieved a status which makes it necessary to recognize it as an effective standard. Subsequently the CODASYL group turned its attention to data base management and specified a data description language (independent of any programming language), along with a COBOL version of the description language; the reports it issued on these have generated even more controversy than has COBOL.[14]

Because of such controversies it takes decades for standards to be accepted by ISO, the International Standards Organization responsible for standards at the world level. Standards are evolved and tested at the national level and spread through multilateral exchanges. In computing, national standards for a large number of items are slowly evolving. For hardware, these include standards for character sets, formats for data exchange, punched cards, punched paper and magnetic tapes, and so on; for software, flow-diagram symbols and agreements on standardized languages, particularly FORTRAN and COBOL.[15] In addition certain other types of standards such as the MARC record for bibliographic exchange[16] and the IFIP glossary are gaining acceptance, although these are a long way from adoption as formal international standards.

What emerges from this examination of antitrust actions, communications, software protection, and standards is that there are political as well as economic forces toward diversification in the production and marketing of computer products and services, and toward governmental regulation on how these services should be allocated. Lacking so far is a clear expression of the public interest which would give direction to government policy. It is true that in the United States there has been a more or less consistent attempt to enforce antitrust legislation. But in practice this has only meant that large companies (IBM and the common carriers) were required to separate certain subsidiary operations from their main business.

[14] For the specification of COBOL see CODASYL COBOL, *Journal of Development* 110-GP-1b, Minister of Supply and Services, Ottawa, Canada (1970). For the specification of the Data Description Language see "Codasyl Data Base Task Group Report," Assoc. for Comput. Machinery, New York, 1971.

[15] See, for example, the following American National Standards Institute's documents: ANSI X 3.2/855, July 1969 (punched cards); ANSI X 3.2.1/400, April 1970 (proposal for recorded magnetic tapes); ANSI X 3.2.2/116, February 1968 (proposal for perforated tape rolls); ANSI X 3.29, 1966 (FORTRAN, the first programing language standardized in the United States). For a description of the functions and composition of the complex network of standard committees in the United States, see "Federal information processing standards index," *Fed. Informat. Processing Std. Publ.* Series no. 12 (January 1971).

[16] "The MARC II Format; A Communications Format for Bibliographic Data," prepared by H. D. Avram, J. F. Knapp, and L. J. Pather, Informat. Syst. Office, U. S. Library of Congress, Washington, D. C., 1968.

Governments outside the United States have wished to guarantee national competence in using computers and build up capability for producing computer hardware and software (if not for designing complete systems). The goals here are essentially economic, namely to provide employment, help maintain a favorable balance of payments, and to share research programs which would yield two-way flows of skilled personnel and royalty payments. The measures taken are those commonly applied in economics, incentives to set up research and production facilities, purchase of locally designed systems, imposition of duties against imports, and so forth. As an example of attempts to frame national policies which take broader issues into account, in Canada there have been a number of government-sponsored studies on the dissemination of scientific and technical information and on computers and communications. One report recommended the construction of a national communication "spine" which would link the country's communications and computer facilities, to act as a unifying force as the railways have for transportation.[17] Concern was voiced in Canada about the need to keep data bases containing information about Canadian people and resources. The most comprehensive study was undertaken by a Task Force of the Department of Communications. The final report of the Task Force contained policy recommendations designed to maintain a strong element of Canadian control over the computer–communications industry, and proposed setting up a "Focal Point" which would monitor developments and coordinate measures to promote such control.[18]

More study is required but it is not sufficient to call for more data and more reports. The massive, undigested data already accumulated for investigations on computers and communications and for antitrust suits emphasize that something else is needed. There must be some way of giving focus to the inquiry. This certainly includes some way of coordinating questions about computers with those on related economic and technological issues. The secondary, less obvious effects of computers on society must be examined, as well as the obvious economic ones. In doing this one is soon led to ask what are the goals of technology and of society as a whole. In addition there is the question of who should carry out the studies. Government is one answer but independent bodies such as the professional organizations could also help if they were prepared to discuss problems other than those which are purely technical,

[17] See "A Policy for Scientific and Technical Information Dissemination," Rep. no. 6 (1969); A Trans-Canada computer communications network, Rep. no. 13, Sci. Council of Canada, Informat. Canada, Ottawa (1971).

[18] "Branching Out," Rep. of the Canad. Comput./Comm. Task Force (H. J. von Baeyer, ed.), Informat. Canada, Ottawa (May 1972).

a role which so far they have undertaken only in a limited way. It is these difficult questions of ends and means to which we turn in the next chapters.

Bibliography

Fed. Informat. Processing Std. Publ. Ser., U. S. Govt. Printing Office, Washington, D. C.

Freed, R. N. (1968). "Materials and Cases on Computers and Law," 2nd ed. Boston Univ. Bookstore, Boston, Massachusetts.

Gilchrist, B., and Wessel, M. R. (1972). "Government Regulation of the Computer Industry," AFIPS Press, Montvale, New Jersey.

Information Canada (1971). "Instant World." Ottawa.

Mathison, S. L., and Walker, P. M. (1970). "Computers and Telecommunications: Issues in Public Policy." Prentice-Hall, Englewood Cliffs, New Jersey.

President's Task Force on Communications Policy (1969). Final Report. U. S. Govt. Printing Office, Washington, D. C.

Sackman, H., and Nie, N., eds. (1970). "The Information Utility and Social Choice." AFIPS Press, Montvale, New Jersey.

United Nations (1964). "The Role of Patents in the Transfer of Technology to Developing Countries." N. 65.II.B.1, New York.

Problems and Further Work

1. Compare and contrast IBM's position in computing with that of the Bell System in telephone communications.

2. Summarize the allegations made by the United States government and by others in their antitrust suits against IBM. What is your opinion as to whether these really constitute unfair practices and restraint of trade? See

Computerworld [Feb. 2, 10 (1972); Dec. 8, Oct. 13, Aug. 11, May 19 (1971); Jan. 21 (1970)]; *Datamation,* Feb. (1972); and also Gilchrist and Wessel (1972, Chapter 7); *Comm. ACM* **16,** 133–136 (1973).

3. Write a scenario based on a day in a home (apartment? cell?) where there is a multiplicity of services provided through a Community Information Utility. Name some science fiction stories based on this theme.

4. What statistics should be collected in a Prototype Community Information Utility about system performance and use of services? What other survey data is needed? Are there any questions of privacy in collecting such statistics?

5. At present, most software companies protect their products as trade secrets. What does this involve?

6. List in detail the arguments for regarding a computer program as an extension to the hardware and therefore capable of being patented. What are the counterarguments? How do these arguments apply to a microprogram (i.e., a control program recorded on a read-only computer memory)?

7. Draw up a table comparing copyrights, patents, trade secrets, and registration of computer programs with respect to (1) justification, (2) duration, (3) cost, (4) protection afforded, and (5) acceptability.

8. There is a market for second-hand computers but it is relatively limited. What factors have accelerated computer obsolescence? Why is it difficult to use (and sell) older computers? What can be done to extend the life of computing equipment? Developing countries have been suspicious that computer manufacturers have wished to dump old equipment on them. What arguments are there for and against using previous-generation equipment in developing countries?

9. There is a serious proposal (in the State of California) that software be considered a "property" subject to taxation. See

Comm. ACM **15,** 855 (1972); *Datamation* **18,** 92–94 (1972),

for continuing developments on taxing software. What arguments can be advanced to support this position?

10. Examine the arguments (technical and otherwise) for and against attempting to standardize a language for describing data bases. In your opinion is it feasible to implement such a (standardized) language? now? later? See the summaries by

R. W. Canning, *EDP Analyzer,* pp. 1–16, March (1972); A Pantages, *Datamation,* pp. 82–84, July (1972).

11. Information utilities could develop or be encouraged to develop in a variety of ways. There can be:

- unrestricted competition
- regulated competition
- a publicly owned total utility, that is, one providing all services
- a total utility owned by one company or a consortium of common carriers, computer manufacturers, and service companies
- an integrated network of utilities

For each of these (and for any others which seem interesting) discuss the distinguishing characteristics, the advantages, and the difficulties of implementation.

Chapter

11

SHIFTS IN POWER

"Information is power" has become accepted as a maxim, and with it the realization that power devolves upon those who gather, process, disseminate, or simply possess information. The increasing value of information as a commodity brings with it the potential to change the bases of power and create new ones. In this chapter we are interested in how the computer affects the relationships between different components of an organization, between components at different levels, and between a component and the individuals within it.

One factor which enters into the influence of the computer is whether the computing facilities are centralized or decentralized. Centralization or decentralization is a question which large corporations and governments both face in trying to weigh the relative importance of cost, effectiveness, and control. Possession of the computer imparts control, a fact which is explicitly acknowledged in many situations. But computers do not necessarily imply more centralized control. It is possible to envisage how they would encourage greater transparency in government administration and a more general participation in politics. Perhaps most far reaching of all is the question on how the changes of power brought about by concentration of information systems will affect the individual. Will they result in a few technocrats gaining power at the expense of a diminishing control for most people? Does it offer more or less opportunity for the individual to make choices that really matter?

11.1. Information as Power

We have already seen a great deal of evidence about the power of information—how it confers an ability to predict in business and plan in government, and how it inevitably affects individual privacy. But it is almost impossible to overemphasize just how strongly information and knowledge are perceived as a source of power by economists, political scientists, and sociologists who examine modern society and attempt to discern the forces at play and the directions it is taking. Throughout most of recorded history land has been the critical resource, and power accrued to those who possessed land; in the last 200 years capital has been the critical resource and those who possessed it have had extraordinary power; now, it is argued, power is conferred upon those who possess and can use knowledge.

Daniel Bell, for example, characterizes the postindustrial society by the evolution of a service-oriented rather than production-oriented economy, and by the central role that knowledge plays in it. He writes[1]:

> What has now become decisive for society is the new centrality of *theoretical* knowledge, the primacy of theory over empiricism, and the codification of knowledge into abstract systems of symbols that can be translated into many different and varied circumstances.

Peter Drucker states that "Knowledge during the last few decades, has become the central capital, the cost center, and the crucial resource of the economy," and he identifies this as the most important of four discontinuities in our society.[2] And again, "The systematic and purposeful acquisition of information and its systematic application, rather than 'science' or 'technology' are emerging as the new foundations for work, productivity and effort throughout the world."[3]

It must be emphasized that the knowledge and information that Bell, Drucker, Galbraith, and others talk about is very general and wide ranging, and includes theoretical and scientific knowledge, practical ap-

[1] D. Bell, Notes on the post-industrial society, Parts I and II, *The Public Interest*, pp. 24–35, Winter (1967); pp. 102–118, Spring (1967).

[2] See Drucker, (1969, p. xi).

[3] See Drucker (1969, p. 266).

plications, management methodology, and activities embraced by teaching, data gathering and processing, publication, news distribution, and information dissemination. This knowledge economy[4] has many practitioners—scientists, engineers, mathematicians, librarians, teachers, reporters, technicians, planners, management consultants, and so forth. Although the computer is only one constituent, it is an important one. In our earlier discussions of files, data banks, and systems we have tended to emphasize factual data, but there is a continuous transition from factual data to procedures and algorithms for manipulating the data, and to management techniques and theoretical knowledge. Computers are involved in all of these forms and play a crucial role in the knowledge economy.[5]

We saw that the factors which motivate companies and governments to install computers are primarily the desire to achieve less costly and better products and services, but that the ability to plan is also important. Other advantages are gained by those who undertake to install computers early, particularly in their dealings with competitors, or with similar divisions in their organization. The value of the competitive edge imparted by computers is sometimes doubted. There are frequent warnings about the vanity of acquiring computers out of desire for prestige. A truth that lies behind such warnings arises from the fact that it is expensive to be a leader in applying a technological innovation; there are inevitably high costs in learning and high risks in failure. But when computers come to any sector of an industry, such as premium accounting in insurance, reservation handling in transportation, typesetting in newspaper preparation, or deposit accounting in banking, they become universal within a remarkably short time, perhaps five years or so, and this is in itself evidence that lack of computers is a serious competitive disadvantage once they become general in industry.

In business and also in government, it makes a difference *where* the computer is. The processing and planning capabilities of the computer impart authority to the division in charge of it, and this is particularly true if, as so often happens, the arrival of the computer is accompanied by a functional reorganization. We can also note how often, in an industrial dispute, the key issue is whether management or the union controls

[4] Chapter 13 of "The Age of Discontinuity" (Drucker, 1969) is entitled the "Knowledge Economy" and it describes the value, size, and growth of the effort devoted to gathering and disseminating knowledge and information.

[5] For a description of the knowledge industry and the part computers are expected to play in it see K. Ando, Growth and development of the Japanese computer industry—philosophy and current trend, *Proc. Aust. Comput. Conf., 5th, 1972*, pp. 39–71. Courier-Mail, Bowen Hills, Australia, 1972.

the extent of computer usage. In our examination of how the computer is creating shifts in authority and power, we therefore turn to consider where the computer is centered.

11.2. Centralization versus Decentralization

In examining the extent to which possession of computers implies ability to control, it is instructive to start by looking at the computer centralization versus decentralization debate in business. It is in this sphere that there has been the most careful analysis of the relative merits, and the arguments about economy, effectiveness, and control also apply elsewhere.

In computing, the general economic rule which favors large production systems over small ones, based on the economy of scale, has come to be known as Grosch's law.[6] This states that the effectiveness of a computing system, as measured by throughput or speed, is proportional to the square of the cost. The effect of this law is that large, multibranch companies can reduce their equipment costs, or alternatively acquire a more effective system for the same cost, by consolidating their computer services into a single facility rather than establishing separate facilities at each branch. As an example, a company that has two plants, each of which has computing requirements which could be met, say, by an IBM 360 model 40 computer, renting at $9000 per month, could instead install an IBM 360 model 50, renting at about $18,000 per month, obtaining about four times the capacity of the model 40, so that it would be able to undertake more sophisticated applications and have reserve capacity for growth. It is just this fact that performance/cost increases as cost goes up which has provided the justification for marketing larger and larger computers.

It is not only hardware costs which show economy of scale. Surveys of installations in which the equipment costs are compared with salaries show that the cost ratio of salaries to equipment decreases as the size of the installation goes up. Table 11-1 shows this ratio as calculated by

[6] This relation, stated by H. R. Grosch, has been disputed and rehabilitated a number of times. See M. B. Solomon, Economics of scale and the IBM system/360, *Comm. ACM* 9, 435–440 (1966); W. F. Sharpe, "The Economics of Computers," p. 315 et seq. Columbia Univ. Press, New York, 1969. Its validity for data processing calculations is disputed by Littrell (R. F. Littrell, "The Cost of Computer Systems," North Carolina State Board of Education, 1972). His benchmark comparisons on the IBM System 360 and 370 series of machines show an advantage for large systems in scientific calculations, but none in data processing applications.

TABLE 11-1
ECONOMIES OF SCALE IN COMPUTER SALARY COSTS[a]

Range of monthly EDP rentals	$1–3K	$3–6K	$6–12K	$12–25K	$25–50K	$50–75K	$75–150K	$150–300K
Number of companies surveyed	201	437	590	462	277	104	75	30
Number of employees	1902	5811	13,444	17,950	19,402	11,120	11,375	6273
Average salary for computer personnel	155	156	160	167	173	178	184	174
Average salary × number of employees	$1466	$2075	$3646	$6488	$12,117	$19,028	$27,905	$36,383
Dollars/week/co. per K of rental	978	462	405	351	324	304	248	162

[a] Excerpt from M. B. Solomon, Economies of scale and computer personnel, *Datamation* **6**, 107–110 (1970).

Solomon[7] from data gathered in a survey of over 2000 companies in the United States, with some 87,000 employees in their computing departments. The average salaries are larger in the companies with the larger installations, but the number of employees per $1000 per month of rental is smaller, and the net effect is a reduced relative labor cost. In addition to these dollar savings Solomon argues that the larger installations are more productive because higher salaries make it possible to attract and retain more experienced programmers, and because with larger staffs it is possible to institute training programs, standardized practices, specialization, better documentation, and research activities, all of which contribute to making the installation more effective. Another argument in favor of the centralized system is that a larger, more versatile machine makes it possible to integrate file systems more effectively and carry out applications which could not be undertaken without large memory and fast processing rates.

Berman[8] disputes the greater effectiveness of large installations for a number of reasons, of which the most important are that the large organization is far less able to provide good service to its users who are necessarily remote, and that the rigid structure generally found in large organizations is not conducive to good performance or attractive to the most competent people. We have here the main argument for decentralizing not only computing systems but also manufacturing complexes, institutions, government, and political systems. A decentralized system is closer to the people whom it serves and therefore its management will be more responsive to needs, both in respect to the work which is undertaken and the speed of service.

In his review of the debate, Glaser[9] further notes that a reason that many industrial organizations adopt decentralized responsibility for operations in general, is that it also makes it possible to assign local responsibility for profit and loss, and that this same argument holds for data processing operations. He points out that it is possible to apply decentralization independently with respect to operations and development.[10] Two trends are working toward increased decentralization. First, the scarcity of experienced data processing personnel is not a permanent

[7] M. B. Solomon, Economics of scale and computer personnel, *Datamation*, pp. 107–110, March (1970); pp. 293–294, June (1970).

[8] P. Berman, A vote against centralized staff, *Datamation*, pp. 289–290, May (1970); Decentralization Again, *Datamation*, pp. 141–142, October 15 (1970).

[9] G. Glaser, The centralization vs. decentralization issue, *IAG J.* **4**, 15–27 (1971).

[10] The operational staff is responsible for rendering services, and the development staff for decisions on long-range objectives, projections, selection and evaluation, hardware and software acquisition, policies regarding cost distribution, use of outside services, and so on.

factor,[11] and second, middle and upper level managers, as they become more familiar with computers, insist on having data processing staff available and responsible to themselves for reasons of independence and safety. These arguments certainly apply for the operational component of data processing, and to them might be added, as we have seen in Chapter 2, that the trend of technological development is to make it much easier to do computing locally. The developments include the growth of time-sharing, the extension of communications facilities which allow satellite computers to be attached to large remote central processors, and the spread of minicomputers.

Governments everywhere are the largest and very often the first user of computers.[12] The question of centralizing or decentralizing government computing services comes up with the same arguments we have just seen about economy of scale when operations are centralized, and better responsiveness to needs when they are decentralized.[13]

Computers may be installed for efficiency, because they enable certain responsibilities to be carried out within specified schedules, or because they offer better control over important operations. This aspect of control, which makes computers attractive to governments everywhere, is especially in evidence in governments with centrally planned economies. The computer literature of the Soviet Union leaves little doubt of the importance of this point of view.[14] Computers are regarded as *the* means of making the hierarchy of state, local, and central bureaus work effectively, and they have been given increasingly high priority in successive five-year plans. A network of computers has been proposed in which vital data on population, housing, production statistics, and traffic flows are captured at the source and transmitted almost instantaneously to centralized computers with large-scale data banks which control the opera-

[11] See footnote 14, Chapter 2.

[12] For details on the extent of use in the United States federal government see "Inventory of Automatic Data Processing Equipment in the Federal Government." Bureau of the Budget, Washington, D. C., June 1965. Note also the distribution of computers in Canada, as shown in Table 2-3, Chapter 2. In developing countries, also, governments are the principal users, as illustrated by Table 1 in United Nations, "The Application of Computer Technology for Development." Dept. of Economic and Social Affairs, E/4800, New York, 1971.

[13] F. G. Kordes, Policy on automation in government departments: Centralization or decentralization, *IAG J.* 3, 179–203 (1970).

[14] *Soviet Cybernetics Rev.* Network systems require "top-down" approach, pp. 27–28, Nov. (1970); State-wide control systems, pp. 5–7, May (1970); A configuration of the state network of computer centres, pp. 39–41, Oct. (1969); The state network of computer centres, pp. 59–75, Sept. (1969); The RAND Corp., Santa Monica, California.

tions of whole industries and production systems. It is difficult to gauge the extent to which Soviet planners see their whole economy as a single system, amenable to computer control; certainly there is a realization that local plants and local decisions must enter into the picture, but the theories of large-scale planning and global optimums are consistent with their philosophy of government.

Although in the past large centralized computer installations have been favored over small decentralized ones, where there was a choice between the two, current trends are making the decentralized operations more attractive. On the basis of cost/effectiveness it is not possible to state unequivocally that one mode is better than the other. Both centralized and decentralized facilities can be made to work, and in the end, the decision to adopt one mode or the other should be, and usually is, based on convictions as to where control of the operations ought to lie—in a centralized body which has an overview of the organization, or in decentralized working groups alive to the needs of users.

It may be that the approach which management consultants are reputed to take on this question of centralization versus decentralization is the correct one. If a consultant finds a centralized structure, he advises decentralization; if he finds a decentralized structure, he advises centralization. This comment is not altogether facetious. What may be needed is a pulsating structure which oscillates between the two modes. At the very least any equilibrium should be dynamic in the sense that the system is constantly adjusting itself in response to changes in its environment, by allowing more autonomy to the satellites or applying more control at the center, as the need arises.

11.3. Computers in the Political Process

Computers can influence the balance of power between the levels of government, an effect which is important in countries such as the United States, Canada, Australia, and Germany with federal systems of government in which there is a continuous tug of war between the central and regional jurisdictions. Because computers, initially at least, were large and very expensive, the first acquisition of computers in government tended to be by large operating units at the federal level, for example, the defense establishment, tax departments, the census division. Although the initial installations were usually for routine data processing, these divisions were also the first to come to the more sophisticated applications in planning and control. The massive data bases and superior analytical power possessed by those who have computers at their disposal confer an advantage, when, for example, negotiations about tax sharing take place.[15]

As computers have become commonplace in state and municipal governments,[16] the advantages are no longer distributed along federal and state lines. There are still unequal bargaining positions, but these will exist between state and municipal levels of government, between the departments within a governmental jurisdiction, or between the different individuals and groups within a department. Between these levels, very definite shifts of power appear. Downs[17] describes the differences as follows.

- Lower and intermediate-level administrators tend to lose power to higher level officials and politicians.
- The government bureaucracy as a whole gains power at the expense of city and state legislators, the general electorate, and nongovernmental groups.
- Well-organized and sophisticated groups gain power at the expense of those which are not well organized or knowledgeable.

It should be noted that no claim is advanced that substantial power is acquired by individuals or groups who did not have it before, but rather that there is a shift of power from some groups to others. To this we

[15] An example of the advantages conferred by having a computer arose in 1951 during the discussions between the hydroelectric power authorities for the State of New York and for the Province of Ontario over the design of the St. Lawrence Seaway. The Ontario group had at its disposal a comprehensive set of computer calculations including alternatives for several joint projects and for an all-Canadian seaway. The possession of these appraisals strengthened its bargaining position.

Another example occurred in the long, detailed negotiations between the provincial and federal governments preceding the substantial revision of the tax law which came into effect in Canada in 1972. For the federal government's initial report (prepared by the Carter Commission) a very general computer program, able to calculate tax yields from census tapes under a variety of assumptions, was written. This produced massive data, but in this instance the provincial governments were not content to be at a disadvantage. Only after some of them carried out their own tax analysis (with the help of the same organization that had worked with the federal government!) were they willing to proceed with the negotiations.

[16] For details of the type and extent of use at these levels see, "Automated Data Processing in State Government," 1965, and also "Automated Data Processing in Municipal Government," 1966, both published by Public Administration Service, Chicago, Illinois.

[17] A. Downs, The political payoffs in urban information systems, *in* "Information Technology in a Democracy" (A. Westin, ed.), pp. 311–321. Harvard Univ. Press, Cambridge, Massachusetts, 1971.

might add that when this tendency is perceived, a well-organized group which already has influence takes steps to ensure that it does not suffer a disadvantage.

The effects of computers on the balance of power between government levels were explicitly acknowledged when the State of Hessen in the Federal Republic of Germany proposed a "data management ombudsman." Among his duties he is "to observe the effects of automatic data processing . . . and note whether they lead to a displacement of the distribution of powers among the State Constitutional bodies, among those of the local government bodies, and between the State and local authorities. He shall be entitled to suggest any measures he thinks fit to prevent such effects."[18]

Must computers imply a greater centralization of information and control on the part of government? Not everyone agrees that it need be so. MacBride, convinced that a unified national computer center is inevitable (in the United States), seeks methods of making it independent of any one of the government arms so it becomes available to Congress, the courts, local and state authorities, and the public.[19] Michael suggests that citizens' groups might hire specialists, unavailable to governments, to exercise a watchdog role on their behalf.[20] Ithiel de Sola Pool *et al.*[21] go further. They say: "The dangers are maximized if there is a monopoly of control over information. There is a widespread misapprehension that the computer centralizes information control." But, they add,

> . . . the information facilities provided by the computer can equally serve as a decentralizing instrument. They can make available to all parts of an organization the kinds of immediate and complete information that is today available only at the center . . . . A society with computerized information facilities can make its choice between centralization and decentralization, because it will have the mechanical capability of moving information either way. An information utility can make information available with unprecedented facility to people working at all levels.

[18] "Data Processing Law," State of Hessen, Federal Republic of Germany, Oct. 7, 1970, Part 1, p. 625, the translation is from Thomas (1971, p. 19).

[19] R. O. MacBride, "The Automated State: Computer Systems as a New Force in Society." Chilton Book, Philadelphia, Pennsylvania, 1967.

[20] D. N. Michael, On coping with complexity: Planning and policies, *Daedalus,* pp. 1179–1193, Fall (1968).

[21] I. de Solo Pool, S. McIntosh, and D. Griffel, Information systems and social knowledge, *in* "Information Technology in a Democracy" (A. Westin, ed.), pp. 241–249. Harvard Univ. Press, Cambridge, Massachusetts, 1971.

There has been some experience with making computers available to community action groups and disadvantaged communities.[22] Not surprisingly, such groups which have acquired or used computers have concentrated on conventional data processing applications—budget control, inventory systems, personnel systems, and so on. Problems with the directors of agencies and other officials not understanding the mechanics or potentialities of the equipment were not uncommon. It will not be simple to develop more imaginative applications such as information retrieval systems which can help direct the client of a social agency to the proper services, or provide a ratepayers' organization with information on zoning laws. Even where there has been a recognized need to serve organized and well-funded groups as in the case of a legal information system for lawyers or an information system for the United States Congress, computerized systems have not emerged. When the data base is too narrow in scope the system is not useful, and when it is enlarged we encounter the problems of trying to design a large-scale, natural language retrieval system, as discussed in Chapter 4.

Transparency of government and its possible influence on public participation are the concluding theme of Thomas in his monograph on data banks in the public administration.[23] He notes the current tradition in most countries to treat as confidential all data not explicitly designed for public release. Computers permit a reversal of this, a more transparent administration, in which all data not designated as confidential can be made accessible. Such accessibility carries a cost and it might be desirable to make a charge for information, especially to private enterprises (legal firms, insurance companies, real estate agents, building contractors, etc.) which would derive substantial benefits from it. But the improved communication could encourage interest in public affairs and invite new ways for individual participation, a desideratum of modern political systems.

The most interesting possibilities for participation in public affairs, perhaps the most far reaching, would occur if the computerized two-way communications systems discussed earlier under information utilities were to be realized. Many persons, in noting the possibilities that this would open for instant mass opinion polls, have questioned whether this would be a desirable development. Eulau examines the potential effects

[22] For a report based on nine case histories see the summary of C. D. Tyson, "The Control of Technology by Disadvantaged Communities," in President and Fellows of Harvard College (1972, pp. 119–124).

[23] Thomas (1971, sec. 6.5).

on decision-makers and elected politicians and concludes that the influence on the representative process would not be beneficial.[24] Democracy works because politicians have different convictions about the merits of an argument supporting some position, and a fair decision is (or should be) reached in debate after these arguments have been presented. If it were expected that every individual representative had to respond to the collective position recorded by an opinion poll, the debate would not be as effective.[25] Certainly a representative would be in a poor position to exercise his own judgment counter to the clearly expressed view of the majority of his constituents. This is, in effect, saying that although opinion polls are useful, it is *informed opinion* which must be taken into consideration when decisions are made.

The effectiveness of Delphi exercises, particularly on-line Delphi, in achieving a consensus or revealing differences in opinion and attitudes about a wide range of subjects was noted in Section 6.2. But those experiments were conducted with carefully selected participants who were at least moderately well informed about the topics, and often were authorities. In hot-line radio shows, where there is no real control on participation, the discussion is usually rambling and it is impossible to attach significance to the opinions expressed. Before computers and communications could be combined into a tool for dynamic and interactive exchange of ideas on a wide scale, new techniques for selecting participants and focusing a discussion would have to evolve.[26] Although this has not taken place with the radio or television media, it has been achieved in opinion polling.

It is only possible to speculate on the response to making more detailed information about legislative actions and proposals available widely and promptly through a computer information utility, or about the political consequences of more frequent and more widely posed public opinion polls on a large number of issues. A new resource is most likely to be exploited by those who are already politically organized. When an on-

[24] H. Eulau, "Some Potential Effects of the Information Utility on Political Decision-Makers, and the Role of the Representative," in Sackman and Nie (1970, pp. 187–189). See also F. B. Ryan, The electronic voting system for the United States House of Representatives, *Computer*, pp. 32–37, Nov.–Dec. (1972).

[25] Note that this is based on the implicit view that if the same detailed arguments were presented to the public they would not listen to them as carefully as would the representative.

[26] For some possibilities see S. Umpleby, Citizen sampling simulations: A method for involving the public in social planning, CERL Rep. X-12, Univ. of Illinois, Urbana, 1970.

line computerized information system containing an environmental data base was made available to university students, faculty, and other scientists, the first to use it were activist law students engaged in fighting pollution.[27]

The long-term political implications of merging computers with communications, if it were to take place, are far from clear.[28] There are suggestions that a new cadre of political scientists might emerge, specialists in collecting and interpreting public opinion.[29] Because of their understanding of how opinion could be brought to bear on issues they might replace the "political pundits" and the lobbyists who are now regarded as the experts on political trends and the means of achieving political ends. Other possibilities are that more effective communications would encourage the formation of small cohesive activist groups, dedicated to achieving specific ends, and also that the emphasis on personality and "political packaging," already noticeably present in television, could be heightened. The political processes in the Western nations are too pluralistic and too complicated for any one development to have a dominating role. But one can envisage how computers and communications might provide a mechanism which will help restore the conviction that individual and small-group voices matter in the governing process.

In summarizing the changes in power brought about by the introduction of computers both in business and government, it is fair to say that the initial effects have been to favor a concentration in power in the larger groupings at the expense of the smaller ones. As computers have become more available there has been some redress in balance. All the larger units of government now have more data and information processing power than they had before and it is not possible for one to claim a decisive advantage. At the lower levels of government the unequal access to and understanding of computers on the part of different groups and different officials still have significance with respect to possession of power. There is some suggestion that the contribution of computers and communications might eventually have profound effects on political

[27] The environmental data base consists of approximately 50,000 references to published materials on aspects of pollution. It is available through the National Science Library of Canada, and can be searched in the batch mode or through an on-line retrieval system. See National Science Library Newsletter, no. 9, May, 1972.

[28] Even the effects of television alone on political participation are difficult to assess. See N. H. Nie, "Future Developments in Mass Communications and Citizen Participation," in Sackman and Nie (1970).

[29] This suggestion and those which follow are made by the contributors to "The Information Utility and Social Choice" (Sackman and Nie, 1970). For an overview see the summary by K. Prewitt.

groupings. At the level of the individual, the inequalities of power assume their greatest significance.

11.4. Computers and the Individual

A central issue in the development of Western political ideology, perhaps the basic issue, whose origins go back to the Greek democracies, arises out of the conflict between the rights of the individual as opposed to the responsibilities collective society has a right to impose on him. Very different balances have been struck between these in different times and in different countries. Do computers alter the balance? We have already explored some facets of this question in our discussions of computers and privacy in Chapter 6. But the question is so important that we must examine it further.

One fear is that the balance has been altered because the new preeminence of social planning by technology results in major power being placed in the hands of a few technocrats. The fear is that such people are ill prepared to exercise power because of their inability to appreciate human values when these run counter to the demands of efficiency, and because their decisions are not subject to the checks imposed by public debate and democratic processes. This concern, which we have already seen in our discussions of systems, comes up repeatedly and it is not raised only by those who are critical of technology.

Meynaud points out that technocrats do not always possess the expertise they claim to have, and they may especially lack experience in dealing with people. Moreover they are prone to forming closed groups which are deaf to outside advice, and which show partiality for the interests of professionals, managers, and other members of the class from which they themselves are drawn. His belief is that, while complete domination of politics by technocrats has not occurred, the process of transfer of power is under way and that technocracy will continue to expand. "The spirit of our day, directed towards the search for maximal productivity, is definitely favorable to technocratic ideology."[30]

Presumably, technocrats derive their power when politicians and decision-makers do not have the expertise to question their conclusions which are based on highly technical arguments. Just as important is the ability to define the set of alternatives that are being considered in a given situation. This issue of the power of technicians came to the fore

[30] J. Meynaud, "Technocracy," Conclusion, p. 296. Faber and Faber, London, 1968.

with the development of nuclear weapons,[31] but it applies also to computer and systems analysts. Boguslaw writes[32]:

> It is in this sense that computer programmers, the designers of computer equipment, and the developers of computer languages possess power. To the extent that decisions made by each of these participants in the design process serve to reduce, limit, or totally eliminate active alternatives, they are applying force and wielding power in the precise sociological meaning of these terms.

But most of those who consider the question, although recognizing the dangers, conclude that there has been no surrender of power to experts and planners, and that the major decisions on the economy, social welfare, and military matters are continuing to be made by those who have the responsibility for them. Westin, in a detailed study of the role of information technology in public decision-making, finds that the traditional professional and political elite are secure in their control and management of government.[33]

Such views are also expressed by Bell,[34] Price, and Wood[35]; and Carl Kaysen, writing on the contribution of economists to economic policy-making,[36] comes to a similar conclusion about the role of the expert in that area.

Others go beyond this to suggest that expert advice now seldom plays any real role in the political process, and that politicians and decision-

[31] R. E. Lapp, "The New Priesthood." Harper, New York, 1965.

[32] R. Boguslaw, Systems of power and the power of systems, *in* "The New Utopians: A Study of System Design and Social Change." Prentice-Hall, Englewood Cliffs, New Jersey, 1965. We may note that with the specialization of labor, the type of social and political choices we have been considering are *not* specified by programmers or the designers of computer equipment and languages; but they are built into the models and simulations of the systems designers and planners who *apply* the computers, and the general point is valid.

[33] A. F. Westin, Information technology and public decision-making, summarized *in* "Harvard University Program on Technology and Society, 1964–1972, Final Review" (President and Fellows of Harvard College, 1972, pp. 59–67). Westin emphasizes the failure of management information systems to achieve promised goals, with the result that information processing technologists have lost rather than gained authority.

[34] D. Bell, Notes on the post-industrial society (1), *The Public Interest,* no. 6, 35 (1967).

[35] For a summary of their views, D. K. Price, "The Scientific Estate," Belknap Press, Cambridge, Massachusetts, 1965, and R. C. Wood, Scientists and politics: The rise of an apolitical elite *in* "Scientists and National Policy Making" (R. Gilpin and C. Wright, eds.). Columbia Univ. Press, New York, 1965; see Technology and the polity, *Res. Rev.* no. 4 of the Harvard Univ. Program on Technol. and Soc., pp. 31–32 (1969).

[36] C. Kaysen, Model-makers and decision-makers: economists and the policy process, *The Public Interest,* no. 12, pp. 80–95 (1968).

makers simply call upon those who will render technical opinions to support positions they have already taken. Thus H. L. Nieburg[37]:

> Increasingly, as the expertise of the scientist is politicized, the real centers of power in federal agencies or in Congress pick and choose those scientists who will proffer the advice they want; the chosen scientists provide a rationale and a justification for policies arrived at by other means. Scientific advice becomes a new species of lawyers brief and advocacy, and a cover for conducting policies in bureaucratic corridors or congressional cloakrooms. In all key post-war decisions, scientists have been present in ancillary roles both in and out of government, but they have made none of the major decisions.

Similar positions are advanced by Daniel Greenberg[38] and Victor Ferkiss.[39] According to them the day of giving special attention to the advice of experts is past,[40] if it was ever here at all.

Because we have such a divergence of views about the power of technocrats, it does not follow that the actual position is in the middle, or indeed close to any one of them. What we would like to see is that technical advice carries different weight in different situations. Where values have been articulated and a framework constructed which makes technical analysis possible and relevant, technical considerations can dominate. Where there are value conflicts and the technical analysis applies to only part of the problem, political considerations should dominate. The prevailing opinion is that decisions about most social and economic problems are still being made as political decisions in which technical experts, including computer experts and systems planners, play useful but minor roles.

But the worry about the place of the individual in a technological society goes much deeper than this. The real concern is not that too much power is held by too few, but rather that too little is held by too many. In other words we must come back to alienation and powerlessness. The belief, highly pessimistic in character, that man has already been diminished almost beyond hope of recovery because of the application of technology, runs through a whole school of technology critics. The indictment is that man no longer has any choice in the way he lives, that decisions

[37] H. L. Nieburg, "In the Name of Science." Quadrangle Books, Chicago, Illinois, 1966. Reprinted with permission.

[38] D. S. Greenberg, The myth of the scientific elite, *The Public Interest*, no. 1, pp. 51–62 (1965).

[39] V. C. Ferkiss, The spectre of the scientific elite, *in* "Public Policy and the Expert." Council on Religious and Internat. Affairs, New York, 1971.

[40] It may be that the influence of an advisor depends on the terminology; technicians are ignored, technocrats are feared, experts are needed, and authorities are respected.

are made to promote economic growth rather than his basic needs, and that what is technically feasible is allowed to happen without regard to consequences. These views, in varying forms and with different degrees of intensity, are expressed by such well-known writers as Jacques Ellul, Hannah Arendt, Herbert Marcuse, Ludwig von Mises, Erich Fromm, and Lewis Mumford.

The degree of choice which man is able to exercise is one of the focal points of the criticism. On this we find the same wide divergence of views that we saw about the influence of experts. At one end there is the despairing view of Herbert Marcuse who believes that society, through technology, co-opts man—it absorbs his energies, ambitions, ideals, and protests, so that he is integrated into it almost without realization that any alternatives exist, and without possibility of escape even if he were to become aware of his plight.[41] In a similar view Erich Fromm,[42] on examining the present technological system and its effects on man, sees two guiding principles: that "can" becomes "right" and that maximal efficiency must be secured. The consequences are to "reduce man to an appendage of the machine, ruled by its very rhythm and demands." When science undermined religious belief, it failed to provide an alternative certainty and as a result there has arisen "the need of what amounts to a blind belief in the efficacy of the method of computerized planning," but "both the religious decision, which is a blind surrender to God's will, and the computer decision, based on the faith in the logic of 'facts,' are forms of alienated decisions in which man surrenders his own insight, knowledge, inquiry, and responsibility to an idol, be it God or the computer."

These views do not go unchallenged. There are others who argue that technology has not resulted in too little choice but rather too much, that the prospects are for *more* not less individuality, that what is required are new mechanisms for exercising the multiplicity of choice, and that *any* solutions for societal problems must be based on the application of more technology, administered of course in the light of human values. Toffler, for example, emphasizes the changes which characterize the multiplicity of choices, and makes the need to live with change, predict it, and ultimately channel it his central thesis.[43] McLuhan takes hope in

[41] H. Marcuse, "One-Dimensional Man," Chapter 1—The new forms of control, pp. 1–18. Beacon Press, Boston, Massachusetts, 1964.

[42] E. Fromm, "The Revolution of Hope: Toward a Humanized Technology," pp. 26–57. Bantam Books, New York, 1968.

[43] A. Toffler, "Future Shock." Random House, New York, 1970.

the new possibilities arising out of cybernation and automation, and suggests that it will repattern the very nature of identity.

> But whereas before the problem of identity had been one of meagerness and poverty, it has now become the problem of abundance and superfluity . . . . It would be a cosmic irony if men proved unable to cope with abundance and riches in both the economic and psychic order. It is not likely to happen.[44]

The range in views about the effects of technology on man and the shades of opinion on what the real problems are, what is likely to happen, and what should be done about them are far wider than has been suggested here.[45] On the whole there is pessimism, particularly on the subject of choices. Why? It is obvious that technology and computers make it possible to record not only quantitative, measurable attributes of people but also qualitative preferences in travel arrangements or car styles. It is even possible to make a case for believing that computers offer the most hopeful mechanism that has appeared so far for taking cognizance of the needs, differences, and preferences of individuals. Admittedly, the difficulties many people have encountered with computerized billing systems (quite aside from questions of confidentiality and privacy) suggest caution with computerized systems which make administrative decisions about people. As such systems become more common, for example, in motor vehicle departments where they are used to issue driver's licenses and record traffic offenses, more attention is being paid to the quality of their decisions as compared with those rendered by traditional means.[46] Are the decisions made as promptly with computers? Are they as fair? Are there as good opportunities for review? There is a recognized need to improve the quality of computer systems, especially those which deal with people, but there are examples of well-designed systems (see airline reservations, Section 4.3) and one can be optimistic that there will be less and less tolerance for poorly designed systems in the future. As more and more administrative practices are automated, it

[44] M. McLuhan, Cybernation and culture *in* "The Social Impact of Cybernetics" (C. R. Deckert, ed.), pp. 95–108. Simon and Schuster, New York, 1967.

[45] For a more complete summary and for some of the principal views see, Harvard Univ. Program on Technol. and Soc., Technology and the individual, *Res. Rev.* no. 6 (1970).

[46] In the United States the Association for Computing Machinery has encouraged chapters to set up ombudsmen who would help people having trouble with mistakes made through use of computers. The International Institute of Administrative Science (whose headquarters is in Brussels) has undertaken a comprehensive study of administrative decisions made by computers.

may be argued that the programs which carry these out will evolve so as not only to be fair but also to include a large number of alternatives. For many of the routine and ordinary matters of everyday life, which in toto nevertheless have an important bearing on life style, it should be possible to take into account character and personality differences.

For more important matters, however, those involving basic choices in life—education, jobs, friends, a place to live—not many would care to have these determined by computers. Thus one key element becomes how to exercise personal control over these. It does not matter that most men have always had only a limited choice about them. Today our expectations are higher. For other matters still, particularly those relating to the political environment, it is not reasonable to expect that one's individual choice will be determinative. It then becomes a question of knowing how the desires of different groups can be reconciled, and how group actions can be effective. We have already seen earlier in this chapter how computers *might* come to have a role in resolving these issues.

Finally for some vital matters, for example, war, overpopulation, and pollution, the collective will is unmistakenly clear. Yet it seems to be incredibly difficult to translate this will into effective action. It is not possible to maintain that computers will have a direct bearing on how to cope with these problems. But technology as a whole does have a crucial role to play, and computers, insofar as they relate to other technologies, are relevant. At least as important as technology is the question of values. What are we prepared to give up to achieve a world in which these environmental factors are not at stake? We return to these questions of technology, values, and trade-offs in Chapter 13.

Bibliography

Bobrow, D. B., and Schwartz, J. L. (1968). "Computers and the Policy-Making Community." Prentice-Hall, Englewood Cliffs, New Jersey.

Drucker, P. F. (1969). "The Age of Discontinuity." Harper, New York.

Galbraith, J. K. (1967). "The New Industrial State." Houghton, Boston, Massachusetts.

Harvard Univ. Program on Technol. and Soc. (1969). Technology and the polity, *Res. Rev.* no. 4.

Harvard Univ. Program on Technol. and Soc. (1970). Technology and the individual, *Res. Rev.* no. 6.

President and Fellows of Harvard College (1972). "Harvard University Program on Technology and Society, 1964–1972, A Final Review." Harvard Information Office, Cambridge, Massachusetts.

Sackman, H., and Nie, N., eds. (1970). "The Informaion Utility and Social Choice." AFIPS Press, Montvale, New Jersey.

Thomas, U. (1971). "Computerised Data Banks in Public Administration." OECD. Informatics Studies 1, Paris.

Westin, A. F. (1971). "Information Technology in a Democracy." Harvard Univ. Press, Cambridge, Massachusetts.

Problems and Further Work

1. A Delphi experiment is to be conducted with participants who are students, teachers, and specialists in educational theory and research. Devise a set of questions designed to elicit opinions on the directions of education. Among other matters it is desired to know:

- which pedagogical techniques (cable TV, CAI, team-teaching, etc.) are likely to grow—how much and how soon
- the future of part-time and continuing education
- the readiness of the public to accept additional expenditures for education
- the social consequences of an increase in the level of education

See

J. R. Salancik, W. Wenger and E. Helfer, The construction of Delphi event statements, *Technlog. Forecasting Social Change* **3**, 65–73 (1971).

2. Should there be a requirement that when someone is given the opportunity to participate in a (computerized) opinion survey, he must first demonstrate some knowledge about the issue? If there are occasions when competency should be established, suggest methods of doing this.

3. Outline the various types of information which would be useful to a legislative body such as Congress or a state assembly. What are the advantages and difficulties in attempting to construct a computerized information system for this purpose? See

E. S. Mesko, Computers and congress, *AFIPS Conf. Proc.* **34**, 351–358 (1969); R. L. Chartrand, Computer technology and the congress, *Informat. Storage Retrieval* **6**, 229–240 (1970).

4. In what specific ways can computers be used to decentralize various branches of government? See footnote 22; also

Nat. Acad. of Eng., "Communications Technology for Urban Improvement Committee on Telecommunications," Chapter III, 1971.

5. Discuss the potential of computerized information utilities for producing a well-informed electorate. How do you envision the extent, organization, and control of such a system? What safeguards are necessary? How would the system be similar to (different from) the news and information services presently coming via newspapers and television?

Chapter

12

PROFESSIONALIZATION AND RESPONSIBILITY

This chapter is concerned with the responsibilities of those who work with computers. We begin with relatively narrow considerations of professional relationships and competence, but are soon led to the wider, ethical aspects of behavior, and finally to the moral responsibility of the scientist, engineer, or for that matter of any individual, for the social consequences of his work.

12.1. Professional Societies

What determines a *profession?* It is common to regard medicine, nursing, law, engineering, journalism, and architecture as professions. One of the connotations of the term is that professionals are distinguished from others doing similar work; for example, draftsmen from architects, medical orderlies from doctors, clerks from accountants. Although there is no universal set of defining characteristics, the following features are generally accepted as evidence of professionalism:

- a definable body of knowledge and a high level of education and skill
- recognition by society that a valuable service is being performed
- formal occupational associations
- standards for competence and behavior, accompanied by public reliance on and acceptance of these standards
- the usual absence of direct supervision; the willingness and ability to take initiatives and supervise others as required
- the existence of confidential relationships with clients and a sense of obligation to identify clients' needs and not only their wants
- a direct sense of responsibility for the quality of work
- a regard for specialized service designed to meet the needs of the client

Reflection makes it obvious that many if not most occupations possess these features to some degree. The extent and the degree of formalization of these characteristics vary with time and culture. We are thus led to the point of view of Vollmer and Mills (1966) who consider *professionalization* as a dynamic process, whereby the work of certain occupational groups acquires such characteristics to an extent generally recognized by society.

In most countries, professionals are either certified or licensed to practice, where licensing implies mandatory government control and certification may only entail a recommended but voluntary procedure. The basic justification for certification or licensing is to protect the public against incompetent practitioners. Standards for competence are established and maintained by professional organizations through examinations administered by the societies or by government.

Protection is the key word in discussing the emergence of professional societies. Four groups can be identified as needing protection.[1] These are the general public, the direct consumer of services, employers, and employees. The professional license, contracts, a code of ethics, as well as unwritten standards of acceptable practice all serve to define the responsibility of the professional.

The different responsibilities can conflict, both for individuals and professional organizations. For an employee a conflict obviously arises if he is asked to carry out a task he believes not to be in the best interests of

[1] "Professionalism in the Computer Field," Report of a Roundtable Meeting (chaired by Willard Wirtz), AFIPS Press, Montvale, New Jersey, 1970.

a consumer–client or of the general public, or if he is expected to act in a way which takes unfair advantage of another person in the profession. Those who are self-employed may find the conflicts to be even greater since their behavioral guidelines are less established than they might be for someone working for a larger company. To balance these various interests, to offer guidelines for resolving disputes, and to protect all concerned, professional societies set up review, discipline, and appeal mechanisms. But professional organizations themselves generate another set of conflicts. In order to ensure high standards of performance, particularly where public safety is involved, they may insist on long education and training programs. For this reason, and also to protect the interests of current members, societies may regulate competition in the field. But it is in the public interest to have some competition. An immediate conflict arises if there are not enough professionals trained and licensed to supply the services needed at a "reasonable" cost.

Currently, there is considerable debate among those engaged in computing and information processing as to whether the subject is a science, an applied science, or a branch of technology, and whether those who work in the field ought to be considered professionals. The distinction often made is that the basic concern in a pure science is knowledge about the nature of our environment and our functioning in that environment, whereas technology is concerned with the application of scientific knowledge to improve the human condition; applied science provides a bridge between pure research and development. Some maintain that the representation and manipulation of information should be considered a (mathematical) science, either pure or applied, and that, like other scientific societies, computer organizations should have a relatively open membership, limiting activities to the dissemination of knowledge to their members and the general public. The computing societies certainly started this way, as exemplified by the Association for Computing Machinery (in the United States), the British Computer Society, and the Canadian Information Processing Society. Computer science (or information science) departments in the universities still basically reflect this viewpoint.

Today most programmers, systems analysts, EDP managers, operators, and others involved with computers are *not* scientists, neither by inclination nor by training. The organizations to which they belong are ceasing to be scientific societies, and as they change, the nonscientific members often show a desire for professionalization and professional status. In the United Kingdom, the British Computer Society has transformed itself into a professional society in which members are graded according to qualifications, determined in part by examination and in part by experience. Similarly, in the United States, the Data Processing Management Association has conducted a certificate examination since 1962. However, in both the United States and Canada, the question of whether information processing societies should take this route to professionalization is still being debated.[2]

Nowhere has a generally recognized professional standing for computing emerged yet; there are no jurisdictions where programmers or analysts must have special certificates or be licensed in order to engage in their work.[3] Substantial reservations have been raised against proposals to move in this direction. It is argued that standards of competence have not yet been established for programming or systems analysis nor have job classifications been well defined, and that certification or licensing will not provide significant additional protection for the public, but rather only serve to make entry into computing careers more difficult. In other words, certification will be mainly a protection and status symbol for those already in the field.[4] It is easy to agree that the public is entitled to protection, especially against massive operational failures (e.g., the case where a bank or insurance company loses all its computerized records). But there are many places where controls may be effectively applied: to individual workers, to companies providing computer services, to the direct consumers of services,[5] or to the manufacturers of software and hardware.

Currently, there is a growing recognition that the range of job types associated with computers necessitates different approaches for different groups. Keypunch operators, junior programmers, and others for whom

[2] We do not suggest that this debate has been fully resolved in the United Kingdom. While the major society (BCS) has moved toward professionalization, the question now is whether these attempts will be effective. There are some indications of government acceptance (e.g., BCS was asked to review a census form, and at least one local government board, the Local Authorities Management and Computer Committee, has recommended that programmers be certified, and recognizes the BCS qualification as appropriate). However, it is still too early to gauge the importance of BCS certification. In Canada, members of the major society (CIPS) defeated a referendum motion to seek professional status.

[3] There is a strong possibility that in Japan the now voluntary examination administered by the Ministry of International Trade and Industry may become a legal requirement [see "Professionalism in the Computer Field" (AFIPS, 1970)].

[4] The most eloquent expositer of the view that entry to skilled jobs should not be barred by artificial restraints is Ivan Illich, see "Deschooling Society." Harper, New York, 1971.

[5] The AFIPS report (1970) makes the interesting suggestion, albeit not too seriously, that the users of computer services (e.g., a company which buys a payroll program) might be licensed in the same way that automobile drivers are licensed.

training and skill are emphasized are being classed as technicians. This has importance in that regulations which normally apply to technician positions, for example, the necessity to record and pay extra for overtime work and often the obligation to join unions, are also applicable here. The more senior programming and analyst jobs, for which a university degree is usually expected and which often carry management responsibilities, are not being included in the technician categorization. Although there are serious efforts to define a body of knowledge, specify entrance requirements, and set up certification procedures for those engaged in the more senior tasks, there has not been a general agreement that professionalization is needed. It may be that the desire, on the part of both management and those working at senior programming tasks, not to be bound by regulations governing overtime work and union affiliation will lead to a more vigorous pursuit of professional status.[6]

Related to but distinct from the issue of technical competence is the question of ethical behavior. The same groups of people still need protection. But ethical practice is even more difficult to define and enforce than technical competence. Those who argue the case for increased professionalization in computing suggest a traditional approach for dealing with these problems, namely, a code of ethics. The most famous code of ethics is the Hippocratic oath in medicine which was assembled about B.C. 400, and for which there are apparently sources dating as far back as B.C. 2000. In the late nineteenth and early twentieth centuries most engineering professions and many social sciences adopted such codes and they are now an accepted feature, perhaps the defining characteristic, of nearly all professional organizations.

In 1966, a set of guidelines for professional conduct in information processing (see Table 12-1) was adopted by the Council of the Association for Computing Machinery in the United States. AFIPS (the American Federation for Information Processing Societies), which embraces a number of computing organizations, has also urged the development of codes of public responsibility.[7] The British Computer Society, which as already mentioned has committed itself to professionalism, also has a code of conduct to which members are expected to subscribe. It was accompanied by a great deal of discussion and correspondence both before and after it appeared. More significantly it was followed by the

[6] An assessment of the present degree of professionalization in computing can be found in Professionalism, *EDP Analyzer,* December (1968). See also J. Titus, Wage and hour laws specified for computer center employers, *Comm. ACM* **15,** 125–128 (1972).

[7] "Professionalism in the Computer Field" (AFIPS, 1970).

TABLE 12-1

ACM GUIDELINES FOR PROFESSIONAL CONDUCT IN INFORMATION PROCESSING

INTRODUCTION

This set of guidelines was adopted by the Council of the Association for Computing Machinery on November 11, 1966 in the spirit of providing a guide to the members of the Association. In the years to come this set of guidelines is expected to evolve into an effective means of preserving a high level of ethical conduct. In the meantime it is planned that ACM members will use these guidelines in their own professional lives. They are urged to refer ethical problems to the proper ACM authorities as specified in the Constitution and Bylaws to receive further guidance and in turn assist in the evolution of the set of guidelines.

PREAMBLE

The professional person, to uphold and advance the honor, dignity and effectiveness of the profession in the arts and sciences of information processing, and in keeping with high standards of competence and ethical conduct: Will be honest, forthright and impartial; will serve with loyalty his employer, clients and the public; will strive to increase the competence and prestige of the profession; will use his special knowledge and skill for the advancement of human welfare.

1. Relations with the Public

1.1 An ACM member will have proper regard for the health, privacy, safety and general welfare of the public in the performance of his professional duties.

1.2 He will endeavor to extend public knowledge, understanding and appreciation of computing machines and information processing and achievements in their application, and will oppose any untrue, inaccurate or exaggerated statement or claims.

1.3 He will express an opinion on a subject within his competence only when it is founded on adequate knowledge and honest conviction, and will properly qualify himself when expressing an opinion outside of his professional field.

1.4 He will preface any partisan statement, criticisms or arguments that he may issue concerning information processing by clearly indicating on whose behalf they are made.

2. Relations with Employers and Clients

2.1 An ACM member will act in professional matters as a faithful agent or trustee for each employer or client and will not disclose private information belonging to any present or former employer or client without his consent.

2.2 He will indicate to his employer or client the consequences to be expected if his professional judgment is over-ruled.

2.3 He will undertake only those professional assignments for which he is qualified and which the state of the art supports.

2.4 He is responsible to his employer or client to meet specifications to which he is committed in tasks he performs and products he produces, and to design and develop systems that adequately perform their function and satisfy his employer's or client's operational needs.

TABLE 12-1 (*Continued*)

3. Relations with Other Professionals

3.1 An ACM member will take care that credit for work is given to those to whom credit is properly due.
3.2 He will endeavor to provide opportunity and encouragement for the professional development and advancement of professionals or those aspiring to become professionals with whom he comes in contact.
3.3 He will not injure maliciously the professional reputation or practice of another person and will conduct professional competition on a high plane. If he has proof that another person has been unethical, illegal or unfair in his professional practice concerning information processing, he should so advise the proper authority.
3.4 He will cooperate in advancing information processing by interchanging information and experience with other professionals and students and by contributing to public communications media and to the efforts of professional and scientific societies and schools.

introduction of a disciplinary procedure which could lead to exclusion, suspension, reprimand, or admonishment of members.[8]

There are those who claim that ethical codes are completely inadequate. Miller writes about the ACM code: "Without intending to be unduly harsh on this particular group, which at least has tried to formulate some professional canon, I must say that provisions of this type are platitudinous; they are somewhat like asking for a pledge of allegiance to milk, motherhood and the American flag."[9]

Even in professions which have long-standing disciplinary procedures and enforcement mechanisms, experience in dealing with so-called ethical problems is not encouraging. For example, the American Society of Civil Engineers considers hundreds of ethical problems every year. Between the years 1951 and 1964, 78 of these problems became formal cases; 48 were dismissed. Of the 78 cases, 26 concerned unethical competitive bidding, about 20 concerned actions regarded as derogatory to the integrity and honor of the profession, 6 involved supplanting another engineer in an engagement, and the remainder arose from a variety of other charges.[10] It is difficult to avoid the conclusion that the main activities centered on the protection of the profession and of professionals,

[8] Explanatory notes on the disciplinary structure, *Comput. Bull.* **14** (11) (1970). The ACM has also proposed a hierarchy of canons, ethical considerations, and disciplinary rules similar to the structure of the American Bar Association. Members who violate disciplinary rules would be subject to suspension or expulsion.

[9] A. R. Miller, "Assault on Privacy," p. 255. Univ. of Michigan Press, Ann Arbor, Michigan, 1971.

[10] D. B. Parker, Rules of ethics in information processing, *Comm. ACM* **11**, 198–201 (1968).

and that *protection of public interests ran a poor third!* In all too many cases, the so-called ethical committee of a profession spends its time debating the size of the sign which a member is permitted to display. The ACM or BCS codes could provide a basic framework for professional conduct but Miller's assessment cannot be dismissed as mere cynicism.

12.2. Professional Imperatives

In trying to determine whether there is a need for professionalism in computing it is useful to examine some of the ways in which those who work with computers might act contrary to the public interest or take unfair advantage of their employers and competitors.

Falsification of Financial Records

Those who are engaged in programming financial applications such as payroll, inventory, or charge account processing have opportunities to alter records, and these may present unusual temptations for theft or misappropriation of funds. For one thing they often have an overview of the data processing operation which makes it possible, in falsifying ledger entries, to change the related entries so as to preserve the consistency of the accounting system. For another, their work is seldom checked in detail by others.

One example of what can occur is the case which led, in January 1967, to the prosecution of a programmer who worked for the National City Bank of Minneapolis. In June 1966, he found himself in financial difficulty. It was relatively easy for him to insert a patch in the banking program, to prevent his checking account, which he maintained with the bank, from being shown as overdrawn. Success led him to continue the deception, and by September 1966 he was overdrawn by $1357, and the "temporary" patch was still in the program. He was discovered when the computer failed one day and a manual operation was carried out.[11]

Van Tassel[12] lists instances of frauds, pointing out that most computer frauds are discovered by accident, and that it is impossible to know how many incidents are never reported in order to avoid publicity. So far relatively few instances of fraud committed by programmers have been reported but the number is bound to grow, especially if we are moving

[11] This case was reported in the Minneapolis Tribune, October 13, 1966. It was prosecuted under Title 18, United States Code 1005 in the United States District Court, Minneapolis.

[12] D. Van Tassel, "Computer Security Management." Prentice-Hall, Englewood Cliffs, New Jersey, 1972 (see Chapter 1).

to the cashless society forecast by many.[13] Although new methods of auditing have to be developed and the rules of evidence relating to machine-readable records have yet to be fully defined, present laws against theft and fraud apply to crimes where computers are involved.

Unauthorized Use or Destruction of Information

We have already seen in the discussions on privacy that in most installations, analysts, programmers, and operators have easy access to personal information such as salaries, medical histories, and employee ratings. It is inevitable that there will be abuses from such access, abuses which could result in gossip, slander, and even blackmail. In Section 4.5 we discussed ways for minimizing the dangers.

Appropriation of Programs

In Section 10.3 it was noted that the legal position with regard to ownership of computer programs is still to be determined in most countries. When purchasing or leasing systems, the customer is usually asked to agree that he will not transfer the program to a third party. But such agreements are difficult to enforce, especially in view of the unclear situation with respect to ownership of programs.[14] Although it is difficult to know to what extent a programmer who transfers from one company to a competitor can be prevented from applying his knowledge in the new situation, there have been prosecutions for theft of programs (see Threat Monitoring, Section 4.5).

Exaggerated Claims

In every human endeavor there are some who make exaggerated claims for their products and skills. Many have captured the public imagination by suggesting that they can solve problems with computers which are,

[13] For further examples of programmer fraud see R. N. Freed, Computer fraud—A management trap, *Business Horizons*, June (1969). For a discussion of the trend to the cashless society see M. Greenberger, Banking and the information utility, *Computers and Automation*, pp. 28–31, April (1965), or A. Anderson, The credit card society, *in* "The Computer Impact" (I. Taviss, ed.), pp. 93–103. Prentice-Hall, Englewood Cliffs, New Jersey, 1970.

[14] One case of suspected theft has occurred in the State of California (January, 1971). A software company, Information Systems Design, has charged (under California Penal Code Section 499c dealing with Theft of Trade Secrets) that their confidential program for remote plotting was illegally accessed and copied from a remote terminal by a consultant to the Shell Corporation which utilizes the services of Information Systems Design. *Computer World*, March 10 (1971). For additional cases see Freed (1969, section I-61).

with our present state of knowledge, intractable—for example, automate a large library, translate natural languages, or make difficult managerial decisions. At what point does optimistic enthusiasm become irresponsible exaggeration? or deliberate deceit? What measure of responsibility should be expected from systems analysts and programmers in their dealings with politicians and managers, when they are engaged in their professional task of planning computing applications? How well should any hardware or software be tested before a company makes its product public?

Companies which market computing equipment and services naturally attempt to protect themselves against possible action for damages arising out of claims that they have misrepresented their products. For example, the IBM software contract contains clauses which limit liability to the amount paid for use of the program, and which state that IBM will not be responsible for consequential damages, that is, costs incurred because failure of the software caused subsequent injuries or loss. Traditionally the courts have not allowed such disclaimer clauses to protect a vendor when there is clear evidence that his product failed to meet its implied performance standard. In the case of computers there have been a few successful suits for both hardware and software failures, but it is far from clear when a performance level is not legally met.[15]

A particular form of exaggerated claim which has resulted in hardship to many is practiced by certain private data processing schools. In many cities in North America and elsewhere, there are schools which promise good jobs to persons with little formal training by offering what amounts to a few weeks of exposure to punched card machines or primitive data processing equipment. The victims are often unemployed, who can ill afford the wasted fees.

Quite aside from practices which border on fraud, there are examples of applications of computers which give one pause to think. What are the legal and ethical situations when computers are used to sell handwriting and character analyses or horoscopes? What is the validity of computer programs for career guidance, dating, and matchmaking? A careful examination of certain computer efforts at job counseling reveals that they do in fact make use of the best techniques available by use of in-depth questionnaires. But is this also true of programs which claim to do character and personality analysis? And if it is not, should there be restrictions against marketing such products?

Unfortunately, it is easier to describe instances of unacceptable performance or unethical behavior than to give workable guidelines which

[15] For a summary on liability see Freed (1968, section I-AR).

can be applied in specific cases. With hindsight, we can analyze errors or misuse, but the experience gained from dependable, effective systems is not always applicable in a new situation.

AFIPS has undertaken a program to systematize review procedures for large-scale EDP systems,[16] with special emphasis on systems in the public interest. The proposal is to build up from specific experiences a base of questions to be asked, good practices, and ideal concepts. System review manuals are to be produced and the aim is to have a set of standards applicable to a wide range of systems and stages of development. There is the hope that eventually these efforts could lead to an accepted methodology of program certification.

Ordinary mistakes, poor planning, deceit, fraud—none of these is unique to computing. The fact that a programming error or a power failure can cause an unfortunate or even dangerous disruption in society is as much a reflection of the general reliance on technology as it is of the failure to provide adequate back-up mechanisms.[17] Nevertheless, we do our best to focus responsibility; individuals and firms can be held responsible for cases of malpractice in medicine, law, accountancy, and other professions, and if a computing profession emerges, it must expect to be held responsible for its performance. Large and complex systems, dependent upon the efforts of many programmers and systems analysts, complicate the problem of individual responsibility, but the concepts of modular design indicate that it is not impossible to assess responsibility.

As already stated in our discussion on privacy, something stronger than a code of ethics adopted by a professional society will be needed. Some of the problems cited above lie well within the domain of present laws and practices—certainly those dealing with financial records do. The extent to which the computing profession can be held strictly accountable for its claims and conduct will in the long run be determined by the courts as the laws with regard to breach of contract and fraudulent misrepresentations are applied to computer situations. Because information processing is a relatively new field, for many situations the boundaries between what is fair, what is misleading but should not be prohibited by law, and what is deceitful to the point of being fraudulent are still being drawn. For the protection of individual privacy, we will need laws which establish safeguards against the misuse of information. To protect

[16] "AFIPS System Improvements Activities," broadcast letter from G. A. Gosden, Montvale, New Jersey, April 5, 1972. See also Draft code of good practice, *Comput. Bull.* **16**, 52–62 (1972).

[17] One example occurred when $290,000 in tax revenue was lost to a small community because of keypunch and programming errors. See *Computerworld*, p. 3, June 7 (1972).

against misappropriation of programs we may need to copyright or patent certain kinds of software. To ensure that systems work as promised, we will need warranties for both software and hardware. For these cases, and in numerous other situations, the law will have to evolve to take account of the changing information technology. Professional organizations or national information processing societies can play an important but not unique role in the evolution of the laws needed to ensure acceptable standards of performance.

12.3. Social Responsibilities

It is not sufficient to discuss responsibility in the narrow professional sense. What is the social responsibility of a scientist, engineer, or any professional? Does it go beyond giving the best service possible to one's client, employer, or country? This question has been raised throughout modern history, but especially in the twentieth century. In the context of war crimes, the Nuremberg trials at the conclusion of World War II were an unequivocal statement that men are held responsible for their part in crimes against humanity even when their actions are directed by higher authorities (i.e., the government). But perhaps righteousness is a prerogative of the victorious. Can we interpret the spirit of the Nuremberg trials in the present context of the moral and social problems (in war or peace) posed by our technology?

More than 25 years after Nuremberg, issues of social responsibility are far from resolved. Among scientists and engineers, two opposing viewpoints are frequently advanced. One opinion holds that the underlying goal of science and technology is to improve the "quality of life." This implies that those closest to the technology have a special *obligation* to question the uses and consequences of their work, to exert as much beneficial influence as possible, to direct technological development and its application, and even to refuse to work on projects deemed not socially constructive. This view is certainly not new, but it has become more and more prominent since the end of World War II, especially during the last decade. Well-articulated statements of this position span two decades in the *Bulletin of the Atomic Scientist.* Many scientific journals have lately been examining these issues; some (e.g., *Science, Environment*) devote sections to discussions of social consequences, and numerous books calling for social responsibility have been written.[18] There is also

[18] For example: (1) "The Social Responsibility of the Scientist" (M. Brown, ed.). The Free Press, New York, 1971; (2) H. L. Nieburg, "In the Name of Science." Quadrangle Books, Chicago, Illinois, 1966; (3) R. E. Lapp, "The New Priesthood." Harper, New York, 1965.

a growing number of groups (e.g., Scientists and Engineers for Social and Political Action, The Committee for Social Responsibility in Engineering, Computer People for Peace) which hold to this position over a broad political spectrum.

The other school of thought also subscribes to belief in the ultimate social benefits of technology. But the view here is that the scientist has no special *rights,* beyond that of any citizen, in determining the uses for his work. Science is (or at least it is argued, should be) neutral, and so must be the scientist. Society alone must decide the direction of the technology. In an extreme statement of this position, the scientist Ernst Chain[19] speaks ot the scientist's role: "I believe that the responsibility is not his, but society's. He has no choice but to assist his nation . . . . Obviously, the scientists cannot be held responsible for the obnoxious effects of their inventions . . . . It is up to society, not to its scientists, to take legal measures to protect privacy and to prevent pollution of the air, water and soil . . . ." Beyond any political or ethical values, Toffler[20] is probably correct when he observes that scientists are often "more interested in the nature of their work than in the success of the project or the ultimate end to which their contributions are put."

Of course, there are all shades of variations and compromises between these positions. Almost everyone subscribes to the opinion that the scientist does have an obligation to keep the public informed of the nature of his work and its possible consequences, and that the scientific ethic demands a search for "truth." But the scientist's role is complicated by the fact that almost all research and development is funded by government or by large industries. Even as the scientific revolution was just beginning Francis Bacon foresaw this institutionalization of science to be inevitable.[21] Paul Goodman[22] and others can only conclude that science has come under political, military, and economic control. While it is true that scientists have, like anybody else, always been under political, religious, and economic pressures, Goodman warns that the subtle and overt pressures today are more controlling than ever before. For example, in 1965, the United States Federal Government spent 16.1 billion dollars for research and development. What is significant is that 7.3 billion came from the Department of the Defense, 5.3 from NASA, 1.5 from

[19] E. Chain, "Social Responsibility and the Scientist in Modern Western Society." The Council of Christians and Jews, London, England, 1970.

[20] "Values and the Future" (K. Baier and N. Rescher, eds.), p. 25. Free Press, New York, 1969.

[21] See Chapter 5 in L. Mumford's "The Myth of the Machine—The Pentagon of Power." Harcourt, New York, 1967, for a discussion of Bacon's insights.

[22] "Like a Conquered Province." Vintage Books, New York, 1968. See also, Can technology be humane, in Brown (1971, pp. 247–265).

the Atomic Energy Commission, and only two billion from the department of Health, Education, and Welfare.[23] Given this type of funding, can scientific research really be neutral? Nieburg makes the accusation explicit when he argues that science has been nationalized—that science and technology are instruments of policy and the contract is the means of directing the policy.[24]

If we accept the thesis (of Bell, Drucker, Galbraith, and others—see Chapter 11) that organization and technical knowledge have become the new strategic factors and power gravitates to the most strategic factor, then the question of how to discharge responsibility becomes that much more urgent for those who have the new power. Any proposal for solutions to a social, economic, or political problem is more and more likely to contain important considerations of technical capabilities. Can the scientist resist the temptation to impart his own biases in giving his technical assessment? Can the expert give his honest opinion without fear of reprisals in the form of loss of funding?

Computers have been used by the United States as a new instrument in the Southeast Asian air war, and as instruments of research have been vital elements in the production of nuclear missiles and other war materials. Computers have also become a central element in police surveillance systems. Do the logical and moral consequences of a code of ethics demand that the professional societies discuss these activities and issue their official approval or disapproval if there is a consensus? Or would such action represent an unfair use of expertise? For example, to those not in the medical profession, it would seem an intolerable misuse of power if doctors refused to practice in order to prevent increasing socialization of medical care, even if their actions were based on sincere convictions about the inferior quality of socialized medicine.

Engineers and scientists are often advised to pass professional judgment only on issues within their technical competence, to separate their citizen and professional roles.[25] But the line between technical judgment and social–political opinion is not as clear as one might wish. There are few guidelines to distinguish between what is impossible and what is unlikely, between what will not work as proposed and what cannot be

[23] The DOD, government and universities, by Lange, *in* "The Social Responsibility of the Scientist" (Brown, 1971, p. 61). Lange obtained these figures from the Committee on Government Operations, House Report 1158, October 1965.

[24] H. L. Nieburg, "In the Name of Science," Quadrangle Books, Chicago, Illinois, 1966.

[25] Recall Robert Hooke's famous injunction to scientists in 1665. "To improve the knowledge of all natural things, and all useful arts, Manufactures, Mechanik Practices, Engines and Inventions by Experiment (not meddling with Divinity, Metaphysics, Morals, Politicks, Grammar, Rhetoric or Logick)." See E. S. Hischocks, Organization of science in the United Kingdom, *Science* **129**, 689–693 (1959).

made to work. Inevitably, conscious and unconscious biases affect these technical judgments.

An interesting study of the conflicts relating to social responsibility can be found in the McCracken (1971) discussion of the formation of Computer Professionals Against the ABM and his testimony before the United States Senate. The specific technical issue raised by this group, which includes many leaders in the computer field, is whether the complex of computer programs required for this massive real-time system (ABM) could be made to work as proposed. They argue that the experience of large computer operating systems and other real-time systems indicates that in such complex projects the concept of success must be clearly defined, the nature of the use must be well understood, and the system must be tested and retested in the actual environment as well as in simulated experiments. These necessary conditions, they argue, are not possible with the ABM, and hence their contention that computing capabilities have been grossly overestimated in the plans for developing antiballistic missile systems.[26]

McCracken openly admits, however, that other considerations played a part in the formation and arguments of the Computer Professionals Against the ABM. For various social, economic, and political reasons, they question the very *purpose* of the development and its effect on national priorities. McCracken describes the conflicts well. There are arguments for and against the formation of such a group along the lines previously discussed; that is, should professionals organize to influence the political process? In addition, we see the difficulties facing the decision-maker who is trying to obtain expert testimony. What are the vested interests of those who testify? When does technical fact give way to technical prediction, then speculation, and finally to opinions not primarily based on technical considerations?

We have already discussed (Section 11.4) the influence of scientific experts on the political process. The general conclusion was that the power of the technologist is effective in day-to-day administration, within both government and industry, rather than in overt public deci-

[26] For a concise argument of why ABM will not work see H. Grosch, Why MAC, MIS, and ABM won't fly (or, sage "advice to the ambitious"), *Datamation,* November (1971). J. Weizenbaum [On the impact of the computer on society, *Science* **176**, May (1972)] extends this distrust to all gigantic systems. He argues that by the time such systems are ready to be used, most of the original programmers have left the project, the system has become incomprehensible to those dependent on it, and it becomes increasingly difficult if not impossible to introduce modifications. Current operating systems provide a good example, and although there is evidence that a better operating system design is possible, Weizenbaum's mistrust of large and sensitive systems in the public domain is well taken.

sions. But technical and administrative decisions can evolve into established standards and guidelines, and it is difficult to assess the full effect of the status quo in making major decisions. Moreover, in specific issues such as the ABM, there is reason to believe that critical scientific groups have had a strong, although in this case not decisive, influence on the Senate vote.[27] We are often reminded that the influence of atomic scientists was decisive (in the United States) in having nuclear research placed under direct civilian (AEC) rather than military control.[28]

Computer specialists have testified on a number of other controversial proposals including widely publicized hearings on data banks and urban transportation. In different areas of science biologists, chemists, and physicists voice their views of the ecological necessities. The social impact of science has become an accepted subject of discussion at national meetings of scientific organizations, and there have been occasions when the topic has gone into areas which are clearly political. At meetings of the American Association for the Advancement of Science, the American Mathematical Society, the American Physical Society, and the Association for Computing Machinery issues such as the conduct of the Viet Nam war, racism, and the boycott of meeting places to protest police behavior have been raised and discussed with fervor. Internationally there has been a public debate on the desirability of avoiding scientific meetings in countries which are dictatorial or authoritarian.[29] Generally speaking, the scientific societies have rejected political issues as not being within their sphere of interests, but there has been a widening in the scope of subjects that are regarded as germane. Thus discussions of government funding, employment opportunities, educational programs, and impact on society are frequently found on conference agenda and in publications. Those wishing to express themselves at a more political level have formed ad hoc groups or special organizations to do so.[30] Independent of the viewpoints expressed, we believe that special advocacy groups (like the Computer Professionals Against the ABM) play a valid and important role in our present democratic process.

[27] See Charles Schwartz's account of political action by physicists and other scientists against the ABM in Brown (1971, pp. 19–35).

[28] Space exploration followed this precedent and was also placed under civilian control.

[29] For an account of these, with details on the debates as they occurred in the American Physical Society, see Friedlander (1972), "The Conduct of Science."

[30] One reason national societies are hesitant to become involved in political issues in the United States is that such a move would jeopardize the societies tax-free status, and might endanger research funding for individual members. There is also a widespread feeling that there are other avenues by which individuals can express their political convictions. Technical, scientific, and professional organizations, for reasons which have some historical justification, tend to be conservative.

Committees on the social implications of computers have been formed in the computer societies of all the English-speaking countries, and also in other countries and in the International Federation for Information Processing. These committees do not elicit the active support of the majority of members, but there is a considerable literature being generated on subjects within their interests. While it is not likely that they will turn to politically charged questions, the domain of subjects considered to be legitimate is being enlarged. The influence exerted on computing by certain companies and industries (e.g., by IBM, the common carriers, or the banking industry), the definition of the public interest, and the desirability and direction of government intervention are examples of controversial subjects which should and are likely to receive more attention.

In summary, it would be wrong to suggest that computer organizations are becoming highly politicized. But like other technical, scientific, and professional organizations, they are moving away from a traditional laissez-faire attitude to a more active position on the implications of their discipline.

Bibliography

AFIPS (1970). "Professionalism in the Computer Field," AFIPS Press, Montvale, New Jersey.

Amer. Assoc. Advan. Sci. (1972). "Science for Society: A Bibliography," 3rd ed. Washington, D. C.

Brown, M., ed. (1971). "The Social Responsibility of the Scientist." The Free Press, New York.

Bulletin of the Atomic Scientist (monthly). Chicago, Illinois.

Communications of the Association for Computing Machinery (monthly). New York.

Computers and Automation (monthly). Berkeley Enterprises, Inc., Newtonville, Massachusetts.

Freed, R. N. (1968). "Materials and Cases on Computers and Law," 2nd ed. Boston Univ. Bookstore, Boston, Massachusetts.

Friedlander, M. W. (1972). "The Conduct of Science." Prentice-Hall, Englewood Cliffs, New Jersey.

McCracken, D. D. (1971). "The Public Policy and the Expert" with commentary by Bruce Arden, Victor Ferkiss, and Roger Shinn. The Council on Religion and Internat. Affairs, Spec. Stud. #212, New York.

Vollmer, H. M., and Mills, D. Z., eds. (1966). "Professionalization." Prentice-Hall, Englewood Cliffs, New Jersey.

Problems and Further Work

1. Computerized tests and computer programs are used and advocated for career guidance. See, for example,

M. Katz, W. Chapman, and W. Godwin: SIGI: A computer-based aid to career decision-making, *Educom* **7**, 12–18 (1972).

What scientific basis is there to justify such an application? Are there ethical or moral considerations involved? Do ethical considerations arise in the use of computers for dating or for choice of a spouse? For casting horoscopes? What arguments are there for and against prohibiting such uses of computers or declining to work on such applications? (See also problem 5, Chapter 5.)

2. During the late 1960s a rosy future was predicted for computerized management information systems. Large systems with integrated data bases would provide valid and timely data to make planning, program evaluation, and policy formulation more effective than ever before. In large measure these systems failed to materialize. Discuss the reasons. Should the failure be regarded as nonprofessional behavior on the part of computer manufacturers, salesmen, consultants, and systems programmers? What steps might be taken to avoid wholesale disillusionment in the future? See the references cited in footnote 14, Chapter 7, and footnote 33, Chapter 11; also,

C. H. Kriebel, MIS technology—A view of the future, *AFIPS Conf. Proc.* **40**, 1173–1180 (1972).

3. Consider some position related to the computing field (e.g., chief operator, data processing applications programmer, senior systems programmer). Describe the duties for this position and design a test to be used as part of an accreditation program. Discuss the effectiveness of such tests.

4. Draw up a list of about 20 specific computer applications and rate them from −5 to +5 according to their social desirability in your opinion (cf. Table 6-5). Compare your ratings with those assigned by someone else. What guidelines are there in the computer Code of Ethics (ACM and BCS) about the propriety or impropriety of working on undesirable applications?

5. What distinctions, if any, can be drawn between ethics in the specific context of computers, "professional" ethics, and ethics in general? Give examples of questions which in your opinion are clearly in the different domains.

Chapter

13

VALUES, TECHNOLOGY, AND COMPUTERS

The effects of computers, automation, and technology can be grouped into intersecting domains of influence. While economic and political considerations may have the most obvious impact on our lives, the less immediate influences on our culture and values often have the most permanent effects. In this chapter, we explore the dynamic nature of values, with emphasis on the relationship between technology and values. We wish to focus attention on the complexity of current value systems and on the fears experienced by critics of technological society. We conclude with some thoughts on the direction of values over the next generation.

13.1. The Nature of Values

In the realm of philosophy and theology there is no mistaking the centrality of values. They also underlie economics, law, political science, and sociology. Our concern is with the relationship of values to science and technology. Technology changes values but it does not destroy them.

Values are preferred outcomes or goals, but this is too simple a definition. They stem from human instincts and emotions and the necessities of social organization,[1] and we use them to formulate attitudes and goals which in turn determine behavior. But one must be cautious about inferring values from behavior; actions are the result of a complex interplay of instinct, emotion, biological and social necessities, and rational thought.

Valuation is a dynamic process. Value systems both produce and are produced by culture; they may change very slowly in comparison with technological change, but they are not eternal. They include not only beliefs and goals which are "universal" but also those operative only for specific cultures, economic or social classes, religions, subcultures, individuals. Values are local in time and space.[2]

But can we reject the notion of an "absolute" value, that is one which is true and valid whether or not it is held by any group, or must we retreat from the dynamic point of view and declare some values to be absolute? To accept absolutes has profound implications. It does not preclude the possibility that they can be reflected in different ways, but it does limit the effects of all changes dependent on science, technology, political–economic systems, population size, and other environmental factors.

The dilemma can be avoided by accepting the presence of a few "universal" values. The difference is more than semantic. Universal values are those that are perceived in some form and degree in *all existing* cultures. This definition acknowledges a certain strength and permanence to them, allowing for substantial differences among societies, but not closing the future to the possibility of complete change in the set of universal values.

What candidates are there for universal values? Indisputable ones are hard to find. First come those most directly associated with emotions and instincts: the desire for human friendships, intimacy, love. To these we should like to add *activeness*[3]; that is, the pursuit of a significant and creative life which transcends biological necessity. This short list does not mean that we are nearly valueless, but rather that our values are to a large extent social; they are largely determined by culture and environ-

[1] We reject the view that there can be no aggregate social values, that there are only subjective individual values.

[2] See C. Kluckhohn, The scientific study of values and contemporary civilization, *Zygon* no. 1, 230–240 (1966). He would say that only "cultural values" are local in time and space; we view universal and individual values in the same way.

[3] See E. Fromm, (1968) for an extensive discussion of this value.

ment. Boulding sees them as another and very essential set of learned preferences.[4]

The concepts of self-reliance, privacy, and other values which emphasize individuality are *not* present in all cultures; nor is the respect for tradition or the quest for rationally confirmable "truth" universally valued. Truth, justice, honor, tolerance, trust, and regard for originality are *cultural* values. In a similar way economic values, the desires for success, fame, and material possessions are not universal, nor is patriotism; all these are often debatable within any society.

A value system, then, is a complex ordering of universal, group, and individual values, not all of which need be consistent.

In studying the relationship between technologies and values, several writers have expressed the belief that a "science of values" is possible.[5] Rescher[6] suggests the following approach: Identify the various ways in which values can be upgraded or downgraded and the forces which can bring about such change, viewing the changes within a cost/benefit framework; that is, measure how technology and other changes force change in the cost of pursuing a given value relative to its benefits. A number of diverse modes of upgrading (downgrading) are specified.

- Acquisition (abandonment) is the most extreme change.
- Increased (decreased) distribution refers to who will be pursuing the value.
- Rescaling upward (downward) is perhaps the most important mode of change. The concern here is with the extent of commitment to the value and with the relative scale of commitments which determines a value system; in other words, how much energy and resources are we willing to invest to maintain, realize, and propagate a given value, and what rewards and sanctions will be applied to ensure compliance.
- Widening (narrowing) redeployment indicates a change in how a value is applied; what cases fall under its operative scope.

[4] K. Boulding, "The Interplay of Technology and Values," in Baier and Rescher (1969).

[5] One of the strongest statements to this effect can be found in H. Sackman, "Computers, System Science, and Evolving Society." Wiley, New York, 1967. Sackman argues that an applied science of values is part of the philosophy of American Pragmatism and he states the following (p. 530): "Viewed as working hypotheses, and cast in operationally specified system contexts, ethics and values are in fact amenable to scientific inquiry—serious experimental endeavor in live social settings along these lines is well within our grasp and is long overdue."

[6] N. Rescher, "What is Value Change? A Framework for Research," in Baier and Rescher (1969).

• Raising (lowering) standards appears to be a most common mode of change. Here we observe that our standards of how successfully a value is being pursued are constantly changing.

Upgrading and downgrading result from a number of forces, including new scientific knowledge, economic and technological change, and ideological and political change. Rescher believes that the cost/benefit approach is particularly attractive to economic, technological, and demographic changes because, compared with scientific discoveries and political changes, they are readily foreseen.

One example of Rescher will help to clarify his framework. In an age of exceedingly explosive and destructive weapons systems, the cost in dollars and fears of maintaining nationalism through military superiority exceeds any realistic appraisal of the benefits involved. Hence it would appear that inevitably, one or more of the following changes must occur: Nationalism is downgraded by an actual rescaling; a redeployment is affected in that nationalism becomes more closely associated with economic or health indicators or even success in Olympic competition; standards are lowered so that superiority may mean just one extra missile.

Not everyone agrees that a science of values is possible. We do not wish to imply that the cost/benefit analysis just illustrated is capable of producing a strict functional relationship between every technological development and the values affected by it. Rather it should be considered as a complement to the System of Social Accounts proposed by Bell,[7] and as a very preliminary attempt to rationalize the study of value change; as such it can be useful.

13.2. Technologies and Values

During the nineteenth century, a great debate focused on values and economic systems. Marx presented the view that the systems of production determine values, while Weber argued that values were primary in shaping the economic system. The same debate exists in our context: Does technology determine values or do values direct technology? Which is primary? Bronowski sees science as the main determinant of modern

[7] D. Bell, Notes on the post-industrial society II, *The Public Interest*, no. 7, 102–118 (1967). A System of Social Accounts is needed to provide a more complete definition of "economic progress," including social costs and net returns (e.g., pollution costs, effects on social mobility, etc.). See also R. Bauer (ed.), "Social Indicators." MIT Press, Cambridge, Massachusetts, 1966; M. Olson, "Toward a Social Report." Dept. of Health, Education, and Welfare, Washington, D. C. (1969); and Anderson (1968).

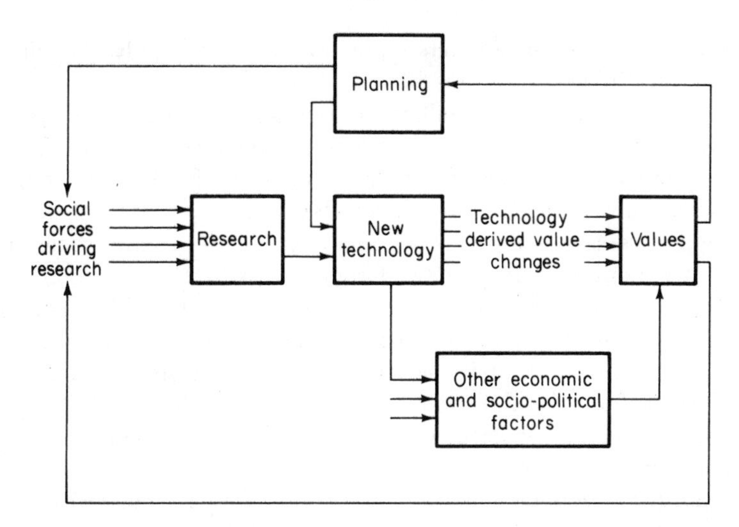

FIG. 13-1. *The feedback between technology and values. (Reprinted with permission of The Macmillan Company from T. Gordon, The feedback between technology and values in "Values and the Future" (K. Baier and N. Rescher, eds.) Free Press, New York, 1969. Copyright 1969 by The Free Press, division of The Macmillan Company.)*

values, and Hazard identifies the main technological developments which he claims are changing present beliefs. On the other hand, de Jouvenal and Powelson assert the primacy of values.[8] Boulding and Toffler correctly dismiss this as a chicken-and-egg question; they and others (Gordon, Heilbroner, Mesthene) call attention to the continuing effect values and technology have on each other without worrying about the question of primacy[9] (see Fig. 13-1).

Society must obviously place a high value on progress, innovation, production, and verifiable knowledge if it is to continue the present rate of scientific and technological development successfully. We have already commented (in Chapter 12) on the institutionalization of science and technology. Massive support of research and development by government and industry reflects deliberate decisions about national goals. If, as is hoped, our planning should become more open and value

[8] J. Bronowski, "Science and Human Values." Harper, New York, 1965; L. Hazard, "Challenges for Urban Policy," B. de Jouvenal, "Technology as a Means," and J. Powelson, "Economic Attitudes in Latin America and the United States," all in Baier and Rescher (1969).

[9] K. Boulding, "The Emerging Superculture," T. Gordon, "The Feedback between Technology and Values," and A. Toffler, "Values Impact Forecaster," all in Baier and Rescher (1969); R. Heilbroner, Do machines make history? *Technol. and Culture,* **8,** 335–345 (1967); E. Mesthene, "Technological Change—Its Impact on Man and Society." Harvard Univ. Press, Cambridge, Massachusetts, 1970.

oriented, it will become much more important to study the effect of values on technology.

Science has had dramatic effects on our world view. The Copernican universe led to an entirely new, less egocentric concept of man. But from another point of view, the accumulation of scientific discoveries has led man to see himself as the controller rather than, as in ancient times, the controlled object of nature. More recently the destructive potential of modern weapons and imprudent tampering with the environment are forcing recognition that man must coexist with nature. As another example of how science changes man's outlook, our world view is not as rigid and deterministic as it was in the eighteenth and nineteenth centuries, but rather probabilistic; this is largely due to twentieth century developments in the physical sciences and the subsequent development of probability and statistical theory.

At least three general scientific fields are acting as major contributors to current value change: biology–medicine, transportation–communication, and computing–automation. We have only to list some of the major developments in the field of biomedicine to sense their impact: Contraceptives, transplants, genetic engineering, and the theory of evolution have all acted to challenge established views on the inviolability and uniqueness of human life. Perhaps the most value-charged development is the possibility of using biomedical techniques to achieve change and control of behavior. We speak here not only of "nonprofessional" drug experimentation but also of the frightening suggestions with regard to personality control made by psychologists such as Skinner.[10]

Technology has had its most pronounced impact indirectly through change in the social structure; for it was the combined technologies (industrialization) which induced urbanization, the effects of which are still being experienced. But as is often pointed out, in spite of all their ill effects industrialization and urbanization spelled the end of serfdom and the beginning of mass political realization. It is ironic that they can now be regarded as a threat to human dignity, a value whose operative strength is due largely to the political freedom technology helped realize.

When we come to study the effect of more recent technologies, while almost everyone agrees that the telephone, television, and so on, have had a profound value impact, it is not so clear what the main effects have been. Television may be making us more insensitive to violence,

[10] B. F. Skinner, "Walden II." Macmillan, New York, 1948. See "Freedom and the Control of Men," in Burke (1966) for a short justification of the "disutopia" proclaimed in "Walden II." Also B. F. Skinner, "Beyond Freedom and Dignity." Knopf, New York, 1971.

cruelty, and death. But it may also be true that modern communications and transportation are leading to a greater tolerance of different value systems; as never before, we are in contact with diverse cultures and systems of belief. Communications may be producing more homogenized tastes; on the other hand, they tend to heighten value conflict in the sense that the confrontations between reality and principle become more visible. In general, communications (and transportation) seem to act in favor of flexibility and mobility over security and stability. The controversial work of McLuhan[11] is perhaps best viewed as a set of probes about the extent to which media shape culture.

Computers and automation are seen by many as the most serious threat to traditional values. They provide the ultimate rationale for precision and efficiency, the new aesthetic which critics see as a dominating force in current behavior and planning. To Mumford and Ellul,[12] *efficiency and technique* in producing have become more important than man, the supposed object of the services and goods. Man has become preoccupied with toolmaking; he has erected new gods: calculability, probability, factuality, efficiency. In this ontological perspective, man has lost sight of his own role, the process takes on its own life and becomes worshiped for itself. The more humanistic values have become downgraded in favor of technique.

Is this a correct assessment? Because of the inadequate framework for studying value changes, only the most circumstantial evidence can be offered for or against the Mumford–Ellul hypothesis. It may be interesting to note that in the previously mentioned AFIPS/Time survey (see Chapter 6), while attitudes about the consequences of computers were generally positive, 54% of the respondents did believe that "computers are dehumanizing people and turning them into numbers." But we seriously question the adequacy of public opinion surveys in assessing value change. On the humanistic side, there is scattered evidence in transportation planning, employment practices, and so on, that narrowly constructed efficiency criteria may not govern; the finality of computer output does not go unchallenged. Perhaps the warnings have had some effect.

Computers have challenged yet another of man's concepts about life by undermining the cherished conviction that intelligence is a unique

[11] M. McLuhan, "The Gutenberg Galaxy." Univ. of Toronto Press, Toronto, 1962; "Understanding Media: The Extensions of Man." McGraw-Hill, New York, 1964.

[12] L. Mumford (1967, 1970); J. Ellul, "The Technological Society." Knopf, New York, 1964. We follow Ellul's use of "technique" to mean more than just machines; it is also organization and the whole way of thinking and doing things.

human quality.[13] Although we have argued (in Chapter 8) that artificial intelligence has not yet become a serious competitor to human intelligence, predictions to the contrary can have a real effect. The seeds of doubt have been planted when Minsky writes: "There is no reason to suppose that machines have any limitations not shared by man."[14] Does that make us try to emphasize our emotions more and surround basic values with mystery so as to reassure ourselves that human existence is still unique?

The most direct impact of computers and automation is on values associated with employment and activity. In Chapter 9, we observed that the present "facts" of automation contradict many myths. Automation has not brought massive unemployment; with automation, alienation in work can be decreased (from that induced by earlier mechanization) if, as can happen, individual responsibility and knowledge of the entire operation increase; and completely automated processes are by far still the exception.

The evidence that automation will not, in time, bring about widespread unemployment is less convincing. While unemployment rates remain fairly constant, productivity rates continue their gradual steady increase and the average workweek continues its gradual steady decrease. The possibility that large segments of the work force will be replaced by machines, that work will be the privilege of the elite, still persists as a nagging, if remote, fear. We are less and less inclined to explain or justify our "human purpose" by the work we do. The Work Ethic represents the value we place on work, and the unknown potential of computers and automation challenges it. Can activity other than work provide a truly human existence? To many this question is *the* central issue in automation and no study of values can avoid discussing the meaning of leisure.

[13] This theme of fundamental challenges to man's identity is developed by a number of authors. Mazlish [see The fourth discontinuity, *Technol. and Culture* **8**, 1–15 (1967)] views the man–machine confrontation as another artificial discontinuity which will be discarded (in favor of symbiosis) in the same way that the discontinuities between man and the universe, between man and the primates, between man and his compulsions were discarded. Our point is that man's self-image was (at least initially) diminished by the discoveries of Copernicus, Darwin, and Freud.

[14] M. Minsky, "Computation: Finite and Infinite Machines," p. vii. Prentice-Hall, Englewood Cliffs, New Jersey, 1967. Minsky's more provocative statement that "the brain is merely a meat machine" has attracted considerable attention. J. Weizenbaum [see On the impact of computer on society, *Science* **176**, 609–614 (1972)] believes that the fact such a statement has caused so much excitement is evidence that we are now at the beginning of "a crisis in the mental life of our civilization"; man's image of himself is in serious danger.

13.3. Leisure

The modern problem of leisure is twofold: first, there is the potential for greatly increased leisure for many, if not most, segments of society; second, the importance of leisure is magnified by the role it may have to play in replacing work as a purposeful activity.

The use of the word *potential* should be noted. Despite early predictions, a mass leisure class is still conjecture, not reality. Table 13-1 shows the gradual but significant decline in the United States for the average number of hours worked per week from 1850 to 1960. Since 1890, the average workweek has been decreasing by 3.5 hours/week every decade. The possibility that many will eventually have large amounts of leisure cannot be ruled out.

Extrapolations of the trend are provocative. Kahn and Wiener[15] project an 1100 working hour year with less than 150 working days of 7.5 hours. A reduction in the number of working days could take the form of a shorter workweek or a longer vacation or sabbatical.

There are alternatives to fewer working days, for example, a shorter working day or earlier retirement. Kreps[16] speculates on these: by 1985, the workweek could drop to 22 hours, there could be 27 full-time (=37.5 hours) workweeks per year, or at 50 full-time weeks per year retirement at age 38 could become common. A definite possibility is that workers will be spending significant periods between jobs in retraining. Wilensky[17] reminds us that this is not the first time in history that there have been large amounts of free time. Recently, free time has only been increasing since the mid-nineteenth century and the trend could be reversed.

The amount of free time and how it is used depends on social class, educational level, financial assets, nationality, religion, geographic region, and age. Wilensky and de Grazia[18] are concerned that free time will come first to those least prepared to cope with it. Clerical workers, craftsmen, factory workers, and non-farm laborers are the occupations in which free time is increasing; the professional and managerial classes

[15] H. Kahn, and A. J. Wiener (1967).

[16] Testimony given by Juanita Kreps to U. S. Senate Special Committee on Aging, see M. Kaplan, Leisure as an issue for the future, *Future* **1** (1), 91–99 (1968).

[17] H. Wilensky, Uneven distribution of leisure: The impact of economic growth on 'Free Time,' *Social Probl.*, pp. 33–35, Summer (1964). Roman citizens had 175 no-work holidays per year. Of course, it is hard to gauge the average free time if the average includes both slaves and citizens.

[18] S. De Grazia, "Of Time, Work, and Leisure." Twentieth Century Fund, New York, 1962.

TABLE 13-1
LENGTH OF AVERAGE WORKWEEK IN AGRICULTURE AND IN NONAGRICULTURAL INDUSTRIES, 1850–1960[a]

Year	All industries	Agriculture	Nonagricultural industries
1850	69.7	72.0	65.7
1860	67.8	71.0	63.3
1870	65.3	70.0	60.0
1880	63.8	69.0	58.8
1890	61.7	68.0	57.1
1900	60.1	67.0	55.9
1910	54.9	65.0	50.3
1920	49.4	60.0	45.5
1930	45.7	55.0	43.2
1940	43.8	54.6	41.1
1941	44.2	53.2	42.2
1942	45.2	55.3	43.1
1943	47.3	58.5	45.1
1944	46.2	54.4	44.6
1945	44.3	50.6	43.1
1946	42.4	50.0	41.1
1947	41.7	48.8	40.5
1948	40.8	48.5	39.6
1949	40.2	48.1	39.0
1950	39.9	47.2	38.8
1951	40.4	47.9	39.4
1952	40.5	47.4	39.6
1953	40.0	47.9	39.2
1954	38.9	47.0	37.9
1955	39.7	46.5	38.9
1956	39.5	44.9	38.8
1957	39.1	44.2	38.6
1958	38.6	43.7	38.1
1959	38.5	43.8	38.0
1960	38.5	44.0	38.0

[a] Reprinted with the permission from S. de Grazia, "Of Time, Work, and Leisure." The Twentieth Century Fund, New York, 1962. Copyright 1962 by The Twentieth Century Fund.

often work disproportionally long hours. Kaplan suggests that not only the various segments of the labor force but also the different unions will approach the alternatives of free time and leisure in basically different ways.[19]

It should be apparent that most definitions of leisure stem from persons belonging to approximately the same class (academics, psycholo-

[19] M. Kaplan, "Leisure as an issue for the Future," *Future* 1 (1), 91–99 (1968).

gists, economists, etc.). Leisure is to be distinguished from free time. For de Grazia, free time is any time not spent at work, but leisure is a freedom—it is the "freedom from the necessity of being occupied." It is inner-directed, the time for contemplation, music, philosophical discussion; leisure does not have to be constructive in societal terms, and leisure is not watching television, shopping, fixing up the house, keeping fit, or taking "adult education" classes—these activities fail to refresh the mind and soul and they are outer-directed by desire for social acceptance or better job opportunities. Using his rather elitist definition, de Grazia argues that leisure time has not increased appreciably. We do not have to accept his definition to agree that time spent waiting (traveling to and from work, queuing for recreational services) is hardly leisure, and we can at least appreciate Smigel's[20] point that compulsory mass education for utilitarian purposes is a form of work, not leisure.

Kranzberg[21] envisions leisure in a functional way. Recreation derives from the word *recreate*, so that leisure is the time to recreate one's skills, knowledge, and beliefs, to reemphasize individuality. In this way leisure can begin to replace work. For others, leisure fulfills the psychological necessity to find new commitments and affiliations.

In all these subjective opinions, there is little mention of pleasure, rest, time with family. And yet this is what leisure means to most people. Consider Faunce's[22] early survey of automobile workers. Asked to respond to a hypothetical increase in leisure time, they showed an almost unanimous desire to work around the house and spend more time with their families. These findings are confirmed in a more recent (1970) survey[23] conducted by Steele and Poor among (a different set of) workers in 13 plants which adopted a four-day workweek. Although there are some interesting differences from the results of Faunce (see Table 13-2), the emphasis is definitely on home relaxation (which of course includes watching television) and recreational activities. The interests of professional groups have been found to be distinctly different.[24] Whose in-

[20] E. O. Smigel, The leisure society, *in* "The Computer Impact" (I. Taviss, ed.). Prentice-Hall, Englewood Cliffs, New Jersey, 1970.

[21] M. Kranzberg, Technology and human values, *Virginia Quart. Rev.* **40** (4), 578–592 (1964); J. Dumazedier, "Toward a Society of Leisure," p. 236. Free Press, New York, 1967.

[22] W. A. Faunce, The automobile industry: A case study in automation, *in* "Automation and Society" (H. B. Jacobson and J. S. Roucek, eds.), Philosophical Library, New York, 1959.

[23] J. L. Steele and R. Poor, The reaction of people at 4-day firms, *in* "4 Days, 40 Hours—Reporting a Revolution in Work and Leisure" (R. Poor, ed.), pp. 105–122. Bursk and Poor Publ., Cambridge, Massachusetts, 1970. The firms surveyed included manufacturing, service, and retail organizations.

TABLE 13-2
USE OF INCREASED LEISURE[a,b]

Activities	Percents[c]	
	Faunce study (N = 125)	Four-day study (N = 138)
1. Work around the house	96.8	84.1
2. Spend time with family	76.8	73.9
3. Travel	53.6	52.9
4. Go to ballgames, fights, hockey games, etc.	48.8	27.5
5. Fishing and hunting	42.4	31.2
6. Other hobbies	25.6	35.6
7. Engage in some form of athletics (bowling, golf, baseball, etc.)	24.8	31.2
8. Read more	24.8	29.7
9. Go back to school or learned a trade	19.2	5.8
10. Active in school boards, P.T.A., Boy Scouts, etc.	17.6	10.1
11. Got another part-time job	16.8	16.7
12. Joined social club	15.2	8.0
13. Engaged in political action work	12.8	4.3
14. Rest, relax, loaf, etc.	11.2	69.6
15. Swimming, boating	4.8	48.6
16. Work on car	2.4	28.3
17. Church activities	1.6	10.1

[a] Reprinted with the permission of R. Poor, from J. L. Steele and R. Poor, The reaction of people at 4-day firms *in* "4 Days, 40 Hours—Reporting a Revolution in Work and Leisure" (R. Poor, ed.). Bursk & Poor, Cambridge, Massachusetts, 1970. Copyright 1970 by Bursk & Poor Publishing and 1972 by Pan Books Ltd.

[b] Proposed use of increased leisure time differs from actual use. People spend more time on unorganized or relaxed activities and less time on organized or disciplined ones.

[c] Entries denote the percentage of those surveyed who expected (achieved) regular participation in the indicated activity. N = number surveyed.

terests will be served if society (government) decides to plan for leisure? Leisure will most certainly be planned because many of the amenities needed (educational facilities, recreational areas, financial and physical access to services) are public goods.

There are serious doubts whether leisure can replace work as a source of activity in our present society. Fromm[25] believes that "if man is passive in the process of production and organization, he will also be passive

[24] For example, J. E. Gerstle, Leisure, taste, and occupational milieu, *Social Probl.*, p. 58, Summer (1961).

[25] E. Fromm (1968, p. 110).

during his leisure time." Reisman[26] agrees with Fromm that industrialization has not only reduced the meaning of work but at the same time has destroyed folk traditions which linked work and leisure and integrated leisure within the community framework. It is not so much the Puritan ethic but rather the loss of folk traditions which makes us cling to work. Leisure can only become more valuable if work becomes more challenging. This can occur only if work is reorganized to give employees more responsibility. But this reorganization that Fromm envisions may be too optimistic. Managers are much more willing to give away time and money than decision-making powers.

There can be no doubt that educational institutions are beginning to play a major role in the use of free time. Enrollment in part-time degree programs and in non-degree courses (photography, languages, etc.) shows an interest which goes beyond the immediate desires for job improvement and financial reward. And in spite of the work aspect of compulsory education, the reintegration of work and leisure (in the form of *self-directed* education) is consistent with the value of activity. Leisure must now be more than a job extension or restorative from work. Dubin's[27] study shows that industrial workers do not consider their central interest to be work, nor do they see their social relations stemming from work.

In the survey previously mentioned, Steele and Poor[28] report that 92% of the workers were pleased or very pleased about their new four-day week. Yet there have been and will probably continue to be rejections of increased leisure. Meyersohn[29] reports that one-third of the respondents (employees in a small manufacturing company) changed their initial acceptance of a four-day week when their "free Mondays" began to be filled with either boredom or household chores. Similarly, when 13-week sabbatical vacations (every five years) were arranged for senior steel-

[26] D. Reisman, "Leisure and Work in Post-Industrial Society," in Burke (1966). Wilensky also agrees that it is unrealistic to expect that creative leisure activities can compensate for unsatisfying work. See Work, careers, and leisure styles, summarized in "Harvard University Program on Technology and Society, 1964–1972, Final Review," pp. 140–147. Harvard Information Office, Cambridge, Massachusetts, 1972.

[27] R. Dubin, Industrial workers' world: A study of the central life interests of workers, *in* "Work and Leisure: A Contemporary Social Problem" (E. O. Smigel, ed.). New Haven College and Univ. Press, New Haven, Connecticut, 1963.

[28] G. Steele and R. Poor (see footnote 23). The general conclusions of "4 Days, 40 Hours—Reporting a Revolution in Work and Leisure" is that the four-day workweek is working well at most places. Customer dissatisfaction and economic hardships have, however, caused some firms to revert back to the longer week.

[29] R. Meyersohn, Changing work and leisure routines, *in* "Work and Leisure: a Contemporary Social Problem" (see footnote 27).

workers, this may have reflected the preferences of the union leadership more than those of the rank and file. In contracts where an alternative savings plan is offered, a majority are choosing money over the sabbatical.[30]

Rather than concluding that the "working class" has failed to cultivate the proper leisure tastes, it is more likely that what is lacking is adequate financial and recreational resources and compatibility with the work and school schedules of children and spouse. There are some serious doubts about government's ability to support a widespread leisure program adequately. Recall Armer's calculation, in Chapter 9, that 30 billion dollars would be needed for a one-year full-time continuing education program for 5% of the work force. Perhaps the computing technology will help by reducing the costs and availability of education (see Section 8.3). Illich,[31] one of the most provocative critics of education and contemporary society, sees computers as a tool in dispensing an open network of educational services. But continuing education, in any form, will not appeal to everyone. If the economics make it feasible, people may choose to participate in volunteer services. Some urbanites may want to grow their own food in a publicly provided agricultural oasis; others may be politically active in reviving a sense of local community. Some will seek increased cultural opportunities. The most immediate demands will most surely be for greater sporting and recreational services.

But in most parts of the world where the problems center on the provision of food and shelter, considerations of increased leisure are remote.

13.4. Value Conflict

Is today's society more alienated than ever before? It is more constructive to ask in what ways various individuals in the society feel alienated, what are the forces which cause or contribute to these feelings, and what changes can be made to improve the situation. We take the view that alienation is to a large extent the reflection of value conflict, and try to identify how present technology affects value conflict.

It is a clear fact that values are in conflict today, but this is hardly a unique feature of postindustrialized twentieth century society. Nor should one assume that value conflict is always undesirable. In many

[30] See Smigel, "The Leisure Society" (see footnote 20).
[31] I. Illich, "Deschooling Society." Harper, New York, 1971.

ways it is endemic to any value system. People want security, stability, and permanence, and yet they also want flexibility, mobility, and innovation. Despite their contradictory nature, these are all values for which we must achieve some dynamic equilibrium. For Bronowski,[32] "the concepts of value are profound and difficult exactly because they do two things at once: they join men into societies and yet they preserve for them a freedom which makes them single men." There are few problems until men want to be both "social animals" and "free men."

Even if we were able to establish an ordering in each individual value system, there are theoretical as well as practical obstacles to combining individual systems into a consistent societal or group value system. To use Arrow's[33] example: if the majority prefer (value) *A* over *B*, and prefer *B* over *C*, it does not follow that the majority value *A* over *C*. That is, pluralistic value systems lead to theoretical limitations in societies' "set of majority preferences."[34]

However, the main issue is that there are factors in a technological society which can and do exaggerate value conflict. Some of these have already been discussed but deserve repetition.

- The rapid rate of technological development has put a strain on the slower rate of value evolution.
- There has been a general scientific challenge to traditional sources of authority. The church, the family, the government—none goes unquestioned; knowledge conflicts with the stability and security of accepted authority.
- In the same way, mobility, mass education, and new expectations about the *right* to have basic physical needs satisfied have challenged the stability of family and community.
- Communications advances have led to a greater awareness of diverse cultural and individual values; this in turn invites questioning of one's own system of beliefs.
- The benefits of knowledge are emphasized but the accumulation of specialized, technical knowledge results in everyone knowing more and more about less and less.
- The need for social structure and public services has been emphasized, while the concept of self-reliance and the areas of choice and action have not been suitably redefined. Beyond the interdependence of today's

[32] J. Bronowski, "Science and Human Values," p. 55. Harper, New York, 1965.

[33] K. Arrow, "Social Choice and Individual Values." Wiley, New York, 1964.

[34] To use algebraic terminology, this set does not constitute a partially ordered set since the ordering relation "prefers" is not transitive.

society, there is a commitment to social planning which seems to oppose values of individual freedom. Long-range strategic planning conflicts with short-term personal orientation. The greatest conflicts hinge on who does the planning.

We have tried to illustrate the central role of computing in all aspects of planning. But we have also indicated in Chapter 7 why systems analysis and planning in the social structure have met with far less success than, say, planning for the space program. This may be a "knowledge society" but fortunately *values are still the basis for decision-making in the social sphere.*[35]

The consequence of attempts at social planning is a gradual but inevitable focus on values. *Good* social planning entails an explicit description of values and the specification of value conflicts, because planning results in a focus for examining values. The more we plan, the more inconsistencies become apparent. In this way, value conflict is a desirable by-product. As Albert[36] explains, value conflict can be constructive if it leads to a reintegration or compromise of values to suit current realities.

Value conflict will not be constructive unless it is an active force in planning, not just a passive accommodation of presumed technological inevitabilities. At the risk of simplification, two major themes can be identified in the criticism against automation and technology. The majority of critics accept the systems approach, the desire to rationalize significant parts of our lives. The objections center around the failure to account for social costs and values properly in the problem formulation; that is, only narrow and quantifiable values are emphasized in determining the goals. But beyond all the thoughtful, forceful, and sometimes pessimistic arguments of writers such as Fromm, Goodman, Mannheim, and Ozbekham,[37] there is still a basic belief in the rational process to the extent that they would accept Bell's System of Social Accounting. The other school of thought distrusts the overemphasis on rationality itself. There is a romanticism about spontaneity and even a belief in the need for certain amounts of irrational and unexplainable behavior. This line of criticism can be found in Ellul, Marcuse, Roszak, and Seidenberg,

[35] This is the view of Bell (see footnote 7) with our own added emphasis.

[36] E. Albert, Conflict and change in American values: A cultural historical approach, *Ethica* **74**, 19–33 (1963).

[37] E. Fromm (1968); P. Goodman, "Like a Conquered Province," Chapter 3. Vintage Books, New York, 1968; K. Mannheim, "Diagnosis of Our Time," Chapter 2. Oxford Univ. Press, London and New York, 1943; H. Ozbekham, "The Triumph of Technology: 'Can' Implies 'Ought'," in Anderson (1968, pp. 204–233).

and in the more recent writings of Mumford as he becomes preoccupied with the ontological being of the "machine" and the process.[38] Humanity, he feels, has or will soon have transferred all its attention to one aspect of its being—it has sacrificed emotion for rational thought.

The first view seems to be the more positive and hopeful, not because it rejects emotions but because it still allows us to decide the value to be placed on the preservation of emotions, spontaneity, diversity, and individuality within our plans. It is in accord with what Cox[39] calls the prophetic tradition of Judeo-Christian thought—that the future is "open and responsible" (that is, there are many possible futures and the future can be directed toward desires and goals).

The danger then is not that we will overplan but that our plans will be too simpleminded and will lack proper consideration for those values and emotions which are not quantifiable.[40] As Ozbekham stresses, the planning must be open, pluralistic, and normative. Gordon and Ikle[41] emphasize that planning must not only consider present values but must predict and adjust for future values. No matter what the techniques used, no matter how improved our perceptions, there can be no finality; values and goals will continue to evolve, and we must be prepared to revise our plans accordingly.

[38] H. Marcuse, "One Dimensional Man: Studies in the Ideology of Advanced Industrial Society." Beacon Press, Boston, Massachusetts, 1964; T. Roszak, "The Making of a Counter Culture." Doubleday, Garden City, New York, 1969; R. Seidenberg, Justice for all, freedom for none, *Center Diary* no. 17, 25–37 (1967); Mumford (1970). In a sense, it is difficult to classify Ellul and Mumford in this group. The humanism of Mumford is surely more closely related to that of Fromm than to that of Roszak. Our distinction, however, is based on the solutions proposed by the respective critics. A related distinction is made in W. Kuhn, "The Post-Industrial Prophets: Interpretations of Technology." Weybright & Talley, New York, 1971. He identifies those who see the machine as an extension to man (McLuhan, Wiener) versus those who see the machine as being largely opposed to man (Ellul, Mumford).

[39] H. Cox, Tradition and the future, I and II, *Christianity and Crisis*, pp. 218–220, Oct. 2 (1967); pp. 227–231, Oct. 16 (1967).

[40] A. Toffler in Baier and Rescher (1969, p. 26). For a specific example see M. Ross, Rule by computer? *University Affairs*, March (1972), published by the Association of Universities and Colleges of Canada, where the implications of applying only quantitative criteria to evaluating the performance of universities are raised.

[41] T. Gordon in Baier and Rescher (1969, p. 156); Ikle, Can social predictions be evaluated? *Daedalus*, Summer (1967). Gordon almost senses a contradiction when he observes: "If planners use today's values in their planning they imply that values will be or should be static, yet values are evolutionary. Do we know what's right for tomorrow? If we do not, how can we plan effectively? If we think we do, what freedom have we left for them?"

13.5. Some Directions

Predictions about the future can take three forms: what is possible, what is desirable, and what is likely. Further, one can be concerned with the short range (the next 5 to 10 or 20 years) or long range (the next 25 to 100 years). We have already discussed technological forecasting in Chapter 6 and our short-range predictions for various aspects of computing and automation can be found throughout the book, particularly in Chapter 8. Bell[42] is one of the few to suggest that sociological forecasting should not be as difficult as technological forecasting because of the constants in human life. The methodologies of Section 6.2 and Chapter 7 have just begun to be applied to social and value structures.[43] It is an open question as to whether the universals in life can ever provide enough illumination for predictive confidence equal to or beyond that attainable in technological forecasting. We close with some opinions on value directions over the next generation (to the year 2000).

In 1966 Rescher[44] conducted a survey among a small group of scientific and future-oriented persons in the United States. Its purpose was twofold: to analyze what would be the likely changes in American values under the impact of foreseeable scientific, technological, political, and socioeconomic developments, and to assess the nature and desirability of such value change. The conclusions from Rescher's survey can be summarized as follows.

- There has not been an erosion in the general commitment to values. However, many significant trends can be identified.
- There will be a general upgrading of values associated with social cooperation. For example, justice, equality, peace, and group affiliations

[42] D. Bell, The nature and limitations of forecasting, *Daedalus*, p. 937, Summer (1967).

[43] For the most part, the forecasts have been intuitive. The Kaiser Aluminum Corporation's "Future Game" inspired by O. Helmer and T. Gordon [see Baier and Rescher (1969, pp. 148–214)] is an interesting experiment in this regard, and they have also emphasized the applicability of Delphi techniques to social planning in O. Helmer: "Social Technology." Basic Books, New York, 1966. However, the Delphi conducted by Gordon and Helmer is basically concerned with technological forecasting. See N. Dalkey, and D. Rourke, "Experimental Assessment of Delphi Procedures with Group Value Judgments." RAND Rep. R-6-12-ARPA, 1971, for a Delphi more concerned with the implications and desirability of potential changes in social and value structures.

[44] N. Rescher, "A Questionnaire Study of American Values by 2000 AD," in Baier and Rescher (1969, pp. 133–147).

will be more highly valued. Values will be, more and more, group rather than individual.

- But there is also a general upgrading of values associated with self-satisfaction (e.g., aesthetics, pleasure, intellectualism, material comfort).
- Many traditional sources of authority will be deemphasized; the nation, the family, religion will become groups for affiliation rather than objects of devotion.
- There will be a downgrading of self-reliance and private property rights.
- The effects of technology are mainly indirect; they act to facilitate value-sensitive developments in the political, sociological, and economic spheres. For example, "omnipresent central planning" is a computer-facilitated development which is seen to have significant effects on economic security (upgraded), and self-reliance, freedom from interference, and privacy (downgraded).
- There are scientific and technological forces which have a direct impact on values; the most important are in biology–medicine (e.g., control of aging, genetic control, psychological engineering). "Massive automation" is seen to have negative effects on economic security but to increase the value of leisure-oriented activities.

Because the survey limited itself to events within the realm of possibility for the year 2000, it did not explicitly try to ascertain the effect of artificial intelligence or man–machine symbiosis. While limiting the range of events provides focus for the survey, there is a serious question as to whether the short list can adequately express certain values. From our point of view, a deficiency in the questionnaire was that no value corresponding to "participation" or "worthwhile activity" was identified (the closest representative in the values listed was self-fulfillment). The respondents are basically optimistic; they see social harmony and the pursuit of individual needs replacing economic insecurity and fear. The potential changes were clearly viewed as progressive trends, the main exceptions being the downgrading of self-reliance and devotion to family.

The Rescher survey is largely in accord with the scenario produced by Kahn. Assuming no surprises, Kahn also foresees a more orderly, unified, utilitarian, affluent, leisure- and knowledge-oriented society; a stable and more cooperative world; an emphasis on social values, and at the same time an increase in self-indulgences; the erosion of traditional societal levers, sources of authority, and focus; a continued commitment to basic humanistic needs and values; and a diversity of life styles and value systems.[45] Kahn makes some more specific predictions. He sees a continuing erosion of work-oriented values and a search for meaning and purpose, the search for new values and meaning being particularly strong among the upper middle class "young" in Western society. He senses a confrontation between the "humanist left" (in search of meaning) and the "responsible center" (constructing and emphasizing the social structure).

The forecasts given here are applicable to Western societies in the process of becoming more and more postindustrialized. They depend on the basic assumption that the present conflicts and imbalances within societies and among nations will be lessened if not resolved. It is the volatile consequences of modern conflict which make social cooperation imperative, perhaps seemingly inevitable. But inevitability may only be a function of one's detachment from the conflict. Survival has different levels: For many (e.g., in the Indian subcontinent) it still means obtaining food, health, and shelter; for others (in urban ghettos or rural shacks) it means securing livelihood and affirming dignity; and for some (the middle class and the affluent) it means preserving one's sense of individual being.

If the problems listed in Section 1.3 can be at least partially resolved, a stable society may be what the next generation will value most. It may be possible to have a society that is affluent, humanistic, leisure-oriented, partly alienated, and at the same time stable.[46] The humanist's concern is that by the twenty-first century, we may not even know what essential part of ourselves we had to sacrifice in attempting to achieve that stability. Whether or not one sees the forecasts presented here as encouraging may be a question of whether one leans more to the "responsible center" or to the "humanist left," but such a sharp dichotomy is not inevitable. True humanistic planning, which is not embarrassed to recognize the beauty and frailty of human life, will not be easy, but by our concerns and actions, the human spirit can insist on its place in the social structure.

[45] Statement of Herman Kahn to the Committee on Science and Astronautics, U. S. House of Representatives, Jan. 27, 1970, U. S. Govt. Printing Office, Washington, D. C., 1970.

The societal levers are sources of stability and purpose in society. They include the Puritan ethic (work and achievement orientation), the martial virtues (duty, honor, patriotism), tradition, and religion.

Kahn's "exhaustive" list of needs and values includes: respect and recognition, balance of change and stability, daily activities, achievement, wealth, power, just rewards, seminal satisfaction, affection and love, self-expression, shared experiences, and satisfaction of basic emotions.

[46] See H. Kahn and A. Wiener, "The Year 2000." Macmillan, New York, 1967.

Bibliography

Anderson, S. (1968). "Planning for Diversity and Choice." MIT Press, Cambridge, Massachusetts.

Baier, K., and Rescher, N., eds. (1969). "Values and the Future." Free Press, New York.

Burke, J. G., ed. (1966). "The New Technology and Human Values." Wadsworth Publ., Belmont, California.

Center Magazine (bimonthly). Center for the Study of Democratic Institutions, Santa Barbara, California.

Daedalus (1967). Toward the year 2000: Work in progress, Amer. Acad. of Arts and Sci., Summer.

de Jouvenal, B., ed. (1962). "Futuribles." Geneva, Switzerland.

Fromm, E. (1968). "The Revolution of Hope. Toward a Humanized Technology." Harper, New York.

Harvard Univ. Program on Technol. and Soc. (1969). Technology and values. *Res. Rev.* no. 3, Cambridge, Massachusetts.

Jungk, R., and Galtung, J., eds. (1969). "Mankind 2000." Norwegian Univ. Press, Oslo.

Kahn, H., and Wiener, A. G. (1967). "The Year 2000: A Framework for Speculation on the Next Thirty-Three Years." Macmillan, New York.

Mumford, L. (1967, 1970). "The Myth of the Machine." Vols. 1 and 2. Harcourt, New York.

Sci. J. (1967). "Forecasting the Future," special issue, October.

Technology and Culture (quarterly). Soc. for the History of Technol., Univ. of Chicago Press, Chicago, Illinois.

The Futurist: A Newsletter for Tomorrow's World (bimonthly). World Future Soc., Washington, D. C.

Appendix

STATISTICAL TESTS

We shall only present a brief discussion of some common statistical tests. For this a few basic definitions are needed (e.g., those for a distribution, a random variable, significance level), and these are to be found in any standard introductory text on probability and statistics.[1]

We can test a hypothesis about an unknown distribution by estimating how probable the sample observations are under the given hypothesis. More precisely, to test a hypothesis H using a sample A of size n, we compute the probability that if H is true, a random sample of size n disagrees with H by as much or more than the given sample does. If this probability is less than a specified *significance level* α, then *we reject* H *at the level* α; otherwise, we accept (or rather we have no reason to reject H) at the level α. The level α is usually chosen at 0.01, 0.05, or 0.10.

We can illustrate hypothesis testing by one of the most widely used statistical methods, the χ^2 (chi-squared) test. Let X be any random variable with mutually exclusive and exhaustive events $E_1, \ldots, E_k$;

[1] For example, M. Hausner, "Elementary Probability Theory." Harper, New York, 1971.

$$\text{prob}(E_j) = p_j, \qquad 1 \leq j \leq k$$

Let there be $n = \Sigma_{i=1}^{k} m_i$ independent determinations of X, where m_i is the number of times E_i occurred in the n trials. Define the statistic

$$\chi^2 = \sum_{j=1}^{k} \frac{(m_j - np_j)^2}{np_j}$$

As $n \to \infty$, the distribution of χ^2 approaches that of the chi-squared distribution with $k - 1$ degrees of freedom. The importance of this result is that one does not need to know anything about the distribution of X. And while analytic estimates of the speed of convergence (to the chi-squared distribution as $n \to \infty$) are not known, experience and numerical computations indicate that the approximation is good as soon as $np_j \geq 5$ for all j, $1 \leq j \leq k$.[2] We can rephrase the χ^2 statistic as follows: Let $t_j = np_j$ denote the theoretical (perhaps hypothesized) value for the number of occurrences of event E_j in n trials. Then we can test a hypothesis on the basis of the theoretical results it yields for the possible events. Suppose we compute

$$\chi^2 = \sum_{j=1}^{k} \frac{(m_j - t_j)^2}{t_j} = v_n$$

(for some sample of size n). Then if $\text{prob}(\chi^2 \geq v_n) < \alpha$ we reject the hypothesis at the level α.

One important modification of χ^2 analysis concerns contingency tables and tests of homogeneity. Let $E_1, \ldots, E_k$ be mutually exclusive and exhaustive events (e.g., attitudes about computers) and $S_1, \ldots, S_r$ allegedly independent samples (e.g., classes of respondents). (See Table A-1, where m_{ij} denotes the number of samples from S_i observed to be in event E_j.) A homogeneity hypothesis would assert that the number of E_j outcomes in sample S_i should theoretically be $t_{ij} = a_i b_j / n$. Suppose the actual outcomes m_{ij} are observed. Then it can be shown that

$$\chi^2 = \sum_i \sum_j \frac{(m_{ij} - t_{ij})^2}{t_{ij}}$$

has the chi-squared distribution with $(r - 1)$ $(k - 1)$ degrees of freedom.

[2] More cautious statisticians may suggest that all $np_j \geq 10$. There are a number of ad hoc techniques which can be used when np_j is small. See A. E. Maxwell, "Analyzing Qualitative Data." Wiley, New York, 1961, for an extended discussion devoted to χ^2 testing.

TABLE A-1
A CONTINGENCY TABLE

	E_1	E_2	...	E_k	Total
S_1	m_{11}	m_{12}	...	m_{1k}	a_1
$\vdots$	$\vdots$	$\vdots$		$\vdots$	$\vdots$
S_r	m_{r1}	m_{r2}		m_{rk}	a_r
Total	b_1	b_2	...	b_k	n

We illustrate the χ^2 test by some specific results from the AFIPS/Time attitude survey as discussed in Section 6.1.[3] We have the following: E_1 = belief that life is much better with computers; E_2 = all beliefs other than E_1 (life is slightly better, life is the same, life is slightly worse, life is much worse); S_1 = respondents with at most a high school education; S_2 = respondents with at least some college education. (See Table A-2.)

We may decide to examine the relationship between formal education and attitudes (somewhat arbitrarily) by testing the homogeneity hypothesis that S_1 and S_2 will have the same distribution. We have $t_{11} = 399/996 \times 534 \simeq 214$, $t_{12} \simeq 320$, $t_{21} \simeq 185$, $t_{22} \simeq 277$.

$$\chi^2 = \frac{(182-214)^2}{214} + \frac{(352-320)^2}{320} + \frac{(217-185)^2}{185} + \frac{(245-277)^2}{277} = 17.2$$

Consulting a χ^2 table we find that $\text{prob}(\chi^2 \geq 17.2)$ for one degree of freedom is less than 0.01 and therefore we reject the hypothesis at the 0.01 level, and conclude that attitude *is* correlated with education. By observation, we can see that more formal education correlates with more

TABLE A-2
A SPECIFIC CONTINGENCY TABLE

	E_1	E_2	Total
S_1	182	352	534
S_2	217	245	462
Total	399	597	996

[3] "A National Survey of the Public's Attitudes Toward Computers," a joint project of the Amer. Fed. of Information Processing Societies and *Time Magazine*, AFIPS Press, Montvale, New Jersey, November, 1971. The survey results that have been distributed do not provide the full information needed to illustrate the χ^2 test in a more complete manner. Also, results were given in percentages and we have had to approximate the m_{ij} values in our example.

optimistic beliefs about computers. If the data were available, we could test the relationship by considering a finer classification of events (E_1 = much improved, ..., E_5 = much worse, E_6 = don't know), and then checking the resulting χ^2 for five degrees of freedom.[4]

We have been careful to say that education and optimistic beliefs are correlated, rather than saying that higher education tends to result in or *cause* more optimistic beliefs. The χ^2 test of homogeneity simply rejects the hypothesis that the responses are independent of education. In some cases, we are strongly led to believe that correlation indicates a direct causal relationship (e.g., cigarette smoking and lung cancer). In the present example it may be that education leads to a greater appreciation of the benefits of computing; or it may be that education is strongly related to economic well-being, which is having the real effect on attitudes. In short, determining the meaning of correlations in any specific case goes beyond the statistical methods involved.

In addition to recognizing a correlation, we may wish to determine some quantitative estimate of the correlation and obtain some description of its nature. A measure of the correlation or dependence between two random variables, X and Y, is provided by the *sample correlation coefficient*

$$r_{XY} = \sum_{i=1}^{n} \frac{(X_i - \bar{X}_n)(Y_i - \bar{Y}_n)}{nS_n{}^X S_n{}^Y}$$

where X_i and Y_i are observations, $\bar{X}_n$ and $\bar{Y}_n$ are means, and $S_n{}^X$ and $S_n{}^Y$ are variances.

It is not difficult to show that $-1 \leq r_{XY} \leq +1$ and that the absolute value $|r_{XY}|$ indicates the strength of the correlation. That is, if r_{XY} is close to 0, then there is little correlation; if r_{XY} is close to ± 1, then X and Y are strongly correlated. For example, let $X_i = 1$ if the ith respondent believes life is much better with computers (0 otherwise) and let $Y_i = 1$ if the ith respondent has some college education (0 otherwise). Or we might obtain a more complete picture of the correlation strength if the values of X_i reflect a range of attitudes (say, much better = 5, ..., much worse = 1) and Y_i reflects a range of formal education (graduate school = 7, complete college = 6, partial college = 5, complete high school = 4, ..., partial grade school = 1).

One is often interested in trying to determine the *true regression curve* of Y on X (or X on Y), i.e., the expected value of Y given an

[4] It is not that the test illustrated is invalid. Rather, the test as given reflects the relationship between enthusiastic beliefs about computers and education, rather than between all attitudes and education.

outcome x of X. Making approximations to the true regression curve is to a large extent an art in that choosing the type of approximating curve is mostly based on intuition and observation.[5] The approximating curves are usually of the form:

(a) $Y = aX + b$ linear regression

(b) $Y = \sum_{i=0} a_i X^i$ polynomial regression

(c) $Y = aX^b$ exponential regression

Having chosen the type of approximating curve, one usually estimates the coefficients by the method of *least squares*. That is, suppose (X_1, Y_1), $\ldots$, (X_n, Y_n) is a sample of size n and $Y = f(a_1, \ldots, a_r, X)$ is chosen as an approximating regression curve. Then the a_i are chosen so that

$$S = \sum_{i=1}^{n} (Y_i - f(a_i, \ldots, a_r, X))^2$$

is a minimum. It should be emphasized that any sample (X_i, Y_i) can be used to compute a least-squares linear regression approximation. Whether or not this approximation is a good estimate of the true nature of the dependence (if any) between X and Y is another matter, which must be subjected to other statistical tests and empirical observations. Curves such as that in Fig. 2-2, showing the trend of reduction in computing costs, were obtained by regression.

[5] A brief, informative discussion of regression can be found in W. F. Sharpe, "The Economics of Computers," pp. 541–556. Columbia Univ. Press, New York, 1969.

INDEX

Computer Science and Applied Mathematics
A SERIES OF MONOGRAPHS AND TEXTBOOKS

Editor
Werner Rheinboldt
University of Maryland

HANS P. KÜNZI, H. G. TZSCHACH, and C. A. ZEHNDER. Numerical Methods of Mathematical Optimization: With ALGOL and FORTRAN Programs, Corrected and Augmented Edition

AZRIEL ROSENFELD. Picture Processing by Computer

JAMES ORTEGA AND WERNER RHEINBOLDT. Iterative Solution of Nonlinear Equations in Several Variables

AZARIA PAZ. Introduction to Probabilistic Automata

DAVID YOUNG. Iterative Solution of Large Linear Systems

ANN YASUHARA. Recursive Function Theory and Logic

JAMES M. ORTEGA. Numerical Analysis: A Second Course

G. W. STEWART. Introduction to Matrix Computations

CHIN-LIANG CHANG AND RICHARD CHAR-TUNG LEE. Symbolic Logic and Mechanical Theorem Proving

C. C. GOTLIEB AND A. BORODIN. Social Issues in Computing

ERWIN ENGELER. Introduction to the Theory of Computation

F. W. J. OLVER. Asymptotics and Special Functions

DIONYSIOS C. TSICHRITZIS AND PHILIP A. BERNSTEIN. Operating Systems

ROBERT R. KORFHAGE. Discrete Computational Structures

In preparation

PHILIP J. DAVIS AND PHILIP RABINOWITZ. Methods of Numerical Integration

A. T. BERZTISS. Data Structures: Theory and Practice, Second Edition (in preparation)

ALBERT NIJENHUIS AND H. S. WILF. Combinatorial Algorithms

5
C 6
D 7
E 8
F 9
G 0
H 1
I 2
J 3